Touch the Archetypes of feminine Power

The runes are more than an ancient alphabet. They comprise a powerful system of divination and a path to the subconscious forces operating in your life. *Northern Mysteries & Magick* is the only book of Nordic magic written by a woman, and it is the first to offer an extensive presentation of rune concepts, mythology and magical applications inspired by Dutch/Friesian traditional lore. Discover how the feminine Mysteries of the North are represented in the runes, and how each of the major deities of Northern Europe still live in the collective consciousness of people of Northern European descent. Chapters on runic divination and magic introduce the use of runes in counseling and healing.

◆ ◆ ◆

"*Northern Mysteries & Magick* provides us with a long overdue, balanced view of Northern Religion that includes the sorely neglected feminine aspects Norse Mythology. Freya Aswynn sketches that (Matriarchal culture) as it once existed before being deliberately suppressed by the prevailing patriarchy, and encourages the reader to reclaim that culture and to give the feminine aspects their due recognition."

—Nancy Smith, *Freya Runestones*

"*Northern Mysteries & Magick* is one of the classic books in the world of rune lore, and Freya Aswynn is one of the classic Teachers of the Elder Northern Mysteries.... All seekers on the Path look for authentic teachers offering accurate knowledge. Freya Aswynn, through her book, articulates the tradition in a most exemplary manner. It is comforting to know that she remains one of the principal leaders in the awakening of runic consciousness in this century and the next."

—Ragnar, Denali Institute of the Northern Tradition

About the Author

Freya Aswynn was born on Wednesday, November ninth in North Holland, in an area that was known in the old days for magical activities of a feminine, pre-Wiccan Nordic religion. Within a family of fourteen children, of which she was ninth, she was soon singled out as different—psychic or crazy, depending on one's point of view. In 1972 she joined the Rosicrucian Order, AMORC. In 1980 she traveled to England to be initiated into Wicca in three days, thanks to Maxine and Alex Sanders. In May of that year, she started her own coven; in 1983 she had a dramatic "meeting" with Odin, known to her as Wodan. Three years later she became perhaps the most innovative thinker and lecturer on the subject of the runes in the UK, as proven by reviews. Aswynn holds regular seminars on runes, and is managing director of an association providing housing and guidance to young people. She currently lives in Scotland.

To Write the Author

If you wish to contact the author or would like more information about this book, please write to Freya Aswynn in care of Llewellyn Worldwide, and we will forward your request. Both the author and publisher appreciate hearing from you and learning of your enjoyment of this book and how it has helped you. Llewellyn Worldwide cannot guarantee that every letter written to the author can be answered, but all will be forwarded. Please write to:

Freya Aswynn
c/o Llewellyn Worldwide
P.O. Box 64383, Dept. K047-7
St. Paul, MN 55164-0383 U.S.A.

Please enclose a self-addressed, stamped envelope for reply or $1.00 to cover costs. If outside the U.S.A., enclose international postal reply coupon.

Many of Llewellyn's authors have websites with additional information and resources. For more information, please visit our website at www.llewellyn.com.

FREYA ASWYNN

NORTHERN MYSTERIES & MAGICK

RUNES & FEMININE POWERS

2002
Llewellyn Publications
St. Paul, Minnesota, 55164-0383, U.S.A.

SECOND EDITION, 1998
Fourth Printing, 2002

(Formerly titled *Leaves of Yggdrasil*)
First Limited Edition published by ASWYNN, 1988
First Edition published by Llewellyn Publications, 1990

Cover design by Kevin R. Brown
Interior illustrations on pages 9-87 by Helen Michaels based on
    originals by Freya Aswynn
All other illustrations by Freya Aswynn
Interior design and layout by Virginia Sutton
Project management by Christine Nell Snow

Library of Congress Cataloging-in-Publication Data
Aswynn, Freya, 1949-
    [Leaves of Yggdrasil]
    Northern mysteries and magick: runes, gods and feminine powers /
Freya Aswynn.—2nd ed.
        p. cm.
    Originally published under title: Leaves of Yggdrasil; in series:
Llewellyn's Teutonic magick series.
    Includes bibliographical references.
    ISBN 1-56718-047-7 (trade paper)
    ISBN 1-56718-047-CD (compact disc)
    1. Runes—Miscellanea. 2. Magic. 3. Fortune-telling by runes.
4. Gods, Norse. I. Title.
    [BF1623.R89A78   1998]
    133.3'3—dc21   98-9832
                                                              CIP

Llewellyn Publications
A Division of Llewellyn Worldwide, Ltd.
P.O. Box 64383, Dept. K047-7
St. Paul, Minnesota 55164-0383
www.llewellyn.com
Printed in the United States of America

Acknowledgments

A special note of thanks to Andrew Clifton for his proofreading of this updated edition. To Phil and Mags for their consistent friendship and support on various levels. To Lawrence for taking care of computer problems. To Kveldulfr Gundarsson for his translation of *Sigdrifumal*. Thanks to Ruth Bayer for the back cover photograph.

European organizations of interest:
  Ring of Troth Europe
  BM Troth
  London, WC1N 3XX
  e-mail: aclifton@enterprise.net

  Scottish Esoteric Network
  "The Source"
  P.O. Box 23085
  Edinburgh, EH36WJ

Recordings by Freya Aswynn

Songs of Yggdrasil
Compact disc featuring shamanic chants from the
Northern Mysteries.

✦ CONTENTS ✦

✦ FOREWORD ✦

This is a book about an ancient alphabet. It is also about magic.

It is easy to pay lip service to the general idea that there is power in words and sounds, but it is also easy to sympathize with Crowley's early objection to the Golden Dawn: that it promised to teach him the secrets of the universe, but all he was given was the Hebrew alphabet. We are only beginning to rediscover the possibility that an alphabet might be a "secret of the universe," that information could be more fundamental than either matter or energy.

If you are new to the runes, or any other alphabet for that matter, you may be attracted by a certain magic and mystery in the very forms of the letters. After you have studied them a little, the magic can either take root and inspire you, as it did to the author of this book, or it can evaporate with familiarity and leave you with a sense of anticlimax and a yearning to explore elsewhere for that elusive magic. If you are prone to thinking "how can an alphabet be any more than just an alphabet?" it would be worth exploring the magical power of language in your imagination before starting this book.

Begin by considering what life might have been like when reading and writing were the preserve of the educated few. Most people would live without maps, without recipe books, without herbals, without calendars, without memo pads, without road signs. This feat of memory would nowadays seem prodigious. It is hard for us to imagine that people used to know their tribal history by heart, could recite the Old Testament or sing their myths. Widespread literacy makes all this unnecessary: the familiarity of writing has released vast mental capacity by making so much memory redundant. What has happened to all that power?

Now go back further, and imagine a time when the written language was so new that most people didn't even know of its existence. Imagine that you are a runner, and that there is a crisis in the land. A wise man has summoned you, given you a tablet of clay and instructions to run to a neighboring land and present this tablet to your king. For some reason beyond your comprehension you are told to guard this tablet with your life and hand it over intact. When you arrive exhausted at your destination, the king takes this tablet in his hands, gazes at it in silent contemplation for a while, then proceeds to fire questions at you. To your astonishment his questions reveal a knowledge of the crisis which has happened several days running distant. By some extraordinary magic this little clay tablet seems to have spoken to the king, conveying knowledge of distant places, telling him that support is needed. Is it surprising that writing was once associated with magic?

Now go back even further, and imagine yourself as a hominid without any language. Suddenly your group is under attack, and you react like an animal, rushing at your attackers, perhaps clutching a stone as a primitive weapon. In your exertion and excitement you bellow and grunt, and you notice that your attackers are also making noises; but there is something odd about the way they do it. Their grunts and bellows have an eerie purposefulness which seems to link to their extraordinary fighting skill: your attacker suddenly and inexplicably retreats, making a babbling noise; you instinctively chase him and find yourself surrounded by attackers who seem to have a single mind. You are in fear and utter awe because you are witnessing something completely beyond comprehension: the use of speech to direct battle tactics. Animal survival is being transformed into the "art of war."

These simple and highly selective examples are meant to make just one general point: that from the very earliest times language and writing would have been associated with mystery and magic of the most awesome kind. The earlier such associations are made, the more deeply they will be embedded in the group mind, or "collective unconsciousness." So when you feel an initial twinge of excitement at the idea of an ancient alphabet, you are experiencing a genuine link with the magical realm. What you must now do is continue your studies in a way that will strengthen that link, before the sword of conscious analysis can sever the link by persuading you it is "nothing but an obsolete alphabet." Fundamental concepts of language are deeply linked to magical power in our minds; that is why it is possible to use ancient alphabets as a key or tap to magical power— provided you can strike the right balance between academic objectivity and subjective participation. A good example of this balance is found in this text.

I remember my first acquaintance with Freya in the early eighties—I'd been told that I must meet this amazing Dutch occultist who didn't speak perfect English, but was able to fill in any gaps with fluent swear words. This book testifies that she has come a long way since discovering the runes! Freya always was a controversial figure, and in writing about the runes she has chosen a controversial subject.

As she explains in her historical chapter, the runes are intimately linked with Norse mythology, a pantheon which was driven underground by Christianity, and it has remained underground for centuries. Another way of saying it is that these ancient gods have been driven down into the collective unconscious and abandoned. The effect of doing this is similar to the effect you would get if you

xiv   ◆ FOREWORD ◆

drove your cats, dogs and other domestic animals back into the jungle: when you set out to rediscover them several generations later,
you find that they have reverted to the wild, grown feral and fierce.
But their essential nature remains unchanged—a cat is still a cat, with
all its potential.

Something like this has happened to the Norse gods. The first
attempts to re-contact them this century had drastic results. Jung,
in his essay on Wotan first published in 1936, describes how the "old
god of storm and frenzy, the long quiescent Wotan" is awakening
"like an extinct volcano, to a new activity, in a civilized country that
had long supposed to have outgrown the Middle Ages." He describes
how the "youth movement" has sacrificed sheep to this old god, and
how the same spirit was now stirring in the Nazi movement. Perhaps
we should compare the resulting havoc in Germany to what would
happen if the people who chased their cats into the wild were to
enter the jungle several years later and say, "Oh, look, there's our
Kitty! Do let's take her back home."

Half a century later there is still something awesome and wild
about the Norse gods. For some people that is reason enough to have
nothing to do with them. Other people, like the worst of the Nazis,
are so fascinated by this aspect that they become obsessed by it—like
people who bait wild creatures because they are intoxicated by their
bestiality, but have no respect for their basic nature. Other people,
like Freya, can look beyond the rough surface and see the essential
nature of a pantheon every bit as complete and noble as any other.
To approach the gods in this manner is to bring them the gift of
our civilization.

Crowley describes three ages of religion. In the eon of Isis, the
age of the great mother goddesses, the gods were primal forces of
nature with little concern for humanity. As with Jehovah, you
obeyed or perished. In the eon of Osiris we met a new type of god,
much more human. Typically these were male gods who actually
cared for humankind and suffered on our behalf. Christ, Dionysus,
and Wotan were examples of this type—gods who did not expect

humankind to bow before the letter of the law so much as to act on the spirit of the law, gods who set an example for humanity to follow. Now we enter the eon of Horus, and we will begin to learn that the gods are not perfect after all: as Freya explains in her chapter "God-Profiles," the gods themselves evolve and change. Now it is our task neither to obey the gods slavishly (as one should in the eon of Isis) nor to try to model ourselves on their example (as one should in the eon of Osiris), but rather to begin to stand up to them as equals. God became Man for our edification, now humankind must realize its own divinity that the gods may become civilized. Fundamentalism or slavish belief has no future: the person who struggles with Horus because his true will happens to be that of a pacifist will eventually earn from Horus greater respect than the person who treads on the weak "because it says so in the Book of the Law."

There is something compelling about the return of wild gods from the underworld. It is perfectly natural to be fascinated by their primitive power, because it is the essence of the underworld itself. What is wrong is to become drunk on that power, just as it is wrong to banish that power by trivializing the gods. There may be danger in the runes, but this is a time when we need dangerous ideas—we need to turn inward to find challenge. What we must learn is to relate from a position of strength: communing with the gods without destroying their essential nature. This is how the Norse pantheon may return in splendor, to take its place beside the other gods without on the one hand becoming just another commercial novelty, or on the other hand driving us to mutual destruction.

To achieve this we need a balance between the power of ecstatic identification with the runes, and the safety of academic analysis. I believe that Freya's approach sets a good example in this respect.

I know little about history, mythology, or the runes, and I offer no guarantee of the truth of Freya's data. But that is just how she would want it to be, for everything in this book must be tested in the reader's own experience. There is a basic honesty here that one can respect: Freya makes no pretense about being privy to "ancient traditions" or "exclusive brotherhoods": this book is the work of someone who has studied the literature and has lived with the runes.

Enjoy this stimulating book in this spirit; and if you should come to disagree with anything in it, well and good. For I know that Freya herself thrives on controversy—and no living tradition can be a static entity.

—Lionel Snell

◆ PREFACE TO ◆
SECOND EDITION

In this edition of *Northern Mysteries & Magick*, I have sought to emphasize the power held in the feminine Mysteries as well as expand the focus I have taken on the matriarchal aspects of the Northern religion. Chapter six especially reflects that focus. More insight is given on the magical practices of women (Seith, Spae Craft) and also on the roles of less well-known goddesses and other feminine beings who have contributed to the tradition. I do this in the hope of continuing the restoration of the Northern Mysteries and re-establishing the prominence of the feminine perspective.

✦ INTRODUCTION ✦

The story of how I came to the runes—or rather how the runes came to me—begins in my early childhood in Holland. As early as the age of four I was dimly aware of what I would later identify as occult forces. One of my first conscious thoughts that might be described as "occult" happened when I was running in the street with my cape wide open to catch the wind, trying to fly. While doing this, which no doubt many children do, it occurred to me how strange it was not to be able to take off from the ground. My body seemed very heavy and I was convinced that I possessed or had once possessed a different body capable of flight. I often seemed to know, or rather feel, what would happen before it actually did happen; these were mostly premonitions of insignificant things, nothing as dramatic as foreseeing deaths or anything of that nature. Nevertheless there was something about me that made me different. My parents also became aware of this and attempted to beat it out of me. I was also bullied and mistreated by my older brothers, until the State intervened and I was made a ward of the Court at the age of four. From that time on, I did not spend much time with my immediate family, being frequently fostered by an aunt or shunted back and forth between her and my parents.

At the age of ten I was so emotionally traumatized that I was declared maladjusted and was placed in a variety of children's homes from then on until I was nineteen. The last institution I was sent to was a very rough place. My incarceration lasted nine years, during which I was locked in isolation cells, doped up with drugs such as largactil, lectured by incompetent social workers, and often subjected to physical violence—which, as I grew older, I learned to dish out myself! When I was released, I had seen a great deal of the shady side of life and was a confirmed anarchist with no formal education. I could read and write and that was all I needed to make my own start in life. (Now, at the age of forty-eight, I realize that this whole experience was the best available equivalent to a warrior's training and was necessary for me to accomplish my wyrd.) Fortunately, I always managed to experience everything from the position of a detached observer, an ability I now consider one of my greatest assets. I never lost touch with the occult forces and always felt a strong protection from them, although at the time I did not really know what they were.

It did not take me more than about two months after my release to become involved with a local Spiritualist group. There I received a basic training in psychometry and also started to explore astrology. During that time, in 1970, I met my future husband, George. He was twenty-one years older than I and was deeply interested in the runes and the music of Richard Wagner. Our time together, however, was brief. In January 1972 George died of stomach cancer, and once more I had to fend for myself. I soon discovered that the people involved in Spiritualism were, for the most part, not quite as genuine as I had at first thought. When, after my husband's death, four people from that spiritualist group approached me with four contradictory messages from him, I decided enough was enough, and quit.

Although I myself was not a medium in spite of the assertion from other mediums that I was gifted, I nevertheless had a wolfish nose for sniffing out "bull," an ability which has since proved very useful in my work with Seith or Spae Craft (more about this in the updated section on the feminine Mysteries). I embarked on my next spiritual adventure also in 1972, this time with the Rosicrucian Order, AMORC, of which I remained a member for seven years. During that time I became interested in Aleister Crowley, but unfortunately his books were all in English. So I decided to educate myself with the help of books and tapes while studying Crowley at the British library in Amsterdam. My husband had left me some money which I invested in education of a more practical kind, eventually gaining a qualification as a chiropodist (podiatrist).

The next step I took was one that I had been contemplating for several years, ever since I found an article in a Dutch magazine about witches and the Witchcraft Museum on the Isle of Man. I took this article and hid it—I was still "inside" at that time—and I think I kept it with me for almost another fifteen years. When I first read the article I swore a holy oath that one day I would become involved. In 1979, I did. While roaming through the bookshops in Amsterdam, I found a book titled *Pagan Rituals*. I bought it and immediately dedicated myself in the following manner. The book contained a dedication ritual to the Goddess and the God, without specifying to which pantheon they belonged. The ritual was written for at least two people. As I was working alone and my partner at the time did not speak English, I recorded the priest's part on a tape, leaving gaps in between for my responses. Believe it or not, it worked. Soon afterwards I received a letter from the Theosophical Society, of which I was an inactive member. The letter mentioned a summer weekend conference in Holland and one of the speakers was to be a Dutchman who claimed to have been initiated into the Craft. I went to hear him but was not impressed. However, I remained undeterred. On New Year's Eve, 1980, I performed a ritual invoking the Goddess and presented her more or less with an ultimatum: either she would help me find a way into the Craft, or else I would give up this idea and join the Alice Bailey movement instead (a sort of upgrade of the theosophical movement in the seventies).

I had no idea where to go or what to look for, and my knowledge of English was only just adequate. Undaunted, I left for England. When I arrived I bought a paperback called *Alternative London,* in which I found the address of Maxine Sanders, a high priestess of one of the English covens. While attending a meeting of her group, I was given the telephone number of her estranged husband, Alex Sanders, who at one time had attained much publicity in the British press as the "King of the Witches." I rang Alex, who immediately urged me to come over right away to see him. Unfortunately he was out when I arrived at his home. On being introduced to his then high priestess, Betty, I was told that Alex had been awaiting the arrival of someone from Holland, and had indeed received an Inner Plane message announcing my arrival a fortnight beforehand. This would have coincided with the time I performed the ritual in Holland on New Year's Eve. Years later when I was active in the Rune Gild, I met up with a member of that coven who told me that throughout 1979, Sanders had been working Germanic ritual within an Alexandrian Wiccan context—right up to the point of my arrival in London in January 1980! The fact that Sanders worked in Germanic magic was, on the Inner Planes, a call for me to go to the UK to meet him. I was meant to work Germanic magic all along but had to be initiated into Wicca to get the proper training, as Asatru was virtually unheard of. At the time, however, I had no interest in Germanic magic—in fact, I didn't even know it existed. On one occasion, when a young man started to enthuse about Wotan and his own previous life as an Nazi SS camp commander, I very nearly walked out of the room (my parents had been active in the resistance and I had been brought up with a deep hatred for the Nazis).

When finally I met Alex in a pub, he put his arms around me and said, "You'll be initiated tomorrow night." I couldn't believe my ears! The next day an American Gardnerian high priest, Jim Bennett, arrived at Alex's house. He carried out the initiation that evening, and the next day I went back to Holland.

While I was on the train back to London, at 10:00 in the evening, within twenty-four hours of my initiation, I was visited by the most horrendous menstrual period I had ever experienced, ten days too early. Now I laugh about it and realize that it was in fact a direct result of the initiation. Two months later, in March, I was again in England to attend a major annual event in London occult circles. There, before the conference began, I met the man with whom I was to share my life for fourteen years—Lionel Hornby. Through him I became acquainted with a very stable, sensible, straightforward coven and from this starting point, we formed our own coven in June 1981. At first I felt at home in the Craft and threw myself enthusiastically into the work of the coven, but after a while I began to ask myself certain questions. Terms such as "old gods" and "old religion" were part of the everyday vocabulary of the Craft, but what did they really mean to me in terms of my own background? The gods mentioned were usually Graeco-Roman, or possibly Celtic, but I was Dutch and I began to wonder whether we had our own gods. I soon discovered that we did. I realized that the Dutch are a Nordic people and their gods are the same as those of the Scandinavians and Anglo-Saxons: Wodan, Donar, Freyja, and so forth, names that called to me with a curiously haunting power. I began a profound search for my own religious roots, for gods that I could feel were truly my own.

It was not long before the gods themselves gave me a helping hand. One day a young man who was a fellow member of the coven took me down to Surrey to introduce me to a woman who was considering joining the Craft. She lived with two delightful cats named Victoria and Albert, who, astonishingly, had lived for twenty years. This woman turned out to be a dabbler in the runes, and she offered to do a reading for me. She had a series of flat pieces of clay on which the runes were inscribed and a piece of paper on which their meanings were written. She invited me to lay the runes out in a circle, and as I touched them something significant happened. I knew with a powerful certainty that the runes were mine. No other system of divination has ever had such an impact on me.

A few months later came the experience that finally led to my embracing the Northern gods. In the spring of 1983 my relationship with my partner was temporarily thrown into a state of crisis when he made a pass at a visiting priestess. I was livid, and immediately moved out of the room we shared into the basement of our house. Needing some higher power to turn to and having lost faith in the gods and goddesses of the Craft, I cried out to Wodan in my despair and he answered. From that moment on I was and still am totally committed to his service.

On the second day of May that year I started a series of runic workings which I realize, as I read back through my magical diary, were of great significance. My method, which I can recommend as a valid technique for getting in touch with the runes, was to bake twenty-four square cakes, each decorated with a rune in futhark order. Each evening I invoked Wodan and Frija to bless a rune, and then ate it. Then I just concentrated on the rune and wrote down whatever came to mind. I still have those notes, about six small pages in all. That was the origin of this book.

Some of the experiences I underwent as I worked through the futhark are especially noteworthy. When I was working with the Thurisaz rune, I felt a shaft of brilliant white light descend from above me, enter the crown of my head and strike down into the ground beneath my feet. When I worked with Kenaz, a close friend died that very day. One of the aspects of Kenaz is that it is a transforming rune and signifies the funeral pyre, or its modern-day equivalent. While working with Jera, I suddenly became interested in my personal correspondences to the Northern tradition and to Wodan in particular. I knew that, among other things, Wodan was a god of sacrifice, as attested by Tacitus, the Roman historian who wrote in the first century. Wodan's day is Wednesday and his magical number is nine. What an astounding surprise it was when I discovered the mystical significance of my date of birth: Wednesday, November 9. November derives from the Latin for "ninth month." Moreover, November was in Anglo-Saxon called *Blotmonath*, the month of sacrifices. Furthermore, I was the ninth of fourteen children. Indeed the number nine has often recurred throughout my life. For instance, I spent almost exactly nine years locked up in children's homes. In all honesty, I believe that I am a naturally born or chosen priestess of Wodan. When we look at the myths, we find various heroes linked with Wodan (or to give him his Scandinavian name, Odin) either through descent or through an act of personal dedication to him. Examples include Siegmund, Sieglinde, and Siegfried, who were all supposed to be descended from Wodan, and Starkadder, who was dedicated to him. These four figures were brought up under extraordinary circumstances, usually without parents, which suggests similarities to my own personal background. This realization was of great psychological value to me and certainly enabled me to come to terms with my childhood.

When I carried out my rune-working with Eihwaz something remarkable happened. For no apparent reason a man living in our housing association community and under the same roof as us started to react nastily towards our beliefs, although he had been previously informed of our interest in the occult. The trouble began when I started working actively with the runes. Perhaps he was psychic and was tuning in to some of the energies emanating from the runes. On Friday, May 13, 1983, my partner Lionel and I returned home at midnight only to discover that the tenant had deposited a double-sided axe in front of the veil outside the room I had converted into a Temple, where I practiced my workings. I went upstairs in a very angry mood and told Lionel what I had found. His suggestion was, "Sling a few runes!," which I did. I went down to the Temple, picking up a felt-tip pen from the kitchen on the way down, took the axe into the Temple, opened the quarters and invoked various gods Wodan, Donar, Freyja, and Hella. Despite having virtually no knowledge of the runes, I worked myself up into a rage and drew on the axe four runes in a certain sequence. The runes were Thurisaz, Nauthiz, Isa, and Hagalaz, a combination now well known in runic circles. I closed the Temple, cleaned up, and went to bed. The next day, in front of at least five eyewitnesses, the man showed signs of possession. What possessed him we never found out. It went on for rather a long time, at least a couple of hours. If what we had been seeing was not genuine, then it was a very convincing act. We will never know for sure, but I am convinced that it was brought about by the power of the runes which I had invoked.

Later in that year, to develop my divination skills, I worked for a short while in the Camden Psychic Centre. This work was quite successful and I was pleased to receive several letters from clients expressing gratitude for the help I had given them, but unfortunately after three months I quit as the cost of renting my booth at the centre was proving prohibitive. After Camden, I concentrated on gathering knowledge and information with the aim of constructing or partially reconstructing a magical system based on traditional knowledge, grafted onto modern twentieth-century occult practices. This book was the result of that research. At the same time, I made myself busy organizing and lecturing at weekend rune courses in London, which proved very popular. Eventually, I was invited to give rune lectures to interested audiences all over the country.

The most recently published books on the runes deal almost exclusively with divination practices. For this reason, only a small part of this book is devoted to divination, mainly to show how it can be done. Divination is an inborn skill which the practitioner has to develop for him or herself in accordance with his or her own nature. As a guideline, I shall present a few techniques in this work which I developed on my own and which I personally found effective.

At this point I would like to state my reasons for writing this book and to explain why I consider it imperative that the research contained in it should be published. There is a glaring lack of occult information on the Northern tradition. That there is, or has been, such a tradition is established by the literature of the period and the various runic finds discovered since then. It is well known that there were various schools of initiation and esoteric practices in ancient

Egypt and Greece. Even medieval Spain boasted the famous School of Magic in Toledo. I am convinced that the esoteric lore of the Northern tradition was well established in Northern Europe in the pre-Christian era. This contention is difficult to prove because no written evidence of, for example, rituals or cult practices has survived. The only major indication of the existence of such an inner mysteries tradition is presented by the runes. A thorough, in-depth understanding of the runes which extends far beyond the mere level of fortune telling or even genuine divination, and the ability to decode the pattern of the runes and the logical sequence of the futhark, allows us to see that the runes encapsulate a profound esoteric thought-system. In addition, when the runes are integrated with the Northern mythology and the relevant connections are properly comprehended, a consistent, coherent system of initiation begins to emerge. In this book I propose to supply evidence in support of this argument. The runes have been fixed and established in a particular form as a code to preserve the ancestral knowledge of the peoples of Northern Europe. I wish to establish beyond any doubt the relationship between the runes and the Northern, Germanic myths, proving once and for all that the runes should not be applied outside the traditional Northern system of mythology.

From the synthesis of the runes and the myths, I have reconstructed a magical system using modern occult training. I hope this synthesis will provide the occult world with a valid alternative for those occultists working in various other traditions and will help to encourage the development of a Northern Mystery way alongside the Western Mysteries. I have also reconstructed a path of runic initiation based on the original material of the futhark and the Eddas and on an old Northern European near-shamanic tradition, because the Northern Mysteries were for the most part an individualistic tradition largely based on personal experience, rather than being a precise and formally established magical tradition such as Druidism. I postulate that, had our native Northern religion been allowed to evolve in a natural progression from primitive animistic concepts through a more sophisticated pagan pantheon, the next step in this evolutionary process would have been a mystery school along lines similar to those which flourished in ancient Greece and Egypt. Alas, we have not been allowed to follow any religious development. Christianity interfered, and within a relatively short space of time virtually all trace of our heritage was lost. So the task at hand is to delve into the original sources as far as is possible, and from there to extrapolate the trend and follow this line of imaginary development up until the present day, thereby to restore the old Northern religion, integrated and acceptable, in a twentieth-century environment, backed up and emphasized by twentieth-century occult techniques (without the questionable benefit of twentieth-century politics!).

The first edition of this book was published privately in 1989, and a year later a more professional edition was published by Llewellyn. Recently, I have been asked to update this personal introduction and as ever I am happy to comply with my publisher's request. Some important personal information was not included in the first edition for reasons of discretion, but as most of the people involved are now either deceased or grazing at greener spiritual pastures, I have incorporated some of this information into this new introduction. I will follow from here with an account of all recent developments.

Following publication of the first edition of this book, supported by the customary helpful promotion by Llewellyn, I received many letters with inquiries from people asking for more of the same. In response I decided to co-write a correspondence course with (at that time) my close friend and co-religionist Bernard King. This was in September 1991. Although this course was fairly successful it soon appeared that it could do with improvements. Bernard could not continue the work for a variety of personal reasons and another colleague, Kveldulfr Gundarsson, re-wrote a substantial section of the course. At the same time Bernard King, whom I had introduced to

"Elements" publishers, had his own book *Elements of the Runes* published, which is doing very well indeed and I wish him every success. As an outgrowth of the correspondence course, a discussion group, the Asatru Folk Runic Workshop, was formed. ("Asatru," meaning "trust in the Aesir" in Old Norse, has become widely used as a name for the Northern tradition.) This eventually mutated into the Rune Gild UK at the request of Edred Thorsson, founder and Irmin Drighten of the Rune Gild in America. However, as always, to quote from the *Norwegian Rune-Poem* (Stanza 1, line two), "the wolf lurks in the forest." To be more accurate, this particular wolf was living in my house accompanied by a wolverine, and no, I don't mean a she-wolf! Suffice it to say that as a result of disruptive influences, my association with the Rune Gild was of a limited duration. The Gild was finally dissolved at the request of the Irmin Drighten and the majority of the membership was incorporated into Wodan's Own Kindred, from which eventually the Ring of Troth UK was formed. (The Anglo-Saxon word *Troth* is equivalent to the Old Norse *tru*, meaning "trust" or "faith.") This followed on from my lecture tour in America in March 1993, after which I was invited by the American Ring of Troth to form a sub-group in Britain. Shortly after this, in November 1993, with the indispensable help of my wolf-Brother Kveldulfr Gundarsson, and the generous consent and cooperation of Lionel who died six weeks after, I obtained the highest achievement of my spiritual ambition in a major rite of personal dedication to Odin. A fitting start to a major new project!

The Ring of Troth UK was soon established as an independent body, affiliated to groups in America and Australia. Later, by majority vote, it was renamed Ring of Troth Europe, having already attracted members in most western and eastern European countries, from Lithuania to Spain. As a direct result of all these changes, the original London group developed into a thriving active Garth (named Oak Harrow Garth after a site they use for ritual work), by now a jewel in the crown of the Troth. I chartered and inaugurated this Garth in December 1995 just before I moved out of London, together with two members of the old Woden's Own Kindred, to form the nucleus of an Asatru community in Scotland. I named this project "Gladsheim" as this is one of Odin's residences in Asgard and it's a much more friendly name than Valhalla!

Now it is 1998 and the wyrd has changed dramatically once again. My two original companions have left Gladsheim, but undaunted, I was able to restart the project in the autumn of 1997. Luckily, I still had a little money left—and a lot of help from a young enthusiastic environmentalist who did not object to contributing financially and has proven willing to do the sorely needed work. Barry does not follow any specific pagan path; he is the son of a friend who works in the Native American tradition. It is increasingly important, nowadays, for all heathens and pagans to bond together when and wherever they can. When I was in a desperate situation domestically, it was Celtic Wiccans who rallied around me—people whom I had not met before—but are too now part of the Gladsheim extended kin. This does not make me any less Asatru, but I reiterate that all free-thinking people should get their act together and cooperate for the sake of Mother Erda (Earth).

As I write this, the Secretary of the United Nations is in Baghdad trying to keep the peace. We heathens and pagans alike cannot afford to close our eyes to what goes on in the world at large—but it is also important to work locally, within the landscapes and communities in which we live. Gladsheim is intended to become a center of learning with a well-stocked Asatru and metaphysical library, a working *hof* (a temple or sacred building in Old Norse) with at least one resident *hof gythia* (priestess, ON) and one *gothi* (priest)—eventually more—serving different needs of different people and their gods and goddesses. In short I attempt to set up a fully operational Hof with a working priesthood, in whatever format the gods dictate. Alongside this, and also under the gods' guidance, we are committed to a wildlife project and the gradual reforestation of Scotland with native trees. All pagans are welcome to participate in this project—all except drug abusers and opportunists.

Although I myself have obtained a certain notoriety within the international Asatru community as an obsessive Odinist, I have always made it clear that the other gods and goddesses had to be acknowledged and worshipped in their own right. Thus, within the Ring of Troth and other Asatru organizations in the UK, there are growing numbers of Hearths (small family groups) which are more centered on the Vanir and Disir (other families of gods). There is also a thriving Thorshof, and no doubt still more diversity will follow. Asatru is now more widespread and has more open adherents than at any time since the arrival of Christianity. It is growing rapidly, and now clearly stands out as one of our most prominent, active, and thriving native religions.

HEILSA!

—Freya Aswynn

February 21, 1998

· 1 ·

THE
NORTHERN TRADITION
IN PERSPECTIVE

An understanding of the runes requires a knowledge of the esoteric, mythological, and religious Northern European traditions indigenous to the British Isles, Scandinavia, Germany, and my own country, Holland. The runes cannot be properly understood or interpreted unless they are integrated into the framework of Northern mythology, of which they form a part. Today this tradition's rich store of esoteric wisdom has been neglected in favor of exotic importations, which often prove to be less well suited to our own specific cultural and spiritual environment. The Celts do seem to have kept at least some of their traditions alive, but what has happened to those of the Anglo-Saxons and Norse peoples who make up a large proportion of the population of the British Isles? We have been here, after all, since the fourth century. The reasons for this neglect are largely due to the historical circumstances of the Northern religion, which, in reality, consisted of a variety of cults centered on the same groups of gods and exhibited regional variations throughout the Northlands.

During the period of its initial forced conversions, Christianity repressed the native religions of Northern Europe far more agressively

than those of Southern Europe. Rome at that time was the center of
the Christian world, and the Romans had been the hereditary enemies of the Germanic peoples since the days of the Roman Empire.
In Norse mythology, at the Ragnarok, Odin fights the Fenris wolf and
is devoured by it. Mythology also has it that the city of Rome was
founded by two brothers, Romulus and Remus, who owed their survival to a she-wolf that suckled them as babies. The wolf Fenris of
which our mythology speaks could very well represent the Roman
Church as the successor of the Roman Empire. According to this
interpretation, the myth describes how the Northern tradition in the
person of Odin was to be swallowed up by his enemy, the Roman
wolf. Where the Roman emperors failed to subdue the Germanic
tribes militarily, the Roman pontiffs succeeded in subduing them
spiritually. The result was the destruction of our folk traditions, of
which our religion was a part.

For the same reasons, very little of our tradition has survived in
writing, apart from a few Icelandic manuscripts. The earliest of these
date from the tenth century; their subject matter is very likely to
have been Christianized. In addition, there exist in various parts of
the Northland remnants of our folklore which, when stripped clean
of the accumulated layers of Christian interference, can lead us in the
right direction in the search to recover our spiritual heritage.

Another, more contemporary reason the Northern heritage has
been looked askance upon is its debasement by the Nazis. It is high
time that this unfair stigma was removed.

The occult movement in the British Isles, which in occult terms is
one of the most spiritually advanced countries in the world, shows
the same neglect of the Northern Mystery tradition. Here we find a
variety of occult currents coexisting with each other. These currents
we can allocate to three of the four quarters or cardinal points:

1. In the West, we find the Western Mysteries, an amalgam of
   Cabbalism and Grail mysticism together with Greek, Roman,
   and Egyptian magic and the homegrown system known
   as Wicca.

2. Eastern traditions such as Buddhism and Hinduism.

3. The Southern current, represented by the African traditions: Yoruba, Voodoo, Santeria, and Macumba.

We are left with an empty space in the North. Consequently, there is an imbalance in the energies emanating from these quarters. This is true not only for the British Isles, but also for the other countries of Northern Europe. Aided by previous occult training and my psychic abilities, I have during the last four years endeavored to reconstruct a valid path of initiation based on Northern European mythology and the runes.

Wicca is an Anglo-Saxon word, cognated with the Gothic word *witegan,* meaning "knowing." In Wicca, or the Craft, as it is more often called, we can distinguish two currents—the Earth Mysteries and the Lunar Path. There are, of course, the three aspects of the Goddess corresponding to the three Norns of the Northern tradition, but in my own Craft experience I have found that, in the main, people worshipped either the Earthmother or the Moon Goddess.

I venture the hypothesis that, hidden within the Craft, there is a third current, that of the Sea Goddess and the Sea Mysteries. This missing link in the Craft could be part of the Northern Mysteries. The Northern gods, and in particular the Vanir, are borne of or descended from sea gods or goddesses. This is not surprising, as all the Northern countries are close to the sea and their seafaring peoples used to make their living from the sea, usually at a high price in human terms. Thus the sea would be the magical element most important to the North. Holland is situated below sea level and protected from the sea by dykes. In this respect, Holland has an occult significance, which we will return to when we deal with the rune Hagalaz.

Another subject which will come under discussion is the feminine or matriarchal part of the Northern tradition. The Norse myths, and certainly the sagas, tend to suggest that the Northern tradition is an overwhelmingly male creation. In the available source material, the feminine influence is not very obvious, and in popular books the

Vikings are portrayed as stereotypes of male aggressiveness. This picture is only partly true and is colored by the fact that most of the literature about the Vikings was written down during the Christian era.

Every argument has at least two sides, but history is always written by the winners, never by the losers, and everything that the Christian scholars wrote down at that time, be it an account of actual events or their interpretation of our beliefs, is biased. It should always be borne in mind that the Northern tradition is far older than the Viking Age, which distorted certain older aspects of the religion, particularly in regard to the goddesses.

• 2 •

ELDER FUTHARK

Origins of the Runes

The earliest origins of the runes as an exoteric alphabet are clouded in obscurity. During the last century, various hypotheses were put forward but, because of lack of evidence, no one has been able to prove any of them conclusively. In the main there are three different theories: the Latin/Greek theory, the Etruscan/North Italic theory, and the Native theory. For the benefit of those who are especially interested in the subject, I shall describe the various theories briefly and mention relevant books and authors.

A Danish scientist, L. F. A. Wimmer, was of the opinion that the runes were an offspring of the Latin alphabet. He based his theory on the parallels that exist between various rune-signs and Latin letters, for example *F, R, H,* and *B.* Furthermore, he also believed that the futhark system was designed by a single individual. The date he suggested for the introduction of the futhark was approximately 300 C.E. This assumption has been shown to be incorrect, because the first runic archaeological finds are dated earlier. The Swedish runologist O. van Friesen put forward the theory that runic writing descended from the Greek cursive script and was carried northward by the Goths around the third century. Again, this date is too late. It is more likely that the Latin, Greek, and runic alphabets all descend from an older system of North Italic origin. This is the opinion of two runologists, C. G. S. Marstrander and M. Hammarstrom. It is not precisely known who the North Italic people were, although they were probably a part of what we now call the Alpine Germanics.

It seems that we are dealing with a fusion of two systems, partly native-Germanic and partly Etruscan in origin. Various runes and rune-like inscriptions and sigils have been found all over Europe. These symbols were somehow developed into the Common Germanic runic futhark system as we know it; whether the system came about through a slow process of growth and integration or as a result of the endeavors of a limited number of initiates, or even of one individual, we shall probably never be able to establish. My personal belief is that the runic system is partly native and partly North Italic.

We cannot tell precisely which German tribe it was that spread the rune-script all over the Germanic territory. It may have been the Marcomanni, a tribe living near the area of present-day Austria, or the Cimbri, or else the Heruli. (It is not even certain whether the Cimbri were a Germanic-speaking tribe, as the evidence supplied by the Gundestrup cauldron suggests that this tribe was Celtic.) Heruli, or Erilaz, appears to be the name of one of the oldest Germanic tribes, which inhabited the area of present-day Denmark. "Heruli" was used in the Viking Age as a title for a type of rune-master and denotes a trained magician or shaman rather than someone who was merely able to chisel runes in stone. The evidence indicates that the Heruli were most probably the people who disseminated knowledge of the futhark, and by so doing their tribal name has been passed down throughout history as a title applied to those with special skills in rune-lore.

In addition to the historical origins of the runes as an esoteric alphabet, we must consider the evolution of occult, spiritual, and ethical principles encapsulated within them. It is therefore necessary to examine how the runes developed in the first place. Initially, the runes were simple, straightforward sigils representing a certain sound, usually a sound derived from the natural features of the environment in which our ancestors dwelt. For example, the first two runes of the futhark were obviously developed as synonyms for bovine creatures, whereas the third rune was a symbol for awesome natural forces which were represented by giants. Thus each rune has its associations built up through time, associations originally derived from a very simple animistic concept from which gradually developed the present complicated system of esoteric thought and a spiritual path of initiation. Sound is one of the ways in which Nature manifests itself, as in the sound of the wind, the sound of the sea, and the sounds of animals. Sound is magic, and it is creative.

The spiritual values of the runes have developed throughout the ages, primarily through the Germanic thought-world, and have a very close connection with the old Germanic religion and mythology. The attributes and qualities ascribed to each rune form a particular part of the Germanic way of thinking, the Germanic experience, and the Germanic way of relating to the environment. As such, the runes can be regarded, from a multidimensional point of view, as the corpus of various symbols of differing origins combined or distilled into a consistent whole. Those peoples who long ago used the runes for magical and spiritual purposes were the spiritual creators of the runic futhark in the form that has been passed on to us, their descendants. The evidence for this is that a substantial part of the runic inscriptions have been preserved in Germania, by which I mean Germany, Frisia, Holland, England, and Scandinavia. Wherever the runes originated from physically, the early Germanic peoples established and expanded the system, developing it as a magical and spiritual discipline which is as relevant and useful nowadays as it was in the past.

It is recorded in the Northern mythology that the runes were given to Odin (i.e., Wodan) when he voluntarily sacrificed himself on the World Tree, Yggdrasil. Certain shamanic techniques were known to various primitive, heathen cultures—such as the Native Americans, Siberians, Swami people, and, no doubt, the ancient Germanic peoples—in which a shaman underwent a similar process of voluntary suffering in order to transcend the barriers between life and death, and thereby gain occult knowledge. It is feasible that the myth that describes Odin hanging on Yggdrasil was, in fact, referring to just such a shaman, who was probably already familiar with some of the rune-signs and who, through initiation on the Tree, attained cosmic consciousness and insight into the spiritual and esoteric qualities of the runes. Thus enlightened, he may have composed the twenty-four-rune futhark. This theory is all the more likely because, as later study will prove, there is a sound reason why the futhark should consist of twenty-four runes, each in its appointed place with the only exceptions being the last two runes, which may be interchanged. To alter the order or position of any of the other runes would invalidate the entire combination of spiritual symbolism presented by the complete futhark. Rune-masters therefore reject the superfluous and unhistorical notion of a twenty-fifth, so-called "blank" rune.

From the elder futhark—as it is technically known—consisting of twenty-four runes, two major futhark variants have developed. Firstly, the Anglo-Saxon futhark arose from an earlier Anglo-Friesian futhark. This development was a direct result of the migration of the Saxons, Angles, Jutes, and Friesians to England. They spoke closely related and mutually intelligible dialects, but subsequently the language underwent certain mutations which necessitated the creation of new runes to represent additional sounds in the language. The futhark was thus expanded to accommodate the sound changes which had occurred. This development began in the middle of the fifth century. Somewhat later, in the eighth century in Scandinavia, the original twenty-four-rune futhark was reduced to a futhark of sixteen runes. This was also a result of linguistic changes. From a magical perspective, it might be considered significant that the development of the Nordic futhark adhered to the division of the futhark into aettir (groups of eight which reflect the ancient mystical numerological tradition of Northern Europe).

In the rest of this chapter I propose to work through the runes in futhark order. The runes are divided into three aettir. After each aett there appears a summary of the significance of that aett in cosmological terms.

In agreement with most authors who have investigated the modern-day relevance of the runes to magical practice, I deal in this work with the elder futhark, or Common Germanic futhark, not only because it has a status of historical primacy, but also because the runes take us back to the earliest origins of the stirrings of magical consciousness among our ancestors. The elder futhark therefore presents this esoteric lore to modern humans in its purest and most authoritative form, devoid of all post-heathen monotheistic influences.

First Aett

Germanic name ◆ FEHU

Anglo-Saxon name ◆ FEOH

Old Norse name ◆ FE

Phonetic value ◆ F

Traditional meaning ◆ cattle, wealth

This is the first rune of the first aett. The classical meaning of Fehu as handed down through various sources is cattle or wealth, in particular, movable wealth. In a so-called primitive society such as existed in Northern Europe when the runes were first developed, cattle represented wealth. The status of the chieftain was usually measured by the number of cattle owned. In those days, cattle provided both a livelihood and a barter medium used in much the same way as money is used nowadays. Hence the present-day association with the modern English word "fee," by which name this rune is also known.

The possession of money or wealth means that a certain level of responsibility is required on the part of the possessor. This is very well expressed in the *Anglo-Saxon Rune-Poem*, quoted here in the translation by R. I. Page:

Wealth is a comfort to all men,
Yet everyone must give it away freely,
If he wants to gain glory in the Lord's sight.

and in the *Norwegian Rune-Poem*:

Wealth causes strife among kinsmen,
The wolf lurks in the forest.

Both of these poems deal with the attitude of the individual towards wealth. In the first poem he is advised not to be attached to wealth but to give it away freely, so improving his own state of being. Mystically speaking, "to cast his lot for judgment before the Lord" is to create positive karma or, in terminology faithful to the Northern tradition, to improve one's individual wyrd. The "Lord" referred to in this poem is the Christian God, but in actual fact the lord of judgment in the Northern tradition is the god Tyr. The *Norwegian Rune-Poem* warns against the misery that wealth can cause in a family. Anyone who has ever witnessed a will being read, or the sharing of an estate when the deceased died intestate, will be aware of the real identity of that wolf lurking in the forest. Greed and envy are the negative connotations related to the concept of wealth. The rune-poems advise a responsible attitude towards wealth.

On a deeper level of kenning, Fehu is related to the Vanir deities Niord, Frey, and Freyja. Niord is the god directly related to wealth. He is the god to invoke if you need help in extricating yourself from financial difficulties. Frey and Freyja are fertility deities directly connected with livestock and especially with the newly born cattle in spring.

Freyja wears a necklace named Brisingamen, which is a symbol of fertility. Tradition tells us that this necklace is of gold or amber, both costly materials. Freyja had to earn her right to this necklace by sleeping with four dwarves, who represent the four elements of earth, air, fire and water which, working together in balance, engender fertility. One of Freyja's nicknames is Syr, which means "sow." A female pig is an excellent fertility symbol. Nowadays, the word "pig" has derogatory connotations, but in the ancient tradition of the North, pigs are sacred. Frey has a golden boar, Gullinbursti, on whose back he travels. Freyja has a battle swine called Hildisvin.

On the next level of kenning, Fehu is the rune that represents the creative fire which emerges from Muspelheim. In its creative mode, the fire of Muspelheim is ever present. The same fire, at the Ragnarok, is encountered in its destructive mode, when Surt and the sons of Muspel devastate the worlds, so completing the cycle. In its creative mode, the fire impregnates the primordial ice and out of this union is born the cosmic cow, Audhumla (again cattle). She is the representation of the Mother Goddess who gives birth to the giants as well as to the Aesir. She nourishes all that lives. Audhumla is depicted with many teats and she feeds all living beings without discrimination. Giants and gods alike are fed by the primordial cow. The rune Fehu therefore has a predominantly female polarity.

Relevant to Fehu is this passage from the *Havamal:*

Cattle die, kindred die,
Every man is mortal:
But the good name never dies
Of one who has done well.

Cattle die, kindred die,
Every man is mortal:
But I know one thing that never dies,
The glory of the great dead.
[TRANSLATION BY W. H. AUDEN AND PAUL B. TAYLOR]

Here we see the idea of wealth conveyed in a non-materialistic sense, that of the reputation which one leaves behind after death. In Teutonic ethics, a person's reputation was his or her most precious commodity, and great store was placed upon the regard in which one was held after one's death.

> *The first charm I know is unknown to rulers*
> *Or any of human kind:*
> *HELP it is named, for help it can give*
> *In hours of sorrow and anguish.*

This translation, by W. H. Auden and P. B. Taylor, is of the first spell in the *Havamal* (stanza 138). Fehu is one of three runes contained in the spell.

In the *Sigdrifumal* is the following verse:

> *Help-runes you should know if you would help loosen*
> *The child from the woman's womb:*
> *Mark them on her hands, take hold of her wrists,*
> *And invoke the aid of the elves.*

This corresponds neatly to the spell mentioned in the *Havamal*.

In divination, one usually interprets the runes on a less enigmatic level of kenning, depending largely on what level the reading is done. Generally, Fehu represents the ability of the individual to create or to maintain wealth. Fehu also applies to the energy to create wealth, which is available at the time the reading takes place. For example, the querent may wish to know his or her present financial state and its possible developments in the near future.

Germanic name ◆ URUZ

Anglo-Saxon name ◆ UR

Old Norse name ◆ UR

Phonetic value ◆ U

Traditional meaning ◆ aurochs

The auroch was a ferocious native species of wild ox which is now extinct. The energy behind this rune is the life force of the masculine polarity, the unconscious drive for manifestation. While the energy of Fehu is the active element in creation, the fire of Muspelheim, the fire of Fehu interacts with the energy of Uruz, which is the element of ice, and life is generated. Uruz contains a primal Earth energy—the inextinguishable impulse *to be,* the energy behind the forms of nature which survives all attempts at destruction, reforming itself in new patterns when the old ones are outworn. So the energy of Uruz is indestructible, raw, primitive, and unbelievably strong. Uruz symbolizes strength, persistence, durability, and adaptability to environmental changes. On a higher plane, Uruz represents healing energy—a strong, restorative, recuperative physical process. This is the energy that manifests itself along ley lines. Fehu and Uruz are closely interlinked, both relating to cattle. They are a pair, and operate together in a process of creating and sustaining the life forms on this plane.

In olden days, in Continental Germania, the young warriors were subjected to a test of strength, an ordeal in which they had to go out armed with only the most basic weapons and single-handedly slay an aurochs, bringing back the horns as proof that they had succeeded. (The horns were highly prized as drinking vessels.) The hunting and slaying of the aurochs was a risky business, and probably the chances of success were not very great.

The *Anglo-Saxon Rune-Poem* tells us that:

The aurochs is a savage beast,
is fierce and has huge horns.
A great roamer of the moorlands,
It fights with its horns.
It is a courageous brute.
    [TRANSLATION BY R. I. PAGE]

The youth who succeeded in this test of strength became accepted in the tribe as an adult male, a warrior. Such a tradition is usual in tribal societies throughout the world. It was necessary for the tribe to select the strong from the weak, because the survival of the tribe depended on the strength of its warriors. Therefore Uruz teaches us patience, endurance, courage, and the application of aggression at the right time and under the right circumstances. In modern society aggression is seen as a solely negative force. People are encouraged to be docile and the weak rule the strong by denying them the right to be strong. However, aggression can also be seen as a creative force, a force that breaks down outworn forms and builds new ones. Aggression expresses itself in the survival instinct, the unconscious force which urges one to struggle and to survive against all odds. The correct application of this force—i.e., when controlled by personal discipline—makes us both resourceful and persistent. In other words, Uruz is the will to live, the primal impulse to be and to become. In German and Dutch, *ur* means "primal" or "ancient"; this is contained in the name of one of the Norns, Urd.

Uruz is very much associated with growth and, through conflict and challenge, the overcoming of obstacles, the force to assert oneself, and to assert one's right to one's own space. This interpretation is also applicable on the inner levels of being. In this context Uruz symbolizes the primeval uncontrolled force in one's own psyche—those baser forces which we try to contact and bring under the control of the will, transforming them into an inexhaustible source of creative energy.

On a subtle level, the force of Uruz can be felt in Nature just before spring, when one can sense the tension of new growth building up. This energy can be felt in trees just before they start sprouting, after which the energy visibly manifests itself in the appearance of the first foliage. On a practical level of working, Uruz is the healing rune, in combination with other runes which we will discuss later. Uruz can bestow rejuvenation and regeneration of physical health. Thus the second charm in the *Havamal* says:

I know a second that the sons of men
Must learn who wish to be leeches [i.e., healers].

A simple and effective way to enhance one's strength at a moment when it is needed is to take a glass of clean water and, with the index and middle fingers, trace an Uruz rune over the surface of the water. Visualize the rune in brilliant red, letting the power of the rune charge the water. Maintain the visualization for several seconds and then drink the water. It is also helpful to chant the rune while visualizing it. Having charged the water by this method, you may find that it tastes different and has acquired a metallic taste. This is fine. It means that the charm has worked!

In divination, Uruz represents the condition of your strength, on both a physical and a psychological level. It can indicate new opportunities and encouragement. Sometimes it means taking a risk. Uruz inverted would mean that the risk should not be taken. Uruz inverted, in general, counsels one to caution, because one is in a weak position.

The Uruz rune is linked with the god Thor, the Thunderer.

Germanic name ◆ THURISAZ

Anglo-Saxon name ◆ THORN

Old Norse name ◆ THURS

Phonetic value ◆ TH

Traditional meaning ◆ giant

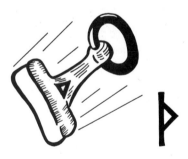

Thurisaz is the third rune in the first aett, and its element is fire. The traditional name of this rune is Thurisaz, which is a very ancient name for Thor and appears in literature alongside the names Wodenaz and Teiwaz. Thurisaz also means "giant." This has been preserved in present-day Icelandic, in which the word *thurs* still means "giant." The Christians chose to translate this as "demon," which seemed to be their stock method of propaganda against anything they wished to eliminate. Thurisaz represents both Thor and the giants. Thor has some characteristics in common with the giants and is certainly the only one of the Aesir who matches the giants in physical strength. In Northern mythology, the giants represent the forces of chaos, and Thor is the one who keeps those forces under control.

The Anglo-Saxon Christians went even further in eliminating knowledge of this rune by renaming it Thorn. Quite possibly they knew what they were doing, considering the enormous powers contained in the Thurisaz rune.

The *Anglo-Saxon Rune-Poem* comments on the Thorn:

> *The Thorn is most sharp: an evil thing*
> *To take a grip on, extremely grim*
> *For any man who rest amongst them.*
> [OSBORN'S TRANSLATION]

Here we are warned that the Thurisaz rune is evil. This is mostly true, as has been proven to me on several occasions. Thurisaz is the most powerful aid in harmful rune workings, but it is so double-sided that it can backfire very easily and very quickly. Conversely, it is just as powerful in procuring protection. Most of the runes have either a neutral mediating position, as in the case of the non-invertibles, or else distinct positive (upright) or negative (inverted) positions, from which the influence of that rune can be deduced in a given reading. Not so with Thurisaz! Although it is reversible and therefore should be clear-cut in its meaning, i.e., either positive or negative, it does not work in the same way as do most of the runes. Thurisaz is either active energy directed outwards, or passive Thurisaz energy contained or directed inwards. The energy of Thurisaz is at once completely neutral and of immense potential. A friend, meditating on this rune, received the visual image of a nuclear explosion. On an occult level, this would describe rather accurately the potential of Thurisaz.

Primarily, this rune is a carrier and can be combined with various other runes to ensure effectiveness in a working. The power of

Thurisaz is easy to tap and the best method of invoking it is through emotion, whatever the nature of that emotion. The more emotion that is put into a working, the more successful the working is likely to be. But make no mistake—Thurisaz is probably the most dangerous rune in the whole futhark. This may be the reason other rune-writers are parsimonious with their information regarding this rune.

Some of our kinsmen have reproached me for giving away too much in my descriptions of the runes. While I fully appreciate their genuine concern, I believe that in the long run it is more beneficial to the people of the North that the knowledge is spread more or less indiscriminately, and I do not feel that it is up to me to make judgments on what is to be taught and what is to be withheld. I believe that each individual of our folk is entitled to all the information available, and I trust in our inherent ability to act responsibly. As far as others are concerned, the runes have excellent Inner Plane guardians and misuse will be most unlikely.

As we have already seen, the first two runes of the futhark, Fehu and Uruz, express a more or less unconscious dynamic force. With regard to human consciousness, the third rune, Thurisaz, is virtually on the borderline of consciousness: neither totally unconscious, nor totally conscious as is the next rune, Ansuz, which governs consciousness. For this purpose, where Thurisaz is concerned, the term "subconsciousness" is appropriate. The Thurisaz rune is submerged on levels of the subconscious mind which are easily accessible. In its most negative form, Thurisaz represents the shadow in the unconscious, the repressed and unacknowledged collection of garbage amassed throughout life or foisted on us by the environment and its social conditions. However, as depth psychologists are aware, once the shadow is acknowledged and integrated in the individual's consciousness, it can be of great value, and can then become a power source and a reliable ally. Thus the Thurisaz rune can be regarded as the true will in an unrealized condition.

Another aspect of Thurisaz is of a sexual, libidinal nature. The shape of the rune is decidedly phallic and has strong fertility connotations. Thor himself is a god much concerned with matters of fertility. His hammer is an unmistakable symbol of life-giving fertility, and the shape of the Thurisaz rune resembles a hammer. The oldest conceived ideas about our gods were much more fertility oriented than the war aspects which developed later. To add weight to the argument that this rune has very strong fertility associations, Thurisaz is the third dynamic aspect of the force of fertility and, as such, relates to the two previous runes, Fehu and Uruz. It represents the combination, or rather the result of the interaction, of Fehu and Uruz. In our mythology, out of the fusion of Muspelheim and Nifelheim, which represent the forces of fire and frost respectively, the first living creature, Audhumla the cow, was brought into being. The next being to be formed was a giant named Ymir. Bearing in mind that Thurisaz means "giant," it is apparent that there is a logical sequence to the runes, a reason they appear in the futhark in the order that they do. It is small wonder that deeper knowledge relating to the many meanings of the Thurisaz rune at various levels had been concealed by the Christians. With their hostile attitudes towards the natural forces, the force that they considered most evil of all was, not surprisingly, sex. The full weight and meaning of the energy that psychologists term libido, which in itself encompasses much more than merely sex, is the energy directly contained in the Thurisaz rune.

In a depth-psychological reading for counseling purposes, an inverted Thurisaz rune is often an indication of blockages in the creative energies and of all sorts of inhibiting forces in the unconscious. Other runes that may appear in such a reading may indicate a means of dealing with the blockage in a constructive manner.

On a magical level, Thurisaz is an excellent binder, or what in our lore is described as a "war-fetter." When skillfully applied in combination with a few other runes, it can be used to stop enemy action and even to feed all negative energies back to their source.

It says in the *Havamal* (stanza 140):

I know a third: in the thick of battle,
If my need be great enough,
It will blunt the edges of enemy swords,
Their weapons will make no wounds.

Of course, nowadays this is more likely to apply to metaphorical weapons such as the pen or the mouth as opposed to real weapons like swords and spears. The phrase "If my need be great enough" means two things. Firstly, the person who is sending the charm must be in a situation so desperate that there is no alternative course of action. If the sender has his "back to the wall," he will be able to muster the psychic energy required for a full performance of this kind of working. Secondly, the quotation from the *Havamal* names another rune, Nauthiz or Need, which usually works very well in combination with Thurisaz in a working of this nature.

The various modes of energies represented by the Thurisaz rune are described in detail in the *Saga of Siegfried* and in the fairy tale of the Sleeping Beauty, who, incidentally, in the Dutch version of the story is called Doornroosje, which translates literally as "Thornrose." In the *Sigdrifumal*, Odin uses a sleep-thorn to send Sigdrifa to sleep, thereby taking away her immortality. The same happens in Wagner's *Ring*, where Wotan sends Brunnhilde to sleep as a punishment for acting as Wotan's true will (as already explained, one of the modes of Thurisaz is the true will). By revoking his earlier order to save Siegmund, Wotan rejects his own true will, submitting instead to the will of his consort Frigg, who in this case represents conventionality. Realizing this, Brunnhilde acts accordingly. Unfortunately, her best intentions are doomed to disaster, as Wotan interferes and himself kills Siegmund. In revenge, the god sends Brunnhilde to sleep, thus rendering her unconscious of her will; and at her own request, Wotan surrounds the place where she lies asleep with a ring of fire.

In *Sleeping Beauty* the heroine pricks her finger on a spindle and falls asleep for a hundred years. The hero has to fight his way through a dense barrier of thorns to reach her.

In both these stories, we see Thurisaz as a protective device reflecting the manner in which the thorn protects the rose. We also see it in its opposite mode as a phallic symbol, when Brunnhilde loses her immortality through the action of Thurisaz, which is symbolized by her loss of virginity to Siegfried. As a virgin, Brunnhilde represents the self-contained, immortal goddess. By surrendering herself to a man, she loses her immortal aspect and her destiny becomes linked with his.

In *Sleeping Beauty,* the thorn is a symbol of masculine creative energy, the rose being the opposite symbol, psychologically speaking. In the *Saga of Siegfried*, Brunnhilde is surrounded by a ring of fire, so that none but the bravest hero dares pass through it. A ring of Thurisaz runes drawn around a circle will certainly keep out anything or anybody undesirable.

Germanic name ◆ ANSUZ

Anglo-Saxon name ◆ OS

Old Norse name ◆ ASS

Phonetic value ◆ A

Traditional meaning ◆ A god

This is the fourth rune of the futhark. Whereas Thurisaz represents the forces of chaos, Ansuz represents order, the defenders of which, in our mythology, are the Aesir. In Norse cosmology, after the creation of the giant Ymir (chaos), another being was created, Buri, who was the ancestor of the Aesir (order). Buri fathered Borr, although it is not mentioned who was Borr's mother. Borr married Bestla, who was also of the giant race.

From this we see that there is a certain amount of integration and cooperation between the two opposing forces of chaos (giants) and order (Aesir). The Norse cosmology is similar in this respect to other constructs of opposition from other parts of the world, such as the Chinese concept of yin and yang.

From the union of Borr and Bestla emerges a triplicity: Odin, Villi, and Ve, who usually are seen as one. (Those familiar with the Craft will notice here that instead of having a triple goddess, we in the North are more acquainted with the concept of a triple god.) Needless to say, our concept of the male triplicity is older than that of the Christian trinity. Furthermore, the integration of the forces of order and chaos explains why Odin, albeit a god of order, has an element of chaos within him and tends to use unconventional means to achieve his ends.

The Ansuz rune represents consciousness, intelligence, communication, and reason. The element of Odin, the godforce behind this rune, is air. Air is a penetrating medium necessary to all life-forms. It is through air that sound becomes audible. In an airless environment, sound cannot be heard, and sound is the other main esoteric feature of the Ansuz rune, including the origins of sound as a medium of communication between people, and the sounds of Nature. The magical use of sound to expand one's consciousness and the chanting of runes in a manner in which sound is closely linked with breath can give amazing results.

One of the most magical sounds is the sound of the wind. In Holland, Odin the wind god is heard loud and clear, but he is little known or appreciated. The howling wind had a special effect on me as a child, especially in autumn. The wind is also largely helpful in spreading seeds from plant to plant, which shows that it acts as a medium for fertilization, and reveals as well yet another aspect of communication. Ideas germinate and are spread through communication. The extra dimension of knowledge gained when discussing the runes with a like-minded individual illustrates the communicative aspect of Odin as the power of consciousness.

The *Anglo-Saxon Rune-Poem* says:

The mouth is origin of every speech,
The support of wisdom and comfort of councillors,
and to every man blessing and confidence.

[KEMBLE'S TRANSLATION]

Speech is one of Odin's attributes, as are poetry and the aforementioned magical uses of sound. It is no coincidence that Odin, the god of words and communication, is credited with giving humankind knowledge of the runes. The philosophy contained in the Northern tradition maintains that we are descendants of the gods; and in this respect, the Ansuz rune relates to the ancestors. On a higher level, Ansuz represents the life energy that is called "prana" in the East, and appropriately "od" or "odic" energy by various German magicians. The old Icelandic name for this energy is to be found in the *Voluspa,* stanza 19:

Breath they had not, nor blood nor senses,
Nor language possessed, nor life-hue:
Odin gave them breath, Hoenir senses,
Blood and life-hue Lothur gave.

In the Icelandic original, the word for breath is *ond,* which means "vital breath." This is the gift of Odin.

On a practical working level, Ansuz is the counterbalance to Thurisaz. As Thurisaz is used to fetter, Ansuz can be used to unfetter. It is said in the fourth spell in the *Havamal:*

I know a fourth one: it will free me quickly
If foes should fetter me fast
With strong chains, a chant that makes
Fetters spring from the feet,
Bonds burst from the hands.

So the Ansuz rune can be used for releasing fetters. This rule is also true for psychological fetters, such as anxieties or phobias in the individual's unconscious mind, which act as a hindrance preventing further personal growth or spiritual progress. In a mundane sense these fetters can be understood as an impediment to a more successful career.

Germanic name ◆ RAIDO

Anglo-Saxon name ◆ RAD

Old Norse name ◆ REID

Phonetic value ◆ R

Traditional meaning ◆ riding

R. W. V. Elliott translates this rune as "riding" or "journey," which has been the accepted interpretation in runic circles as the meaning of this rune. Riding has the more symbolic connotations of creating movement, generating motion, taking charge of situations, being in control, taking the initiative, starting a new venture, decision-making or directing a course of action.

Rad, the Anglo-Saxon name of the rune, is cognated with the German *Rat* and Dutch *raad,* meaning "counsel" or "advice," which is one of the meanings of Raido. It gives sound advice in a reading. The governing body of a community is often called *de raad* in Dutch, which literally translates as "the council." There happens to be another word of Gothic origin, *raiht,* which in my opinion is closely related to *rad* or Raido. This word means "right," or in Dutch *recht,* the related verb being *rechten,* meaning in English "to do right, to dispense judgment, to litigate." The Dutch word for "judge" is *rechter. Raiht* is linked to the institute of kingship. In the old days kings had the task of determining what was right or wrong. The Latin word for king, *rex,* derives from the same source as *raiht.* Thus we can clearly establish that the Raido rune is a rune that speaks to us of leadership and nobility. In olden times, nobility was not something which was automatically acquired by virtue of birth. Rather, it was a position which was earned or held by merit, and it implied moral responsibility and integrity. In Dutch and German, the words for knight are *ridder* and *Ritter* respectively, which are again related to Raido. The traditional image of a knight is strongly associated with the aforementioned virtues of honorable conduct and chivalrous behavior. Raido refers to the correct balance between respecting the rights of others in the tribe and maintaining one's own individual rights; "tribe" is to be understood in the old sense as a group of people of similar descent sharing more or less the same social and spiritual values.

Furthermore, by extrapolating from the foregoing ideas, a magical and depth-psychological interpretation of the Raido rune can be obtained. The magical significance of this rune relates to the ability to move within one's natural limits and, consequently, to become aware of what these limits are. The rune also refers to the power of making a conscious decision and the discipline to carry it out. This rune can also be used in a magical working to establish control over one's own circumstances, and to put things in order and make them subject to one's will. Here the concept of will is used in the Thelemic sense, that is, as the higher magical will.

Inherent in Raido are the ideas of freedom and moral responsibility to the Self (even if this conflicts with the norms prevailing in the present-day social structure), as well as the knowledge of right and wrong in the personal developed conscience and the courage to act accordingly. Thus, working with the force of Raido means to be in charge of your own path in life; to keep your own counsel; to ride, not to be ridden; as far as is possible, to be master of your own circumstances; to extend gradually the degree of control that you exercise over these circumstances; and finally to make a conscious choice of the direction you wish to follow. How much of yourself is being ridden, so to speak, depends on your magical control, i.e., the conscious controlling the ego as a rider controls his horse, or a driver his vehicle.

Raido inverted can simply mean the opposite of what it means in the upright position: the opposite of right, or whatever is wrong. Sometimes this quite literally shows up in a reading as a warning, especially when the question asked implies a certain choice or involves decision-making. The inverted Raido rune tells you unmistakably, "No! This is wrong. Do not take this path." On a more complex psychological level, Raido inverted often implies domination by influences outside your control. The more you allow external factors to dominate you and to take control of your life, the more you create weakness, a lack of strength, an empty space, a vacuum. Once this weakness, or vacuum, has been produced, something else can then step in and take control. This something else can be a negative influence from the personal unconscious or, equally possible, someone with a stronger will ruling your life for you.

From the preceding arguments, we can deduce that the Raido rune is a rune of order. (I would almost say law and order, were it not that these concepts in present-day society have connotations of enforcing the state's authority, rather than referring to the ordered cycles and laws of Nature.) As was stated in the section on the Ansuz rune, the Aesir created order out of chaos, as is illustrated in the *Voluspa*, verses 9 and 10:

> *Sun turned from the south, sister of Moon,*
> *Her right arm rested on the rim of Heaven;*
> *She had no inkling where her hall was,*
> *Nor Moon a notion of what might he had,*
> *The planets knew not where their places were.*

> *The High Gods gathered in council*
> *In their Hall of judgment, all the rulers:*
> *To Night and to Nightfall their names gave,*
> *The Morning they named and the Mid-Day, Mid-Winter,*
>   *Mid-Summer, for the assigning of years.*
> [TRANSLATION BY W. H. AUDEN AND PAUL B. TAYLOR]

These verses from the *Voluspa* state that the gods set the Sun and Moon in their appropriate course, and, in so doing, instituted the order of time, namely day and night, and the seasons of the year. Thus the first act of the gods is to create order out of chaos. The notion of a cyclical motion of the Sun and the Moon around the Earth invokes the image of a wheel. (The word for "wheel" is *rad* in Dutch, and we know that the Anglo-Saxon name for this rune is Rad.)

The gods established a clear division of the year, and in most magical traditions the year can be divided into eight equal parts, like an eight-spoked wheel. The eight spokes are connected to the eight directions of the wind representing the four quarters and the four cross-quarters, at which are held the eight festivals of the heathen year, namely two solstices, two equinoxes, and the four other festivals, which in this country are named Lammas, Samhain, Candlemas, and Beltane. (See the Runic Calendar on page 148.) In virtually all ancient magical traditions these festivals were celebrated with religious ceremonies and rituals. Remnants of these pagan festivals which survived throughout Christian times include both Yule and Easter. At the Yule Celebration in the eastern part of Holland, a burning eight-spoked wheel was rolled down a hill to celebrate the return of the Sun.

Besides being a rune of control movement and direction, Raido is also a rune of repetitive movement and thus of ritual. Edred Thorsson mentions this aspect of the Raido rune in *Futhark: A Handbook of Rune Magic*. However, it might be worthwhile expanding on this information by giving more details of the use of ritual and of its relevance to the Northern tradition. Ritual can be a repetitive series of actions designed to create a specific effect on the human mind. It is a psychological tool used to shut off the mundane self and tune the mind into the more subtle vibrations. A well-constructed ritual can clear a space and a time for magical work without outside interference. Moreover, it is a means of magical control, which as we have seen is one of the associations of the Raido rune.

The verse on Raido in the *Anglo-Saxon Rune-Poem* is as follows:

In the hall Rad is pleasant
For every warrior
And very energetic for the man
Who sits on the back of a powerful horse
Covering the mile long road.
 [PAGE'S TRANSLATION]

The meaning of this verse is obscure. It is possibly a censored version of an older, bawdier verse. The phrase "In the hall Rad is pleasant" could very well have had sexual overtones.

Finally, on a very esoteric level Raido can also be used for shamanic traveling to the underworld. Our myths relate that after Baldur was slain, Hermod, another son of Odin, rode to Hel to negotiate the conditions for Baldur's return. The Hel-ride took nine days and nine nights, the same length of time that Odin hung on the Yggdrasil. *Ygg* is another name for Odin, and *drasil* is usually translated as "horse" or "steed." In Old Norse, kenning Yggdrasil is also taken to mean "gallows." This is relevant to the admittedly barbaric custom that our ancestors had of hanging their enemies as a sacrifice to Odin, albeit with the mitigating factor that, rather than allowing their prisoners to suffocate slowly to death for twenty minutes, it was the usual custom to dispatch them quickly with a spear as they were hanging from the gallows. The nine days' and nights' duration of the Hel-ride, as well as the nine nights and days of Odin's ordeal on the Tree, suggest an ancient Northern initiation practice.

Hermod's ride to Hel has obvious connotations with Raido. Raido is indeed a rune which we would expect to lend the ability to travel in other realms of consciousness, as Raido represents the ability to travel to other realms of reality (symbolized in the Northern mythology as the nine worlds). Raido could, for example, be used in conjunction with Ehwaz as the vehicle of travel to, for example, Hagalaz, symbolizing the realm of the underworld; but more will be offered on this when we discuss Ehwaz and Hagalaz later.

Germanic name ♦ KENAZ

Anglo-Saxon name ♦ CEN

Old Norse name ♦ KAUN

Phonetic value ♦ K or hard C

Traditional meaning ♦ torch, light

The verse in the *Anglo-Saxon Rune-Poem* says:

> *The Torch familiar*
> *To the living, a flame*
> *Is blinding and brilliant.*
> *It bums most often*
> *Where royal folk*
> *Are at rest within.*
>
> [Translation by Osborne]

Most rune-workers interpret the meaning of the Kenaz rune as "torch," which has always been regarded as a symbol of knowledge, consciousness, and intellect. Kenaz means "to know"; the English dialect verb *ken* and the Dutch and German *kennen* all mean "to know, to be familiar with."

Furthermore, it means not only "to know" but "to be able to." Another Dutch word related to Kenaz is *kunst,* which can be translated as "art" or "craft" and to which the English word "cunning" corresponds. Kenaz indicates the ability to seek, gain, apply, and recognize. It also indicates the learning and teaching process.

The primary aspect of Kenaz is the torch, that is, the torch of knowledge which is to be passed on to the next generation of kin or *cyn* (both these words are of Anglo-Saxon origin and related to Kenaz). The basic meaning of the word "kin" indicates members of the same family or blood relatives. However, "kin" may also be interpreted in a wider concept as like-minded people of the same tribal origins. The Old English word *cyning* is also related to Kenaz. *Cyning* meant "king"—the royal folk referred to in the *Anglo-Saxon Rune-Poem*. The king, according to the esoteric tradition, had to be a descendant of Woden. He acted as the focal point of the collective folk-soul, for the king was the torch-bearer of the folk's conscious-ness and conscience. He was also the carrier of the hamingja or "luck" of his people. In other old mystery traditions, such as that of ancient Egypt, we often find evidence that the king was also the high priest of the mysteries.

Although most of our ancient knowledge has disappeared, there is no reason to assume that there was not a similar practice in the oldest traditions of our folk. Viewed in a more contemporary man-ner, the "royalty" referred to in the rune-poem may very well have a more spiritual meaning, referring to the initiates who are the spiri-tual descendants of Woden and who carry aloft the torch of enlight-enment by virtue of their esoteric knowledge. Kenaz represents the light within; confidence in the knowledge that one is descended from the gods, kings, and tribal chieftains; and the responsibility to hand over the torch to the next generation, or else to share its light by teaching.

On a psychological level, the attributes of Kenaz are clarity of thought, insight, consciousness of the self, inborn or hereditary knowledge, confidence and trust in one's own intuition, and finally concentration and determined effort. Together with Raido, which is the rune which directs us towards the right path, Kenaz will shed light on this path that we may know where we are going. Together, they can guide us in the right direction.

The rune's element is fire in its contained form, that is to say the fire of enthusiasm and inspiration, also the fire employed by the blacksmith, for example, Weland. One of the gods who can be suc-cessfully invoked with a Kenaz working is Heimdal, who is known as the "Shining Ase." He is the Ase who teaches the runic mysteries to Kon, who is a human descendant of his. (Reference to this is made in the *Song of Rig*, which is one of the Eddaic poems which needs to be studied in order to acquire a proper working knowledge of the runes.) So it is Heimdal who taught the runes to humankind in Midgard.

The magical uses of this rune are quite varied. The most obvious use is the gaining of knowledge, by which is meant occult knowledge. In divination, Kenaz can be used to investigate the deeper background of problems encountered in a reading, the life situation, hidden reasons and origins, and the underlying causes of the effects. Kenaz can function as the light within—as a guiding torch when one wishes to explore the unknown territories of the inner realms. It can be used as a weapon to expel any unwanted influences, just as light expels darkness. Equally, it can be used to attract the right kind of influences. It all depends on the nature of the working and the other runes involved. Another aspect of Kenaz is the exposure of hidden, unknown or unacknowledged aspects of the self or of one's own or someone else's hidden motives.

The Kenaz rune can be used as an astral doorway—as a symbol which can be projected through "the veil," as it is known in the occult world. This rune will make the message clear to all concerned beyond the veil that the purpose of the journey is to gain knowledge or to obtain an answer to a specific question.

Kenaz also represents the transforming fire of the funeral pyre, for example, Baldur's. Thus Kenaz can be used as a beacon, a symbol for our own inner light, to take with us when we travel into the underworld to gain knowledge or information. It will guide us safely back; for traveling into the underworld can be dangerous—it is the realm of the dead. In the Eddas, Odin conjures up a dead volva and questions her about Baldur's fate. There are various ways of entering into an altered state of consciousness. Whatever method is used, Kenaz can be very helpful in recalling the experience after returning to normal consciousness.

Raido stands for traveling; Ehwaz can be used for the vehicle of travel; Hagalaz for Hel, a realm which may be the desired destination of the traveler; and Kenaz for one's own inner guidance while passing through other realities or in altered states of consciousness. This set of runes can serve as a formula for a bind-rune to help you in your traveling.

There are some German authorities, like Gorsleben, who state that the goddess Freyja has a connection with Kenaz. It took me a long time to understand his reasoning. However, there is an obscure link with the feminine Mysteries which can be explained in the following way: Freyja teaches Odin seidr, which is a form of witchcraft and includes "sex magic." Already we have seen that the teaching principle is part of the Kenaz complex. The Middle English word *cunt* relates to cunning. It is likely that this word is in fact far older than Middle English and is of Common Germanic origin. There is some evidence on this subject, in the form of related words and concepts. In *Sign and Design,* Alfred Kallir wrote that "...the rune Cen, its basic sense comes to the fore in the Old English *cennan,* with its two meanings: 'to beget' and 'to bring forth from the mind.'" In the same book, Cen is described as having a shape similar to that of female genitals. There is food for thought here.

Germanic name ♦ GEBO

Anglo-Saxon name ♦ GIFU

Old Norse name ♦ none

Phonetic value ♦ G

Traditional meaning ♦ gift

The god primarily associated with this rune is Odin, although some people allocate this rune to Thor. In fact, there are certain aspects of Gebo connected with marriage contracts and boundary markers which are indeed attributes of Thor. The element of this rune is air.

Giving, as well as receiving, has always been an important part of Northern European customs, as is well documented in the following stanzas quoted from the *Havamal.*

No man is so generous he will jibe at accepting
A gift in return for a gift,
No man so rich that it really gives him
Pain to be repaid.

With presents, friends should please each other,
With a shield or a costly coat:
Mutual giving makes for friendship
So long as life goes well.

A man should be loyal through life to friends,
And return gift for gift,
Laugh when they laugh, but with lies repay
A false foe who lies.

If you find a friend you fully trust
And wish for his good-will,
Exchange thoughts, exchange gifts,
Go often to his house.

[Translation by W. H. Auden and Paul B. Taylor]

These verses tell us of the social obligations attached to giving gifts, a custom widespread throughout the whole of the Northland, as is shown by the following verse of the *Anglo-Saxon Rune-Poem*:

Men's generosity is a grace and an honour,
As support and glory,
And help and sustenance to any outcast,
Who is deprived of them.

[Translation by R. I. Page]

These quotations make one point obvious: giving was not a one-sided affair. The implication is that a gift was given on the understanding that a gift was to be received in return. It is therefore not only a matter of giving, but also of receiving. Everything points to balance and equilibrium. The shape of the rune confirms this: two crossed bars, their arms of equal length. These verses deal with various attitudes and motives implicit in the acts of giving and receiving. The central theme is the preservation of balance, which applies equally to a "negative gift," as is clearly illustrated in the relevant stanza from the *Havamal* quoted on page 34. Although our people were renowned for their sense of honor and hospitality, I do not believe they were what we would nowadays describe as philanthropists. When a gift was made, it definitely had an obligation attached to it. The exchange of gifts was a serious matter. The best example of this attitude was the custom according to which the king acted as "giver of rings" on the understanding that the recipient of the ring was prepared to give his life in battle for the king, if required.

The aforementioned verse from the *Anglo-Saxon Rune-Poem* implies that an outcast could be rehabilitated by being offered a gift, which he would be expected to return. By this means he would be reintegrated into society. On this level, the Gebo rune is represented, in its most mundane function, as the law of compensation, in which nothing is given for nothing and there is always a price to pay. In present-day society there are too many people who are willing to take, but reluctant to give. Superficially they seem to get away with it quite comfortably, but on a deep psychological level they are paying for it with a loss of self-respect and consequently a loss of respect for and from others and for the rights of others. This inevitably results in the loss of hamingja in one's personal life. An illustration of this syndrome is the present high level of crime. It is again a question of equilibrium, where input equals output. On one level or another, an exchange of energy will occur.

In the most practical sense this rune refers to agreements, settlements, legal matters, and the honoring of contracts. A pleasant aspect of this rune is betrothal. The X-shaped sign representing a kiss at the end of a letter is in fact the Gebo rune. Furthermore, this rune was used by our people as a boundary marker. Virtues related to this rune include hospitality, generosity, and the ability to accept and give gifts with honor, for it is in most cases easier to give than to receive well.

The *Havamal* states:

Better not to ask than to overpledge
As a gift demands a gift,
Better not to send than to slay too many.

[TRANSLATION BY W. H. AUDEN AND PAUL B. TAYLOR]

This verse warns against the use of runes as a "negative gift," known in the sagas as a "sending." For each sending, a price has to be paid. In all kinds of magic, energy used has to be compensated for, and as each working changes the consciousness of the operator, it follows that each kind of energy invoked will affect the individual. Thus too many negative workings may contaminate your *wyrd*.

The concept of wyrd roughly corresponds in our mythology to the more widely accepted occult principle known as karma. Whenever a Gebo rune is included in a sending it should be borne in mind that a gift demands a gift in return; so do consider very carefully before you embark on any destructive working, as there will be an equal and opposite reaction. This warning is not a moralizing piece of quasi-Christian weakness, as is found so often in other occult traditions, but is rather a plain fact of the technicalities involved. One must be prepared to accept the consequences of one's actions, without any feelings of guilt or recrimination, which derive from Christianity and have no place in the Northern ethos. Of course, in a similar manner the Gebo rune can be employed in an act of positive giving. In accordance with the same law of a gift for a gift, there should also be something given by way of compensation. Unfortunately, this seems not always to be the case. The equal and opposite reaction can very well occur on a different level from that of normal consciousness or later in time.

In a magical working, Gebo is also very useful in binding two or more runes together. The overall magical principle of Gebo is the reconciliation of opposing forces, or the integration of complementary forces such as the male-female polarity.

On the esoteric level, the Gebo rune represents the gifts given by the gods to man. In the *Voluspa*, the story is told of how the three gods Odin, Hoenir, and Lodur encounter two trees, Ask (male tree) and Embla (female tree). Each of the gods gives a gift of life, by which Ask becomes the first man and Embla the first woman. The Gebo rune also implies the gifts that man gives to the gods in return. This principle is stated beautifully in the Gnostic Mass written by Aleister Crowley: "There is no part of me that is not of the gods." Man's gifts to the gods include service, loyalty, and dedication to whatever is conceived to be "the gods." In this sense Gebo implies sacrifice, although not in the sense of self-negation, which is yet one more attribute our culture acquired through the intervention of the Christian doctrine. Rather, Gebo implies the voluntary sacrifice of one's resources, time, and energy to whatever one holds sacred, without an expectation of reward other than the development of one's own potential. In extreme cases, this gift is the supreme sacrifice, made when someone gives up his or her life for their ideals, whatever they may be. On the highest level, the gift transcends both giver and receiver, thus implying the synthesis of gift, giver, and receiver of the gift in a unity; the result is the dissolving of barriers between all, the mystical union through complete giving, and the surrender of one's ego to the divine consciousness, which is also known as the higher Self. The giving of Self to Self is the core mystery of Odinic initiation.

Germanic name ♦ WUNJO

Anglo-Saxon name ♦ WYNN

Old Norse name ♦ none

Phonetic value ♦ W and sometimes V

Traditional meaning ♦ perfection

The god primarily associated with this rune is Wodan. Secondly, there is an obscure magical tradition from an Anglo-Saxon source connecting this rune with the god Uller or, to give him his Anglo-Saxon name, Wuldor.

The name of this rune is usually translated by other rune-workers as "joy" or "pasture." This association with joy is evidently derived from the rune-name's similarity to the modern German word *Wonne,* which may indeed be cognate with the Common Germanic word *Wunjo.* Although this interpretation is not altogether wrong, more light will be shed on our understanding of this rune if we first investigate the original meaning of Wunjo; in the oldest Germanic language known to us the word means "perfection," according to the philologist Jacob Grim.

In all pagan traditions, gods are seen as being partly good and partly bad, just like us—except that these characteristics are portrayed in the gods on a grander scale.

The Odinic aspects of Wunjo are more beneficial than is implied by the Christian writers of the Eddas, in which Odin is usually depicted as a warmonger or an evil sorcerer.

Wunjo contains all that is beautiful and lovable in Odin/Wodan. One of Odin's bynames is Oski, which means "fulfiller of wishes." This corresponds to the German tradition expressed by the word *Wunsch,* which has since taken on a narrower meaning and now means "wish." The German word *Wunsch,* English "wish," and Dutch *wens* all derive from the primitive Germanic word Wunjo, which meant "perfection." However, in a more esoteric sense this is to be understood as the wish to strive towards that perfection. Although perfection is never achieved in reality, it is an ideal to be aimed at. Wodan was also the giver of blessings and fertility. These aspects belong to the ancient continental Germanic tradition, very little of which was passed on to the Viking Age, when Odin was exalted as god of war to the detriment of his original attributes.

Vestiges of Wodan's role as a bearer of gifts and fulfiller of wishes have survived in Holland, Germany, and other countries on the continent in the Feast of St. Nicholas, celebrated on December 6. This festival was until recently the most popular one in Holland and elsewhere, especially for children. It is yet another example (like Yule and Easter) of the Christian Church borrowing its customs from heathenism and even transforming heathen gods into Christian saints.

It also illustrates Wodan's more kindly and endearing characteristics. In the children's version of this festival, St. Nicholas rides over
the rooftops dropping presents down the chimneys for those children who have been well behaved throughout the year. For those
who have misbehaved, he sends a bunch of birch twigs for them to be
spanked with. In the more extreme cases of naughtiness, children were
told that St. Nicholas would put them in a bag and take them away.

How does this relate to Wodan? St. Nicholas has various attributes
in common with Wodan, although some changes have been introduced. Firstly, St. Nicholas rides on a dapple-gray or white horse over
the rooftops of the houses. He is accompanied by two blackamoors,
both called *Zwarte Piet,* or in English, "Black Peter," who are his ser-
vants. Furthermore, he sports a long staff, a red cloak, and a bishop's
mitre. It is quite easy to visualize the underlying image of Wodan riding on Sleipnir, accompanied by his two ravens, and his staff, cloak,
and floppy hat. St. Nicholas is, in particular, associated with children,
which makes it interesting to consider the relationship between Wodan
and children. In the olden days, unwanted children were exposed at
birth by being placed at crossroads and were considered the property
of Wodan and the goddess Holda, who would take them to join their
retinues. In this the twentieth century social system I would suggest
that unwanted children placed in institutions are the equivalent of the
exposed children and therefore also would enjoy special interest of
Wodan and/or Holda. In Wodan's case, they became participants in the
wild hunt. The hood and staff have even today survived as the typical
props of a stage magician. In Holland we are familiar with the wish-
inghood, which survives today as the stage magician's top hat. The
term "wishing-rod," which is another name for a magical wand, occurs
frequently in Germanic literature in folklore and mythology. This is
correctly identified with Wodan's (or Odin's) spear or staff, which is a
phallic symbol. The birch twigs which St. Nicholas is said to drop
down the chimneys of naughty children are also reminiscent of a fertility festival, at which Wodan supplied birch twigs used by the
engaged couple to scourge each other in the hope of increasing the like-
lihood of pregnancy. The birch twig, of course, is associated with the

Berkana rune which, together with Wunjo, can be employed in a fertility spell. So the most important function of Wodan in this rune is to fulfill wishes.

In the *Anglo-Saxon Nine Herbs Charm* we find this reference to glory twigs:

> *A worm came crawling, it killed nothing*
> *For Woden took nine glory twigs*
> *He smote the adder that it flew apart into nine parts.*

Glory twigs in Anglo-Saxon are named *wuldortanas*. In this word we find the name Wuldor, and this is none other than Uller, the stepson of Thor. Tradition has it that Uller reigns in Odin's absence and that at one time he was a very important god. (We will discuss Uller in more detail in Chapter 5.) Glory twigs, at any rate, are connected with acts of magic and acts of will. The fact that there are nine glory twigs is sufficient to indicate that we are dealing with a magical tradition, because the number nine in Northern mythology is the most magical number. Glory twigs also refer to a certain type of rune-stave. In the *Havamal,* Odin tells us, "Nine lays of power I learned from Bolthorn, Bestla's father." There are nine worlds mentioned in Northern mythology, each of which is associated with a non-invertible rune. These nine runes may well be the nine glory twigs.

Evidently Wunjo is one of the most magically powerful runes. Its connotation of wishes and wishing implies that the power behind this rune is what is known in modern-day occultism as the power or realization of the true will. In the Thurisaz rune, this power is no more than a potential in the subconscious. If correctly applied Wunjo can put us in touch with this power and therefore raise it to manifest consciousness. Pictographically, this is made visible in the difference between the shape of these two runes ᚦ and ᚹ : the triangle rises from the middle in Thurisaz to the top in Wunjo. It makes logical sense to conclude that if the Wunjo rune should appear inverted in a reading dealing with questions concerning magic, then this means that the power of the true will is inaccessible at that particular moment.

The Anglo-Saxon name for this rune is Wynn, or in modern English, "winning." The original meaning of the word *wynn* was "peaceful." Odin, who controls the power of this rune, has three aspects: Odin, Vili, and Ve. The name Vili, in Germanic Wili, fits the concept of the magical application of the Wunjo rune and the art of correct wishing, or in other words, the use of the power of the magical will. Since all magic is fundamentally an act of will, we see that this rune can be extremely useful in realizing one's objectives, whatever these may be. Wunjo combines very well with Raido in that Raido operates as a means of controlling and directing the will symbolized by Wunjo.

From an esoteric and spiritual point of view, Wunjo can mean joy when it is combined with Gebo, which symbolizes the gift of one's own will to the gods, and in particular the alignment of one's own individual will with the will of the god or goddess one serves.

THE COSMOLOGY OF THE FIRST AETT

When I was teaching the Runic Gild in 1984, I intuitively received an insight into the way the runes in the elder futhark are related to the mythology, especially with regards to the myths dealing with the creation and destruction of the cosmos. The reader is advised to obtain a copy of the *Poetic Edda* and study the *Voluspa*. A part of the following paragraphs appeared in articles written by me and published in the magazine *Godismal* in 1984.*

As we know, there are three aettir in the futhark, each consisting of eight runes in a specific order. The futhark sequence of the runes was originally established as a code to enable future generations of

---

*These articles were copyrighted by me under the name Aeswynn. This is proof that the original idea, that there is a correspondence between the runes and the *Voluspa*, is mine and mine alone. Unfortunately I also used this material at weekend courses in the summer and autumn of 1986; as a result it was later paraphrased and published in another magazine in September 1987, despite my copyright, without prior notice or permission, and with no acknowledgment given to me for the original idea.

our people to acquire the knowledge we once possessed. The incoming influence of Christianity was foreseen and precautions were taken to ensure the survival of our religious tradition, which is derived from the original indigenous Asatru faith based on the runes and the mythology.

Most of the following information has already been touched upon in the sections on the appropriate runes. However, in order to show that the cosmology is a consistent whole and that the runes are set out in a logical sequence, I felt it was worthwhile to include an overall resume of each aett.

We can roughly divide the cosmology of the North into three divisions or planes. The first is the plane of creation, the primeval drive that causes the ordered universe to come into existence. This is linked with the first aett, illustrated by the first four runes. Fehu represents the primordial fire of Muspelheim, and Uruz represents the eternal ice of Nifelheim. These two worlds contain totally opposed elements; from the conflict between fire and frost originated all that exists. The two opposing forces met in the Ginnungagap, the abyss. The first being to be created was a cosmic cow, Audhumla, which is the first feminine creative principle in Nature and therefore the first incarnation of the Mother Goddess. This principle is accurately covered by the meaning of the first two runes when viewed as a pair of complementary opposites, Fehu and Uruz, which both relate to bovine creatures.

From the same matter the giant Ymir was subsequently formed. While Ymir slept, a son and a daughter were born from the sweat under his armpit. From these descended all the giants, who are evoked by the Thurisaz rune (*Thurs* means "giant"). Audhumla then licked the ice and from this produced the first of the Aesir, Buri, the ancestor of Odin—as is illustrated by the fourth rune, Ansuz, which means "Ase" or "god." The Aesir then started to take control of the creative process; their first act was to kill Ymir and to create the Earth from his corpse. The Aesir also set the Sun and Moon in place and created the cycle of night and day. This principle is represented by the Raido rune.

We can imagine the Sun and the Moon as heavenly torches. This is linked with the Kenaz rune, for Kenaz means "torch." In addition, there is a reference here to the knowledge gained by the Aesir from their participation in the creation. It may well have been at this stage that the Vanir began to play their part in the scheme of things; in particular Freyja, who taught Odin the secrets of magic, enters the stage of events. Freyja also corresponds to Kenaz. So far we have seen the subsequent movement of creation in the form of the elements, the giants and the Aesir. Once the Aesir had created Midgard and Asgard, everything was set for the next development in this cosmic drama.

Gebo is the next rune and it informs us about the gift of life which the three Aesir, Odin, Hoenir, and Lodur, gave to two trees shaped in human form, who were called Ask and Embla. Ask and Embla became the first human couple. Humankind multiplied, took possession of Midgard, and all was well. Wunjo, the last rune of this aett, indicates that the first stage of creation was completed in perfection, for perfection is the hidden meaning of Wunjo. This is known in our mythology as the "Golden Age." Humanity lived in innocent bliss and joy, and the Aesir were content to make beautiful objects of gold as playthings. No evil had yet come to pass.

This outline of the creation myth, as it is related to the logical sequence of the futhark, is resumed at the end of the sections on the two remaining aettir.

Second Aett

Germanic name ♦ HAGALAZ

Anglo-Saxon name ♦ HAEGL

Old Norse name ♦ HAGALL

Phonetic value ♦ H

Traditional meaning ♦ hail

This is the first rune of the second aett: the aett of Hagalaz. This aett is named after an element, whereas the others are named after gods—Frey and Freyja for the first aett and Tyr for the third. Some rune-workers have tried to apply the same idea to the second aett by allocating this one either to Odin or to Thor. I shall try to prove that most of the runes in this aett are largely concerned with the goddesses, in particular the Norns.

As has already been shown, the first aett deals with the emergence of order from chaos and the establishment of the cosmic routine. In the second aett, we shall investigate those antagonistic forces which attempt to disrupt this order, thereby creating necessary change and evolution. Even on the most superficial level it can be seen that the meaning of Hagalaz is negative. Hagalaz means "hail" and hail is a substance consisting of frozen water and air, although it is not as hard or dense as ice. Every farmer knows what hail can do to the crops: it is a destructive natural force.

In order to understand the more esoteric meaning of Hagalaz it is necessary to discuss it in conjunction with two other runes, Isa and Nauthiz. These three runes, which are the first three in this aett, are related magically and semantically.

In the cosmology of our religion we are informed about the nine realms of Yggdrasil. These three runes correspond to the three lower realms of those nine worlds which form a group known in shamanic terms as the underworld. Hagalaz rules Hel. Nifelheim, which literally means "fogworld," with its connotations of the elements of water and air which make up both fog and hail, is ruled by Nauthiz. The realm of Nifelheim is an extension of Hel and is situated beyond it. The world of the giants, the frost giants in particular, is called Jotunheim and is ruled by the rune Isa.

The name Hel derives from the primitive Germanic *halja*, meaning "covering," and has none of the connotations evoked by the Christian concept of "hell," which has been translated from the Hebrew "Gehenna." (Hel is thus often only thought of as a realm of extreme heat. This misunderstanding is easily explained if it is realized that, whereas in the Middle East heat is seen as potentially life-threatening, in Northern Europe it is the excess of cold which jeopardizes the survival of all living things.) Hel is ruled by the goddess Hella. Although the description given of this place in the Eddas seems grim, it is by no means a place of torment. All who do not die in battle or at sea go there first. Even Baldur, when he was accidentally killed by Hodur, went there and was joined by his wife, Nanna.

The goddess Hella is a later Scandinavian development of the friendly Germanic goddess Holda, also known in folklore as Dame Holle. Incidentally, Holland was named after her. Large parts of this country are below sea level and Holland is nowadays called the Netherlands, meaning "low countries" or "underworld." Holland is a very foggy and misty country and the images of Hel and Nifelhel do correspond to it. The name Holle is linguistically related to the oldest name known for the realm of Hel, Halja. She is also the goddess who covers the land with snow. When it snows in my country, Holland, we say, "Dame Holle is shaking her bed."

The occult and depth-psychological implications of Hagalaz are also noteworthy. Hel is the realm of the dead, and to us who are the living, the dead are part of our past. We have followed the previous runes in futhark order and linked them with the creation myth as expressed in the *Voluspa*. We left them at Wunjo with the Golden Age. At that point the creation myth tells us that there came three giant maidens from Jotunheim. These three are, in fact, the three Norns, the goddesses of fate who collectively represent time: Urd represents the past; Verdandi the present; and Skuld the future. The goddess Urd is the esoteric ruler of the Hagalaz rune.

The psychological meaning of the Hagalaz rune in a reading usually relates to disruptive forces operating in the unconscious, creating necessary change. Moreover, recognizing that the Norn Urd is the power behind this rune, we can deduce that these disruptive forces originate from the individual's past; in most cases this involves

unlearned lessons and unsolved problems from the past, and suppressed negative memories too painful to be dealt with which still
influence the present behavior pattern. However, it is possible that
in complicated cases these disruptive forces originate from a more
distant past—in other words, from a previous existence.

The realm of Hel can be equated with the personal unconscious,
the deepest part of which is connected with the collective unconscious. In this realm resides the capacity for ultimate good, and also
for total destruction. Hagalaz contains a lot of dark feminine power,
and has a strong connection with negative witchcraft, such as
destructive female magic. The first witch known in our mythology
is a lady called Gullveig. Like Hella, she represents the dark aspect of
the Goddess. Gullveig introduced to Valhalla the lust for gold. The
Aesir looked upon gold as a plaything. Gullveig introduced greed
and evil sorcery to the gods and was burned three times: "Three
times she was burned and still she lives."

However, Gullveig did not survive in the normal sense of the
word. After she had endured the triple burning, Loki ate her heart
and so absorbed the evil that was in her. (Alternatively, we can
assume that the triple death of Gullveig gave birth to the three
Norns, who come to the fore shortly afterwards.) No male god can
kill the Goddess, evil or not. This was Odin's mistake. To make things
worse, he refused to pay wergild to the Vanir, who are related to
Gullveig, and thus started the war between the Aesir and the Vanir.
Wergild was a compulsory payment of compensation for manslaugh-
ter, which in the ancient Northern society was defined as an openly
performed act of killing. The wergild system did not function as a
license to kill, because murder plotted and carried out in secret was
virtually unheard of in the Teutonic social structure.

The High German word *Hachel* is related to Hagalaz and means
"witch." It corresponds to the Anglo-Saxon *haegtessa,* from which
the modern English word "hag" is derived. The Old Dutch equivalent of *haegtessa* was *hagedisse,* which meant both "witch" and

"lizard." The lizard is an animal with particularly shamanic associations and the latter meaning is still current in modern Dutch.

Hail is a composition of two elements, air and water. In Holland it was well known that witches worked with the weather and could raise hailstorms to blight their enemies or crops. Folklore belief had it that witches contained those storms in a bag until they were to be released. Two Scandinavian demi-goddesses, Thorgerd and Irpa, were said to be very active in this. The Hagalaz rune can thus be used for extremely negative magic. I have used it in combination with Thurisaz and the result was disastrous for the person who received it. In this working the rune brought to this person's conscious mind all the suppressed garbage in his unconscious. The symptoms he displayed would, to an uneducated mind, suggest demonic possession. If you leave Hagalaz alone and do not consciously invoke its powers, it generates discomfort as a precondition of change. Through it, disruptive elements become consciously received, so that they can be dealt with in a constructive manner.

The realm of Hel is the equivalent of the shamanic underworld and can be reached by shamanic means through traveling while in altered states of consciousness. Both Odin and Hermod travel to Hel on a quest, but strangely enough only Odin's horse Sleipnir can accomplish these journeys. No other horse will do.

Enough about the negative aspects of Hagalaz! There is an alternative form of this rune which is very protective and is especially used to provide protection against bad weather. For this purpose it used to be displayed in a prominent position in farmsteads, especially over doorways or on top of the house. The protective aspect of Hagalaz, or Hail, is mostly referred to as "heil," which can be used as both a blessing and a greeting. This form of the rune was particularly used as a marriage blessing and, as one can see, the shape of this rune looks like the two forms of the Algiz rune intertwined, indicating the union between the male and the female form of Algiz: ⅄.

Germanic name ♦ NAUTHIZ

Anglo-Saxon name ♦ NEED

Old Norse name ♦ NAUDR

Phonetic value ♦ N

Traditional meaning ♦ need

Nauthiz is another rune closely associated with one of the three Norns, in this case Skuld, who rules the future. The futhark order of the three runes Hagalaz, Nauthiz, and Isa does not correspond to the usual given sequence of the Norns Urd, Verdandi, and Skuld. Thus the second rune of this aett corresponds to the third Norn, Skuld.

The word *Skuld* relates to the Dutch and German word *Schuld*, meaning "debt," i.e., that which is owed. It can mean in traditional Nordic terms *wergild*. *Wer* is Old Germanic for "man" and *gild* means both "money" and "guilt"; hence, man-guilt. These associations combine to form a Norse version of what is commonly known as karma. This is expressed in the myth of the war between the Aesir and the Vanir, in which Odin's refusal to pay the Vanir wergild as compensation for the death of Gullveig provided the cause of war. The actions in the past (Hagalaz) created the conditions prevailing in the future (Nauthiz = need). (In Dutch, the word for "war" is *oorlog*. The similar word *orlog* in Old Norse means "fate.")

Skuld is the youngest of the three Norns. She cuts the thread of life when it comes to its end. The fate created during that life will be meted out accordingly. Skuld is usually portrayed as wearing a veil, whereas Urd and Verdandi's faces are uncovered. This clearly means that the future fate is hidden from vision. Skuld is particularly important in divination for the obvious reason that she personifies the future. If she is approached in a friendly and reverential manner, she will lift the veil and provide a glimpse into the future.

The spiritual concept of this rune is necessity, which is also implied by the *Anglo-Saxon Rune-Poem*:

Need constricts the heart, but it often serves as a help
and salvation to the sons of man,
if they attend to it in time.
[TRANSLATION BY R. I. PAGE]

This stanza can be interpreted at various levels. First, the need may originate from the past, constricting the present and placing restrictions on the future. Need in this context can represent guilt, not in the conventional Christian sense, but in a more personal manner. Anyone who evolves along a spiritual path, whatever that path may be, will develop a set of personal ethical values to live by. However, human nature being what it is, we do not always live up to our self-imposed standards and consequently experience a sense of failure. This sense of failure puts a dent in our self-esteem and restricts us in our creativity. All this is necessary, however, and is unavoidable if we are to learn from our mistakes. A second and more psychological interpretation of Nauthiz relates to the individual's own unacknowledged needs, which have to be made conscious and should be attended to. Either they are fulfilled according to Crowley's axiom "Do what thou wilt," or else they should be consciously rejected. Whatever choice is made, one has to be aware of these needs.

In a reading, the runes that follow Nauthiz indicate what is needed or required. Until you attend to the problem, that need will restrict you from doing something constructive. It can also appear in a reading as a warning. On the other hand, this rune was turned up once as an answer to the question, "Shall I do something about my problem?" And I felt strongly that the Nauthiz rune in that particular context meant there was no need to do so.

Magically, Nauthiz can be used successfully to restrict other people. In one of the Eddaic poems, the *Sigdrifumal*, Sigurd is advised to scratch Need (Nauthiz) on his fingernails for protection. Nauthiz, like Thurisaz, may be used to fetter another person and render his actions impotent.

Of the nine worlds, Hagalaz rules Hel, whereas Nauthiz rules Nifelhel, the realm of the dragon Nidhog, whose name means "gnawer from beneath." Nidhog paws at the roots of Yggdrasil in an attempt to destroy the Tree. We can interpret this myth psychologically: Nidhog can be viewed as the shadow in the unconscious, gnawing at or undermining the sense of self symbolized by Yggdrasil. Hel, as we have seen, is not an entirely unpleasant place or state of mind. On the other hand, Nifelhel is. Each of the nine worlds represents a plane or world to which one can travel shamanically or astrally, as well as a psychological principle in the individual human condition. Nifelhel is where all fears reside. There is nothing as restrictive as fear, nothing as inhibiting as the feeling that whatever one wishes to accomplish is doomed to failure in advance. The positive aspect of these fears is that they can be turned into an omen of help when attended to early. In other words, these fears are part of the survival instinct which warns us about imminent dangers. Thus there is a protecting, warning aspect of the Nauthiz rune that teaches us the skill of self-preservation.

An old Germanic association links the Nauthiz rune with the element of fire. The "need-fire" was originally a ritual kindling of fire associated with various festivals such as Beltane, Midsummer, Yule, and Samhain. It originates from a cult of fire-worship and evidence shows that this cult is older than the religion of the Aesir. Fire rituals were used for a variety of purposes, including sacrifices, healing and cleansing. In the need-fire ritual, two fires were kindled a distance apart from each other by two chaste youngsters, one male and one female. Each made a fire by rubbing dry wood together until it caught light. Cattle were then driven between the two fires to ensure their fertility and health. (The custom of engaged couples leaping over a bonfire is a remnant of this rite.) The need-fire was usually kindled in times of need such as dearth, drought, and disease.

It is easily understandable why fire was held to be sacred, for the climate in which the Northern folk live is prone to extremes of cold. Therefore fire, which is associated with the Sun, was regarded as a source of life. However, our lands at that time were covered in dense forests and therefore fire could easily become a destructive and inimical force. Hence, one kenning for fire used by the poets was "forestdread."

Nauthiz also relates to the binding of Loki, who is the god of fire. When he became destructive the Aesir captured and bound him. The underlying principle of this tale is that the power of fire can be controlled by its intelligent use. Moreover, the custom of crossing fingers for good luck is possibly connected with Nauthiz, as the crossed fingers of the right hand form a Nauthiz rune.

Germanic name ♦ ISA

Anglo-Saxon name ♦ IS

Old Norse name ♦ IS

Phonetic value ♦ I

Traditional meaning ♦ ice

Isa is the third rune of the second aett. Like the first two runes in this aett, Isa is also associated with an element—the element of ice. Ice is water in its densest frozen state. Water is fluid; ice is solid and static. Isa therefore represents the principle of preservation and resistance to change. It is the counter-force to evolution, slowing down change; as such it performs a function equivalent to the principle expressed in occult terminology as "the ring pass not." Isa is a necessarily antagonistic force whose controlling effect is essential in order to prevent evolution from running riot in unrestrained and random growth.

Ice is inimical to life and hostile to the environment. Nevertheless, our ancestors saw it as a challenge, and not only succeeded in the struggle for survival in unfavorable conditions, but were also spurred on by Isa to evolve faster than others. Thus necessity proved to be the mother of invention. Our ancestors also had to develop as a sturdy warrior race. Unfortunately, one disadvantage of our native inventiveness is a descent into materialism, which has stultified the evolution of our spiritual values. Most of our Northern people accepted Christianity, an alien religion imported from the Middle East. They did so primarily because they were given no choice and the result is that we are left with little more than vestiges of our own spiritual heritage.

Isa represents the forces used in the pursuit of materialism. It crystallizes spirit into matter. It is the rune of self-preservation and self-containment, the positive aspect of which is our individualism and the ability to survive against all odds; the negative aspect is self-centeredness and the "each for his own" mentality. The Northern people lost their sense of community, and on the whole, are nowadays only interested in short-term profit or pleasure; by contrast, so-called primitive nations from warmer climates who did not have the same pressing need to invent nevertheless retained their sense of community and belonging. Our materialistic selfishness will be our own undoing unless instead of selling out to others or exploiting them, as we continue to do, we learn how to cooperate with each other and with Nature for the greater good of the whole of our folk, and consequently, for all of humanity.

Isa is connected with Verdandi, the Norn who rules the present. As already mentioned, Isa is static—it "is." Its function is to keep things as they are, to maintain whatever "is." On its own, it is an inert rune which merely preserves and conserves. Communication with this rune poses difficulties, as it is cold, hard and unyielding. It represents the darker side of the Goddess, the sterile barren goddess who in our mythology is called Rind and who refused three times to give Odin the son he needed to avenge Baldur, the Sun god, who represents the principle opposite to Isa. In this myth, Rind symbolizes the frozen Earth unwilling to yield to the embrace of the Sun, represented by Odin. The Isa rune also controls the realm of Jotunheim and the frost giants who are personifications of the destructive aspect of the winter weather.

Psychologically, Isa represents the "I" in the most mundane sense, and the capacity for personal survival through concentrated effort. Isa can be a great help in concentrating the will in a single-minded action. In a depth-psychological reading it reveals areas of the unconscious that have been imprinted with a particular pattern. Whatever the pattern is, it is usually very difficult and often impossible to change, as is often the case with habits or ingrained, unconscious attitudes. In most cases it is better to leave these areas alone, as activating them could cause even more trouble, unless one knows exactly what one is doing. A technique of exploring these areas is to use Sowulo or even Thurisaz as a force opposing Isa, which helps to melt the Isa influence. Either of these fire runes should give access to those patterns residing in the unconscious in a frozen condition; the object of this being that the energy of fire is used to symbolically melt these patterns, which can then be altered in accordance with will. Even better is the use of the Kenaz rune as Kenaz represents a more controlled form of fire and also facilitates the gaining of knowledge in these areas.

In divination Isa usually displays a frustrating influence and most often indicates that whatever the question asked or the problem discussed, there is no immediate possibility of change. It might take as much as three months, the equivalent of a season, to effect the required change, although again this can be counterbalanced by invoking one of the fire runes.

There are some positive uses of Isa. It can be used to cancel any disruptive or aggressive forces employed either through magic or in a heated debate. In either case a projection of Isa can soon cool the situation down. The concentrated force of Isa is the only force strong enough to negate Thurisaz. Isa can be used for self-defense and can render any magical attack harmless. Isa can also be used preemptively to freeze another person's action. Magical warfare is very rare and it is certainly not a common practice of rune-masters or other magicians to attack people willy-nilly; but in the rare cases where one is subjected to an attack, Isa will act as a protective barrier against it.

Germanic name ◆ JERA

Anglo-Saxon name ◆ GER

Old Norse name ◆ AR

Phonetic value ◆ J or Y

Traditional meaning ◆ year, harvest

That this rune is the fourth in the aett of Hagalaz and the twelfth in the futhark is a good example of synchronicity, since there are twelve months in the year and twice twelve hours in a day. The name of this rune indicates that it has an important bearing on time and the divisions of time.

Each of the previous three runes was associated with one of the Norns. The *Voluspa* mentions the three giant maidens from Jotunheim, who appear on the scene after the killing of Gullveig, and since Gullveig was burned three times, yet survived, it can be deduced that these three Nornir or giant-maidens are the three aspects of Gullveig. As already stated, each of the Norns represents an aspect of time: past, present, and future. This rune, following immediately after the three Norn-related runes, represents time itself.

The two halves of the Jera rune clearly portray two halves of a year circling around each other in a perpetual swirling motion from light to darkness and back again. The Jera rune is associated, in particular, with the turning of the year at Yuletide, when the Sun returns. Jera also contains the mystery of Baldur and Hodur, who are killed and reborn. Baldur was killed at midsummer and reborn at Yuletide, whereas Hodur was killed at Yuletide and reborn at midsummer. If the year is represented in the form of a circular calendar and the Jera rune is inscribed on the circumference of the circle to represent Yule, with the other runes placed on the circumference equidistantly and in futhark order, then it will be seen that Dagaz is positioned diametrically opposite Jera, or at the point on the calendar that represents midsummer. This reveals the relationship between Jera and

Dagaz and the fact that they complement each other. (Jera relates to the division of the year; Dagaz relates to the division of the day.)

Jera represents the cycle of the year and the return of the seasons. It is a hopeful rune that shows that everything is on the move and nothing stays the same. This rune can create a gentle change, a bending of the web of wyrd. In a reading it is usually an indication of a change for the better—the end of a cycle and the beginning of another one. This rune contains the mystery of the eternal return.

The element related to this rune is earth; the gods who are associated with it (apart from Baldur and Hodur, who have already been mentioned) are the Vanir twins, Frey and Freyja. The Jera rune is strongly connected with fertility, in particular the fertility of crops. Thor also has some connection with this rune. Yuletide has been traditionally his festival, at least in some areas of the Northland; in other areas, it was Frey to whom the Yule feast was sacred. Thor also was traditionally a friend of the farmers or peasants and was considered to be important in matters relating to agricultural fertility.

On a personal level, Jera, being a rune of return, often indicates that which one can expect to return as a result of a previous action. My personal feeling towards Jera is that it is a very friendly and encouraging rune, less harsh than Isa and Nauthiz. Magically the Jera rune can be used in a spell either to speed processes up or to slow them down. It depends on how it is drawn. Look at the rune drawing at the beginning of this section. When the rune is drawn with this shape it will create a progressive motion in forward time, but if this drawing is reversed it can be used in a spell to slow things down. Thus: ᚼ.

This might be useful when confronted with events which are rapidly escalating beyond control.

Whereas Isa represents the deepest descent into matter, with Jera things start turning around. From Fehu to Jera we have seen an involution of energy, or spirit, into matter. Now with Jera the evolution and the motion of return has started and is further enhanced in the next rune, Eihwaz.

Germanic name ◆ EIHWAZ

Anglo-Saxon name ◆ EOH

Old Norse name ◆ none

Phonetic value ◆ E

Traditional meaning ◆ yew

For a long time my personal attempts to communicate with this rune met with great difficulty. I am indebted to Edred Thorsson and Thorolf Wardle, who postulated the idea that the yew tree is Yggdrasil. Since my aim in this work is to present my own personal understanding of and communication from the runes themselves, I will avoid making the mistake of copying from other works on the runes and plagiarizing other authors. Wherever it is unavoidable to repeat others' ideas, I will state this clearly and give credit where it is due. Therefore the following notes represent the result of my own personal research into this rune.

Eihwaz represents Yggdrasil. However, it also resembles the human spine or backbone, which supports the rest of the body. Eihwaz is the psychic equivalent of the backbone, as Yggdrasil, supporting creation, resembles a cosmic spine. The spine has twenty-four independent vertebrae and this fact shows a clear correspondence to the runes of the Common Germanic futhark. Furthermore, Yggdrasil contains the nine worlds, eight of which could be seen to relate to the psychic centers in the body known in traditional occultism by their Eastern name, "chakras," which seem to be responsible for the energy exchanges from the psychic to the physical levels. The physical body is represented by the ninth world, Midgard. These centers also correspond to the main endocrine glands. In occult tradition it is commonly assumed that there are seven chakras functioning as transmitters of psychic energy. The Old Norse word for this would be *hvel* or "wheel," a term that is mentioned in this context in the writings of Rudolf Gorsleben. My theory is that there are, in fact, eight chakras. In addition to the seven well-known ones, there is another chakra situated below the feet. Eight of the nine worlds can be allocated to a chakra, which can then be activated by using the corresponding runes given in Chapter 4. As this technique is advanced magic and at an experimental stage I cannot yet give examples of concrete results of this magical theory, but he who dares wins. Are the Northern peoples not renowned for their spirit of daring?

Now, daring certainly is a concept linked with this rune. Eihwaz is traditionally associated with hunting, especially by means of a bow, for bows used to be made of yew, and hunting is a daring business and was especially so in olden days. The power of this rune is a strong and assertive power. It can give you the necessary impetus to take a headlong plunge into the deep end. It is an outgoing rune of action, striving, persistence, and endurance. On the magical path, Eihwaz is a testing force. My own research with Eihwaz demonstrates that it often occurs in a reading when a querent expresses doubt about a certain venture. In these cases Eihwaz invariably advises that a risk should be taken. It says, "Go for it!"

The association with Odin's ordeal on Yggdrasil has given us a folk-game in Holland. It is a contest known as *Paaltje Zitten,* which can be translated as "pole-sitting," which explains exactly what is done. Huge poles are set up on a common and men climb on to the top of the pole and sit there. The object of this exercise is, of course, to see who remains the longest on the top of the pole. Would it be too far-fetched to suggest that this may be a survival from some forgotten ancient ritual? Another far older custom existed in Frisia, which encompassed a large part of the provinces of north and south Holland in tribal days of old. Whenever danger threatened, a sword of burnt yew was passed from village to village to summon help. A sword made of yew has been found by archaeologists in Friesland, dating from the eighth century.

The element pertaining to Eihwaz is difficult to define, since Yggdrasil partakes of all the elements. It is rooted in the Earth and extends into the sky; thus the elements air and earth are the most significant ones pertaining to the Eihwaz rune.

Two gods are associated with Eihwaz—Odin and Uller. We know that Odin is associated with Eihwaz/Yggdrasil because he transcended the barriers of life and death and partook of both conditions while being suspended between the two. It is this sacrificial act of Odin's that gave him knowledge of the runes, and he retained the ability to travel between the realms of life and death, becoming the "wild hunter." Uller is associated with Eihwaz because he is the god identified with hunting. Bows were made of yew and Uller dwells in Ydalir, or the Valley of Yews. Furthermore Odin and Uller are the opposite of each other and therefore complement each other. There is a myth older than the Eddas in which Odin is usurped and driven away by Uller or Mithodin. This happens at the autumn equinox when Uller takes over and reigns through the winter. At the spring equinox Odin regains control and rules during the summer. This myth is related to the agricultural year.

As we have seen, Jera is the turning point where involution, the descent of spirit into matter, turns to evolution, the conversion of matter into spirit. Eihwaz is the driving force of evolution at this point in the cosmology. Odin, observing the state of creation, subjects himself to his ordeal on Yggdrasil. He was the first being to take an active step along the path of evolution and it was then that he transcended from Ygg into Odin. Eihwaz psychologically will often place the individual in the difficult position of being in a state of suspension, either as a result of conflicting emotions, which have to be synthesized and transcended, or by leaving the individual with a difficult choice between two equally valued opposites.

Eihwaz is one of the most powerful runes, to be used like a backbone in a bind rune. The most beautiful symbol I have been given is Jera spinning around Eihwaz. Meditation on this bind-rune can be a very uplifting experience. The bind-rune looks like:

A combination that is particularly helpful in invoking Uller is Eihwaz and Wunjo. To use Eihwaz magically, visualize it, feel it inside you from head to "tail," and link this sensation with your will to move between the unconscious and the higher conscious. As you do this, partake of and integrate the information coming through from both states of consciousness. This is not as difficult as it sounds since both these states are reflections of each other. This can be seen if a line is drawn horizontally through the middle of Eihwaz, creating two halves which reflect each other and form an upright and an inverted Laguz rune.

Germanic name ♦ PERTHO

Anglo-Saxon name ♦ PEORTH

Old Norse name ♦ none

Phonetic value ♦ P

Traditional meaning ♦ birth?

The traditional meaning of this rune has not been established, but various suggestions have been made, including "secret" and "chess piece." This is the sixth rune of the second aett and it is one of the most obscure runes in the futhark. Often it has been left unexplained and described as a secret by uninformed authors. Yet it really should not be that difficult to tune in to the mysteries of this rune.

Many years ago, when I was meditating on Pertho, I immediately and intuitively sensed an association of Pertho with birth. Pertho, when rotated ⊔ resembles the natural birthing crouch position. I was therefore delighted when I found in a small but sensible booklet on runes, *Runelore* by Thorolf Wardle, the exact information explaining why this is a birth-rune. I will make an exception to my general rule of not quoting from other authors, because this information is too valuable not to be shared. Thorolf Wardle puts forth the suggestion that the *Anglo-Saxon Rune-Poem* has been altered, which seems very likely in view of the fact that it was recorded by Christians who had their own religious objections to some of the poem's implications.

The traditional version of the *Anglo-Saxon Rune-Poem* is:

Peorth byth symble plega and hlehter wlancum
Thor wigan sittath on beorsele blithe aetsomne.

This can be translated into modern English as follows:

Peorth is always play and laughter to the proud ones
Where warriors sit in the beerhall blithely together.

According to Thorolf, two Anglo-Saxon words have been changed from the original. These words are *wigan* (warriors) and *beorsele* (beerhall), which were originally *wifan* (wives) and *beorthsele* (birth-hall), respectively. The original version would have been thus:

Peorth is always play and laughter to the proud ones
Where wives sit in the birthhall blithely together.

The first time that I contacted the Pertho rune, my initial impression was that it was the womb of the Great Goddess, or space. I felt simultaneously that space is also the well of Mimir, where Odin sacrificed his eye. This eye is the Moon in the night sky, whereas his all-seeing eye, which he retained, is the Sun in the daytime sky.

This rune follows Eihwaz when at that stage in the mythology Odin undertook his ordeal on Yggdrasil, after which, once he had gained knowledge of the runes, he still needed the wisdom to use them and the total knowledge of the past and future. This wisdom and knowledge is what he gained from the well of Mimir, which is the equivalent of what is known in other occult schools as the "Akashic records." The well contains all the memory of the ancestors and the racial collective unconscious, the group-soul. It is the place where all knowledge has been preserved and can be recovered. I see my own research into runelore as part of the process of recovering knowledge from the collective unconscious—the well of Mimir.

In some modern rune-work, the twenty-four-rune futhark has been mistakenly extended with a so-called blank rune. This practice is completely superfluous, because the futhark has been constructed on the numerological basis of twenty-four for specific reasons. The so-called blank rune has been erroneously allocated to represent fate by the same authors who associate the Pertho rune with secrecy. In fact, the Pertho rune is the true rune of fate, as is Nauthiz. Pertho is controlled jointly by the three Norns. It is the well of Urd in addition to being the well of Mimir. The Norns weave the web of the individual's fate, including that of the gods.

The Norns are weavers. Frigga is known to be the goddess of spinning and her weapon or tool is a distaff. It is she who spins the raw material from which the Norns weave fate. In the myths she is the goddess who knows all but does not speak. She keeps her secrets. In this context, the Pertho rune does indeed have connotations of secretiveness.

So far we have only considered the Pertho rune in the normal position, facing towards the right. However, if this rune is reversed and faces left, the meaning would be reversed. Instead of a symbol of birth, Pertho would symbolize death. When this rune is facing towards the right, its creative energy can be envisaged flowing outwards. In the leftward-facing position it can be imagined flowing in the opposite direction, turning in on itself and blocking the free flow of energy. The goddess who is first and foremost patroness of the Pertho rune is Frigga. This is so for two reasons. Firstly, she is the goddess who governs births, and secondly she is the power behind the Norns and is involved in creating fate.

From the combination of Jera, Eihwaz, and Pertho, a magical model of thought can be constructed in the following manner: Jera represents time, Pertho indicates space, and Eihwaz stands for Yggdrasil, which is suspended between the other two as the symbol of the created universe, maintained through the interacting and balancing forces of time and space.

The psychological implications of the Pertho rune in its positive form represent those talents and hidden potential possessed by the individual which have not yet been manifested, as well as those innate abilities inherited from one's ancestors, acquired through the hamingja or else possessed in a previous existence. Meditation and magical work conducted to investigate hidden matters of this nature can be successfully carried out through working with Pertho.

In a reading, Pertho usually has esoteric meanings relating, for example, to an initiation experience or to the discovery of a hidden aspect within oneself. The appropriate interpretation depends totally on the level of the reading. In one reading performed, the Pertho rune occurred in a significant place which told the querent, to her astonishment, that there was a mystery surrounding the birth of her granddaughter. This proved to be true, as it was later discovered that the child's father was not the husband of the child's mother, as she had believed. This was a typical experience of Pertho. When a direct question is asked and Pertho is given as the answer, I often find this means "You are not supposed to know." Posing further questions will only result in Pertho turning up yet again. Because of this irritating habit of Pertho, we called it the "f*** o**" rune.

Germanic name ♦ ALGIZ

Anglo-Saxon name ♦ EOLH

Old Norse name ♦ YR

Phonetic value ♦ Z

Traditional meaning ♦ protection

This rune has two forms: upright ᛉ and upside down ᛦ. In the Common Germanic futhark and the Anglo-Saxon futhark the only one used is the upright form: ᛉ. However, in the majority of Scandinavian futharks, both forms occur, the upright form representing the phonetic value of M; the name is given as MannaR, which is identical with Mannaz. In the Scandinavian rune-rows, the inverted form represents a sound somewhere between *r* and *z,* which contributes a magical sound value to the word. For example, in Icelandic the word *AsgardR* would be spelled by the following sequence of runes: Ansuz, Sowulo, Gebo, Ansuz, Dagaz, and Algiz, with the Algiz rune being drawn in its inverted form but slightly bigger. Presumably this was done to differentiate between a normal letter rune and a magical sound rune.

The primary meaning of the Algiz rune is protection. The sign itself looks like a splayed hand, and is reminiscent of Tyr's hand, which he sacrificed in order to bind Fenris the wolf. The Old Germanic word *alhs* means "temple" or "sanctuary." Because all the magical accoutrements and ritual equipment were kept in the alhs, these sacred places of worship had to be strongly defended. Alcis, according to Tacitus, was the name of the divine twins worshipped by Germanic people. Although no one has yet been able to identify these twins, suggestions have been put forward that they were the Northern equivalent of Castor and Pollux. Some workers have suggested that the twins were in fact Baldur and Hodur. My research indicates that since Algiz has a female and male form, the twins also may be male and female. The assumption that these twins are male is probably due to the fact that most serious rune-workers have been male. They have overlooked the possibility that the twins could be Frey and Freyja. Alternatively, as this sign is one of the oldest of all the extant runes, it may even represent the original twin divinity, from which all others have been extrapolated. Other twin deities include Niord and Nerthus, and Ziu and Zisa.

In the Scandinavian futhark the upright version of Algiz is given the name MannaR, which suggests that the upright form of the Algiz rune is male and represents the striving upwards of consciousness. This is symbolized by the upper branches of Yggdrasil extending high above the Earth and reaching out into the sky. The inverted form of Algiz, however, portrays the roots of Yggdrasil delving into the Earth, down into the realms of death. In the occult tradition the inner Earth is regarded as female. The highest branches represent the worlds of light: Vanaheim, Asgard, and Lightalfheim. The lower branches give access to the netherworlds of Jotunheim, Hel, and Swartalfheim. Projected into the center, Midgard is poised between the two sets of branches and flanked by Muspelheim and Nifelheim. These latter two regions are not visibly portrayed by the shape of the rune, as they are governed by the primal forces of fire and ice and represent the hidden support system of all the worlds. This cosmogony can be expressed in a bind-rune: ⵋ.

On a physical level the polarities are reversed, so that the female form of Algiz in its upright shape represents life, whereas the upside-down form represents death. Females give life, and in a warrior society it is often the males who deal out death. It has been a historical custom in Germany to use Algiz runes on gravestones in the following manner:

ⵕ Date of birth ⵔ Date of death

The upright form has a female shape, and the upside-down form a male shape. Indeed these two forms of the rune can be interpreted as simplified diagrams portraying the female and male genitalia, respectively. In Northern mythology it is related that the gods discovered two trees called Ask and Embla, which were respectively male and female. The gods gave them the gift of life and from them the human race is descended. Likewise, after Ragnarok life will again emerge from Yggdrasil, in whose branches a man and a woman named Lif and Liftrasir will have been hiding. Thus there is a well-justified association of trees with life in the myths.

Another bind-rune combining both forms of Algiz is: ⵋ, which is identical to the Scandinavian version of the Hagalaz rune. In

Holland this sign has been traditionally used to symbolize marriage or the union between the male and female principle.

Algiz is the rune often associated with protection and defense, and as such it implies the idea of "shielding," hence its connection with the Valkyries. These are also known as "shield maidens." In addition to choosing the slain on the battlefield, their function is to shield and protect the warrior in the thick of battle. They are known to adopt the shapes of swans and (less well known) ravens. If the pictographic sign of Algiz is laid flat on the ground, it clearly resembles the footprint of a bird, such as a raven or a swan. In fact, in certain areas of witchcraft and among the Gypsies, the Algiz rune is known as a crow's foot, thus: ⤚. (Another function of the Valkyries is that of psychopomps who conduct the slain warriors to Valhalla.)

In its normal upright form the Algiz rune can be used in practical work of a devotional nature, such as when invoking other runes or expanding one's consciousness to the higher realms symbolized by Asgard. It acts as a powerful conductor, channeling energies from man to the gods and from the gods to man. Algiz has been associated with the rainbow bridge, which is the path between Asgard and Midgard and the only way to travel between these two realms. Heimdal, a god especially invoked for protection, is the guardian of the rainbow bridge; he mediates energies from one realm to the other in a fashion similar to that of the Algiz rune. Heimdal therefore can be considered the hidden god-power behind Algiz.

The Algiz rune can be used for healing. By standing upright with the arms raised in the traditional position of Algiz and calling down Uruz, Sowulo, and Ansuz, I have been endowed with such a capacity for healing that the power flowing through my hands could be felt physically. Magically Algiz is one of the strongest runes to be used on four or eight quarters, because it shields, protects, and defends any working done within the circle.

Germanic name ♦ SOWULO

Anglo-Saxon name ♦ SIGIL

Old Norse name ♦ SOL

Phonetic value ♦ S

Traditional meaning ♦ Sun

The ancient Northern peoples, like all primitive peoples, regarded the Sun as a life-giving force. It should, however, be emphasized that they regarded the Sun as feminine. Even in modern German the grammatical gender of *Sonne* is feminine. By way of contrast, in most other magical traditions, such as the Greek and the modern Celtic schools and in Wicca, the Sun is considered masculine. Having advanced from Wicca to Asatru, it took me a considerable time to adjust magically in this respect. The idea that the Sun is feminine is evidently very old and may well stem from a more ancient matriarchal magical tradition. This supposition is corroborated by evidence that in Shinto, the indigenous religion of Japan, and in the oldest Egyptian tradition, the Sun is also viewed as a goddess. The Sun was probably the most important object of worship for primitive man. Life itself depends on it, far more than it does on the Moon. The female principle in primitive culture, which existed a long time before the development of the futhark, was perceived as life-giving, whereas the male role in procreation was not originally known or understood. The notion that the Sun is female is therefore very ancient; this incidentally proves that the Northern myths are far older than the Viking Age, when the Eddas were recorded.

In Holland's oldest tradition, three goddesses were known long before the Aesir or even the Vanir. They were Anbet, who represented the Earth; Wilbet, governing the Moon; and Barbet, ruling the Sun. Traces of worship of Barbet, the Sun goddess, lingered on into the Christian era, when she was Christianized as St. Barbara. In Northern mythology the deity associated with the Sun is the goddess Sunna, who is the conductor or chariot driver of the Sun's life-force. Chariots on which Sun-disks have been mounted have been found in Scandinavia and mostly date from the Bronze Age. The combination of chariot and Sun-disk hints at a relationship between the complementary runes Raido and Sowulo. Raido is the principle of control, or the act of controlling—whereas Sowulo can be the higher spiritual force which is in control.

One reason the Germanic peoples associated a different gender with the Sun is that in the South, the heat of the Sun is often harsh and destructive, whereas the Moon, with its cooling effect in the evening after a day of sweaty labor in the fields, was thought of as a nurturing, comforting, feminine force. In the North, on the other hand, we have always valued the Sun more, simply because we see less of it. Therefore we tend to emphasize its warm, nurturing, and feminine qualities and value it highly for promoting growth. In the South the Sun often causes drought and famine. In the North the lack of Sun would have been a more likely cause of famine.

Sowulo represents the higher will or intent as well as the sense of self and self-worth. It is the highest force in the self, directing the individual's evolution along a specific path. In Jungian terms it represents the process of individuation. In modern occult philosophy, the Sun is a symbol of consciousness—the inner self—and is the polar opposite to the self-image projected upon the outside world, which would be runically expressed best by Isa. Sowulo is associated with spiritual guidance and leadership. In divination Sowulo can direct a course of action or state a positive purpose, although it must always be interpreted in conjunction with the other adjacent runes.

There is nevertheless a destructive element in this rune. It is shaped like a lightning flash. Like lightning, Sowulo strikes suddenly, sweeping aside everything in its way, usually in order to prepare for something better (just as when the atmosphere exudes negative ions following a thunderstorm). This aspect belongs to Thor, the god of lightning. Sowulo therefore can be used to invoke Thor, especially when swift retribution is required. Although the rune is not invertable and keeps the same shape if placed upside down, it can be reversed from left ϟ to right ᚱ. This fact may indicate that there are male and female forms of the rune, or else an introverted and an extroverted form. The introverted form would, in that event, draw power in, whereas the other form would radiate power outwards.

Sowulo is related to the Sun's progress throughout the year, which is divided into two equal halves by the summer and winter solstices. In one half of the year, while the days lengthen, the Sun grows daily in strength; in the other half of the year, the Sun becomes weaker while the days grow shorter. In Northern mythology this mystery is symbolized in the narrative of the death of Baldur, the Sun god, by the hand of his dark twin, Hodur, who in turn is slain at Yuletide when Baldur returns. Baldur is the god most closely associated with Sowulo.

If two Sowulo runes are joined together, we obtain a Sun-wheel or *Fylfot,* one of the world's oldest symbols of the Sun and found in virtually every human culture. In the North the Sun-wheel is associated with Thor. There are two forms: ⌖ and ⌖, one spinning sunwise, the other one widdershins. Magically the former is used to draw power in, the latter is used to expel it.

In addition to Sunna, Baldur, and Thor, Sowulo has a tenuous connection with Odin, as the Sun represents one of Odin's eyes. The eye he sacrificed represents the Moon, the other one the Sun. The latter is visible; the former is hidden in the well of Mimir and thus stands for the Moon shining in the night sky—for the Moon's light is merely a reflection of the Sun's. Through the sacrifice of his eye, Odin became the driving force behind the evolution of our collective folk-soul.

COSMOLOGY OF THE SECOND AETT

The first aett is a description of the forces of creation, which must be counter-balanced by the forces of destruction. We concluded our cosmological résumé of the first aett with the establishment of the Golden Age. We now arrive at the next stage of the cycle of involution and evolution.

The term "Golden Age" refers to the time when gold was used solely as an object of beauty, almost like a toy, and had no specific monetary or fiscal value. The myths describe how the gods fashioned objects of gold for pure enjoyment. The lady named Gullveig, whose name can be translated as "Goldlust," introduced the negative aspect of gold and sowed corruption among the Aesir; for this Gullveig was condemned to death by them. She was burned three times, yet she survived. In one of the myths, Loki devours her heart and thus absorbs the "evil" initiated by Gullveig.

My interpretation of the myth of thrice-burned Gullveig is that at each burning she gave birth to a Norn. Thus the three Norns came into existence. Gullveig was, however, a member of the god-clan of the Vanir. They consequently demanded wergild for her death from the Aesir, which Odin refused to pay. This refusal led to the war between the Vanir and the Aesir. In this war, according to some sources, the Vanir were the victors and occupied Asgard for a period of nine years. According to other authorities, their occupation lasted seven years. Eventually both the Aesir and Vanir realized that they needed to make an alliance against the frost giants. They agreed to a truce and hostages were exchanged. All was well for a time. Frey, Freyja and Niord made their residence in Asgard, while Mimir and Hoenir joined the Vanir in Vanaheim.

How does this myth relate to the second aett? The first rune of this aett, Hagalaz, represents disruptive forces of a particularly female nature. Therefore I am inclined to associate this rune both with Gullveig and more importantly with Urd, the Norn of the past and the guardian of the well of wyrd (or Urd). The Nauthiz rune represents the third Norn, Skuld. Similarly, Isa is the third rune of this aett and is associated with the second Norn, Verdandi. These three runes collectively refer to the passage and measure of time.

Whereas the Aesir established cosmic time and the division of day from night by setting the Sun and Moon in place, the three Norns introduced and governed time as a biological reality. The Norns, in other words, give us the awareness of the passing of time in years, from youth to old age. After their creation of time as the duration of consciousness and experience, everything had a beginning and an end, and everything that was born was doomed to die. At this stage involution of spirit has reached its deepest descent into matter and there is only one way out, expressed in the meaning of the Jera rune.

Involution became evolution when Odin, personifying the collective consciousness of the Northern folk, began his quest for knowledge. The first step in Odin's quest for knowledge was sacrificing himself on Yggdrasil, which is represented by the Eihwaz rune. Through his sacrifice he gained the knowledge of the runes and an understanding of the mysteries underlying the runic signs. He transcended the border between life and death and henceforth gained access to the realms of the dead, becoming the "wild hunter."

He then sacrificed his eye in the well of Mimir, represented by Pertho, and gained knowledge of the past, present, and future. However, he realized the limitations of his power, for he could see into the future without being able to alter what has been destined. He descended to the realm of the dead and conjured up the volva. (Heid is her name in the Eddas. In the West Germanic version of the myth, her name is known to the old Germanic tribes as Erda.) Odin made love to her. Their children are the Valkyries, represented runically by Algiz. The Valkyries are especially endowed with the power to protect and shield, and also act on Odin's behalf in choosing the warriors who will go to Valhalla.

This aett concludes with the Sowulo rune, which symbolizes the return of consciousness in evolution. The first half of this aett is a continuation of the first aett, in the sense that all the runes as far as Jera symbolize a creation process and a progressive descent or involution of consciousness into matter, captured and made subject to the conditions of time and space imposed by the three Norns.

Jera symbolizes the midpoint between involution and evolution. It is here that the wheel of time turns and Odin, through his sacrifices, initiates the process of the return of consciousness. In this function he becomes the personification of the Sun, leading the folk-soul in the direction of evolution.

Third Aett

Germanic name ♦ TEIWAZ

Anglo-Saxon name ♦ TYR

Old Norse name ♦ TYR

Phonetic value ♦ T

Traditional meaning ♦ the god Tyr

This is the first rune of the third aett, which is named after it: the aett of Tyr. Teiwaz is the oldest name known for the god Tyr; its origin is contemporaneous with Wodenaz and Thurisaz. The shape of the Teiwaz rune is like a spear. It also resembles the traditional astrological sign of the planet Mars, identified with the Roman god of war.

Tyr resembles this god in some respects. Both are associated with war and battle. Tyr was the original god of battle in the Northern pantheon, although this attribute was later assumed by Odin. There are significant differences between Mars and Tyr, however; whereas Mars is a warrior purely for the sake of conquest and blood lust, Tyr is a warrior motivated by a sense of justice. He is more of a god of law and order, governing social values, legal contracts and oaths.

The Teiwaz rune should be used in workings to gain justice or to win victory in a conflict. My personal experience of using this rune in order to obtain justice has not always been successful. This may be because I have never found Tyr to be a god with whom I have a strong or natural sympathy. Gods are like people: some you get along with, others you find less in common with. It is as simple as that. Despite Odin's reputation for double-dealing, I have always found him to be fair. Possibly Odin's reputed perfidy was originally one of Tyr's attributes, which Odin inherited when he succeeded Tyr as the supreme god in the pantheon. After all, it was Tyr who swore a false oath when Fenris was to be bound. No one else was prepared to do this. In so doing he lost his sword-hand. Nevertheless,

Tyr is a god of valor and bravery, for it takes great courage to sacrifice a hand.

The psychological values and principles of this rune relate to its role as a rune of conflict and confrontation, implying courage and honor, especially honorable conduct in warfare. It encourages bravery and can provide the initial impetus to set out to tackle a difficult situation. Very often this rune in divination can pertain to legal conflicts or a court action. In a reading it often indicates the assertive energies available and where to direct these energies. In combination with Raido it can create a powerful bind-rune to ensure the favorable outcome of a conflict, legal or otherwise.

On the spiritual level of interpretation, the Teiwaz rune embodies the values of the spiritual warrior. This rune also has an association with death, especially death in battle. In the rune-charms of the *Havamal* it is meant to be part of the twelfth rune-charm, designed to communicate with the dead. Although the Teiwaz rune is evidently the rune of Tyr, it was in Odin's name that a spear used to be thrown over the enemy on the battlefield as an act of dedication to Odin. Teiwaz also has connotations of fertility, implying the active, impregnating male force which is illustrated by the shape of the rune. Tyr was the original Skyfather; the following rune, Berkana, is related to the Earthmother and to the process of birth. The shape of the Teiwaz rune resembles the Irminsul, which is a symbolic representation of Yggdrasil as the cosmic axis.

Germanic name ♦ BERKANA

Anglo-Saxon name ♦ BEORC

Old Norse name ♦ BJARKAN

Phonetic value ♦ B

Traditional meaning ♦ birch

In most of the Germanic languages this rune has the meaning of "birch." However, the Anglo-Saxons translated it as "poplar."

First and foremost this is a goddess-rune. Pictographically, it resembles a pair of breasts when viewed sideways from on top. This rune especially relates to the goddess Berchta, who is the patron of mothers and children. She resides in the underworld; there she has a beautiful garden where the young children who die in infancy are said to go. The goddess Berchta has some aspects in common with Frigga and might indeed be a different form of the same goddess. The Berkana rune, in particular, refers to the processes of gestation and birth. Pertho looks like an opened-up Berkana, which suggests that what remains a hidden promise in Berkana will be brought into the open by Pertho. Frigga, the goddess who more than any other is associated with the Pertho rune, consequently also governs Berkana. Frigga and the Berkana rune have the qualities of secrecy and protectiveness in common. Frigga also resembles Berchta in her protection of children. Unlike Frigga, however, Berchta does not give birth; instead she cares for abandoned children. This aspect would identify her with Holda.

The Berkana rune is very beneficial for women and especially for women's problems. It has a pronounced healing effect when applied to female troubles such as difficult menstrual periods. It also has a rejuvenating effect; in Holland a liquid made from birch leaves is rubbed on the scalp as a remedy for baldness.

According to an old Dutch May Day custom, boys used to dress up in disguise and chase the young women of the village with birch twigs. If the women failed to escape their pursuers, they received a good spanking with the twigs. This custom originated as a fertility ritual. Another customary use of birch twigs survives in Holland to this day: on the feast day of St. Nicholas, a saint who derives many of his attributes from Wodan, children who have been naughty during the year receive, instead of a present, bunches of birch twigs with which they may be given a hiding (spanking). In some areas of Holland, when a couple married and moved into their new house, friends and neighbors would tie a bunch of birch twigs to the door as a token of good luck. This practice was also intended to ensure fertility for the couple.

The Germanic tribes, like their Celtic neighbors, were tree-worshippers, and birch is one of the sacred trees. Berkana is a symbol of the world of plants and trees; in Northern thinking this rune represents the emergence of an agricultural society, based on settled villages, which replaced the hunting and gathering society. To the Lapps, whose tradition has much in common with the Germanic culture, the birch tree was a "tree of life." They would erect a northward-leaning pole made of birch wood; a nail placed at the top of the pole symbolized the Pole Star. In Siberia, shamans regarded the birch tree as shamanically associated with the underworld. According to an old heathen custom in that area, a birch tree would be buried upside down in the ground in the belief that so doing would give one the ability to climb the tree upside down and thus reach the nether realms.

Furthermore, below the birch tree often grows the *Amanita muscaria,* a well-known "magic" mushroom used in rituals to achieve altered states of consciousness, in which "soul journeys" to the underworld were undertaken. Both Teiwaz and Berkana represent aspects of the Tree of Life, Teiwaz as the Irminsul and Berkana as its female counterpart.

Both Teiwaz and Berkana are associated with an ancient Germanic initiation rite in which the candidate was symbolically slain by being "hanged" on Yggdrasil. Two sacred words were whispered into the candidate's ear during this ceremony. These words were Mannaz and Berkana, which together symbolized rebirth. Then the twelfth rune-charm of the *Havamal* was recited and the candidate was ceremonially considered reborn as an *einherjar* or hero. Traces of this ritual survive in Masonic ceremonies. The birch was seen as a magical tree in early medieval Christianity and witches were accused of riding on broomsticks made of branches and twigs of birch. In divination, Berkana indicates a process of growth, a caring, maternal influence, and creativity. Creativity here includes the process of childbirth and motherhood, although the meaning of creativity may equally extend to a creative or artistic project.

For children, and for young girls in particular, the Berkana rune is a lovely, protective symbol. I often advise parents to obtain a silver nameplate or bracelet inscribed with their daughter's name on the outside and with three Berkana runes on the inside. This amulet, which invokes the protection of the Goddess in all her aspects, has produced favorable results. One of my earliest regular clients had a girl who was very accident-prone and was always falling and hurting herself. The problem was solved by the use of such a bracelet.

Germanic name ♦ EHWAZ

Anglo-Saxon name ♦ EOH

Old Norse name ♦ none

Phonetic value ♦ E

Traditional meaning ♦ horse

Most runologists agree that this rune indicates a pair of horses. Edred Thorsson, in his *Futhark: A Handbook of Rune Magic,* has pointed out that this may symbolize divine or heroic pairs, such as Hengest and Horsa, traditionally the leaders of the first Germanic settlers in England. These names respectively mean "stallion" and "horse." A stallion is a male horse, so the name Hengest indicates clearly that the person bearing this name was male. I suggest that the word *horsa* ("horse") could equally well be female; in this case, Horsa was Hengest's female sister, rather than his brother.

The most obvious meaning of Ehwaz implies vehicles and control of vehicles. In the olden days a horse and chariot were common vehicles. In modern days this rune could refer to a car or, more probably, a motorbike. Ehwaz also represents the physical vehicle and may be incorporated in a healing working. On a deeper level, the Ehwaz rune represents the vehicle, or in psychological terms the persona, which is used to relate the external world to one's own emotional attitudes. In other words, it stands for one's ability to adjust to various situations.

Ehwaz, moreover, emphatically relates to Sleipnir, Odin's eight-legged horse. C. G. Jung stated in *Symbols of Transformation* that the oldest image of Odin was a centaur-like creature who was part-man and part-horse.

My first impression of this rune was that it represented a mare. Unlike most warriors who rode stallions, priests of the old faith of the Aesir rode a mare. There are also associations with Sleipnir's parents, one of whom was Loki, who had adopted the form of a mare. This myth of Sleipnir is, in all probability, derived from an older, lost myth which originated from the prehistorical period in Northern Europe, where a horse-cult practiced. Evidence for the existence of this cult is found in the *Saga of St. Olaf*, which describes a group of women in tenth-century Norway performing rituals over a preserved horse's penis. This object of veneration was called a *volsi,* and this cultic practice was an aspect of seidr magic. There are also two demi-goddesses, Thorgerd and Irpa, who are said to have been involved in various practices of this nature. This cult met with the strong disapproval of the Christian Church and consequently was quashed. The name Volsi appears as one of the bynames for Odin in Wagner's operas and it is significant that in one version of the *Volsung Saga,* the Volsi dynasty (or, as we should probably say to be more correct, the Volsi tribe) is described as being directly descended from Odin himself. These facts may shed light on the meaning of another of Odin's titles, that of "Gelding." However, no myth has survived explaining this term fully.

Tacitus recorded some divinatory practices of the Germanic tribes involving horses; for example, the behavior of a horse was held to predict the outcome of a battle. Horses have always been thought of as highly sacred among the Germanic peoples and there may well have existed a secret, primitive horse-cult of fertility worship. Horseflesh was only eaten during ritual sacrifices and was never part of the normal diet. According to Scandinavian sources, Frey, the god of male fertility, was associated with the horse-cult, as was his sister Freyja, the patroness of volvas. They were said to wear horse-masks and supposedly had the ability to assume mare-shapes, in which they could roam about as "nightmares." In the continental Germanic tradition, Wodan was worshipped as the god of horses; Even in recent times rumors have been circulated about the existence of a society of "horse whispers" who were a magical fraternity. This may well be a vestige of one of the horse-cults.

Horses were also used in more mundane practices. A traditional way of cursing was to use a "nithing-pole" or "pole of insult" on top of which a horse's head was set. A well-known example of this custom can be found in *Egil's Saga*, in which Egil successfully constructed a nithing-pole against the King and Queen of Norway with the intention of forcing them to leave the country.

Traditionally, the Ehwaz rune has been interpreted by other rune-workers as particularly relevant to marriage. If the Ehwaz rune is cut in two vertically, we can see that it is a double Laguz rune. Laguz has been associated with love. I suggest that apart from being a significant rune for marriage, Ehwaz has a great bearing on partnerships and joint enterprises of all kinds. It is a rune that can unify two people in a strong cooperative relationship such as marriage or even a business partnership.

Ehwaz therefore symbolizes partnership and cooperation, such as exists between a horse and its rider. It can thus be understood why Ehwaz has been regarded by other rune-workers as being particularly relevant to fertility as well as marriage, for horses are well known to be very caring towards their offspring. The mating of two horses is a very beautiful event, for the male is very gentle and careful in his approach towards the female.

Psychologically, the Ehwaz rune can teach us the art of adjusting. Whereas Raido, a rune strong in sympathy with Ehwaz, enables us to take control of a situation, Ehwaz enables us to adjust to a situation and make the best of it. Magically this would be a very powerful rune force to invoke good luck for any shared enterprises. In occult practice, Ehwaz represents the astral or etheric body, or that part of the self which can be projected outside the physical body. A shape-shift can be performed in a negative aspect. In this manner one projects the astral body and assumes the shape of a horse, in which a magical attack can be carried out. The effect is commonly known as a nightmare. Ehwaz in a bind-rune with Eihwaz can be used for a "soul hunt"; both runes combined can successfully invoke Wodan in his aspect of the wild hunter.

In divination this rune almost always indicates something of a female nature, and often relates to one's own mother or other older females. This interpretation is based on experience rather than on the myths. Horses in general are understood in psychology as symbols of the instinctual drives. The Ehwaz rune has a strong bearing on the female libido in psychology. Often in readings this rune in inverted form indicates a loss of some sort or the breakup of a relationship. Also, false friends have been indicated by the rune in various readings.

Germanic name ♦ MANNAZ

Anglo-Saxon name ♦ MAN

Old Norse name ♦ MADR

Phonetic value ♦ M

Traditional meaning ♦ man

The term *men* in old Germanic languages, for example in Anglo-Saxon, denoted not just the male section of the folk. The words for "man" and "woman" were *weapmen* and *weavemen* respectively;

clearly the former means "men with weapons," and the latter translates literally as "men who weave," i.e., women. Thus the word ending -*men* was used for both sexes and it is in this context that the
Mannaz rune should be viewed. This rune not only means "man" or
"mankind," it is also the name of mankind's ancestor and progenitor.

Within the vast field of Northern European mythology, various
accounts of the creation of the human race are provided. The myth
of Ask and Embla is one version which has already been discussed;
we will now examine some other versions.

In the Continental Germanic tradition Mannaz, who is mentioned
by Tacitus as the progenitor of the Germanic people, was the son of
Tuisco, who was Earth-born. Tuisco is an older form of Tyr; thus
Mannaz was a tribal ancestor god. He, in turn, had three sons:
Ingvio, whose name appeared in the Inguz rune, Irmio, and Istio.
These are also the names of the three main branches of the West
Germanic tribes: the Ingaevones, who inhabited the coastal areas of
the North Sea; the Herminones, who lived near the middle and lower
Elbe; and the Istaevones, who were found between the Rhine and
the Weser. (This threefold division is another example of the occur-
rence of three as a magical number.)

Another narrative relating to the origins of the human race is the
Rigsthula, one of the poems of the Eddas. This poem describes how
Heimdal sets off on a journey to Midgard and is the guest of three
married couples in turn. He spends the night with each couple,
sleeping between the man and the woman; later all three women
give birth to his sons. Each couple represents one of the social classes. Although Mannaz is not directly mentioned in this story, it is
clearly an alternative variation of the myth mentioned above; by
comparing the two myths, it can be established that Heimdal is the
equivalent of Mannaz. Indeed, Heimdal is the god primarily associated with the Mannaz rune. Just as Mannaz is the progenitor of the
three tribes, Heimdal is the ancestor of the three classes. Of course,
this class system cannot be interpreted in Marxist terms. In the old

days, each class had its value and its own place in relationship to the others, which precluded exploitation. (We could probably learn a lot from this social structure.) This rune is precisely about social structure and its implications for the tribe and for the individual. For this reason there is a connection with the Raido rune.

The previous rune, Ehwaz, was mainly related to animals, in particular to horses. The Mannaz rune is similar in shape to the Ehwaz rune, which makes sense—man is after all an animal with above-average intelligence. Mannaz, therefore, is one of the "hug" runes mentioned in the *Sigdrifumal*. That these runes are positioned next to each other in the futhark is further evidence that whoever constructed the futhark knew what he was doing in establishing their sequence. Man and animals share the same environment and are mutually dependent on each other. The image of Odin as a centaur denotes the development of humans out of animals, the differentiation between mind and instinct, and the modern-day alienation from nature.

The Mannaz rune signifies cooperation between people sharing the same environment for the benefit of the whole of the tribe. Mannaz is a double Wunjo. Wunjo is associated with perfection and the conscious application of the will; Mannaz is the cooperative effort in exerting the will for the common good of the tribe.

The first two stanzas of the *Havamal* read as follows:

Young and alone on a long road
Once I lost my way.
Rich I felt when I found another,
Man rejoices in man.

A kind word need not cost much.
The price of praise can be cheap,
With half a loaf and an empty cup
I found myself a friend.
     [TRANSLATION BY W. H. AUDEN AND PAUL B. TAYLOR]

In divination this rune refers to people in general. The sort of people referred to and their relationship with the querent can be deduced from the other runes appearing with it in a reading. Inverted Mannaz sometimes indicates an enemy, although I have seen it denoting a male homosexual. In readings Mannaz can indicate legal affairs and matters of mutual cooperation, especially when it occurs in conjunction with Ehwaz. Together with Raido, it will indicate assistance from people or counsel given.

Magically, this rune can be of great help in attracting support from one's peer group in a dispute. Combined in a bind-rune with Ansuz, it can be employed to win an intellectual argument or pass an examination. Both runes strengthen the mind when necessity arises. An even stronger sigil for this purpose can be constructed by adding Raido and Ehwaz to the bind-rune.

In the cosmological interpretation of the futhark sequence Mannaz expresses the development of humankind's intellectual powers and awareness as co-creator of Nature. Initially primitive and subject to the environment, humans now unfortunately have too much control over Nature and are exploiting their environment.

Germanic name ♦ LAGUZ

Anglo-Saxon name ♦ LAGU

Old Norse name ♦ LOGR

Phonetic value ♦ L

Traditional meaning ♦ lake

This rune is feminine. The goddess associated with Laguz is Nerthus. She is probably the oldest goddess known from Germanic sources and she was worshipped on an island in a lake, possibly in Frisia. She was supposed to bestow blessings wherever she visited. Once a

year, everyone laid down their weapons while her wagon was ritually driven around the mainland. It is not clear whether this ritual
took place in spring or in autumn; a remnant of it was observed in
medieval Holland, where a decorated ship was used in processions.
Eventually, however, the church put a stop to this practice, which
was also probably connected with the custom of ship burial. Nerthus
corresponds to the Scandinavian god Niord, who is also the patron of
the sea and harbors. Indeed they may be either one and the same
god, or else husband and wife to each other. Both possibilities have
been suggested by various writers on the mythology of the North.

In Holland we know of a native goddess named Nehelennia. A
statue of her dating from the first century has been found in
Walcheren, one of the islands now forming the Dutch province of
Zealand. She is portrayed with a dog and a basket of apples, and she
was sometimes described as holding a horn of plenty. Niord is comparable in this respect, for he is also invoked for peace and plenty.

Niord and consequently Nerthus are the parents of Frey and
Freyja. Their rune, Laguz, precedes the Inguz rune, which is primarily the rune of Frey and secondarily the rune of Freyja. (This
again shows that there is a coherent system in the sequence of the
futhark. Indeed, if we refer back to the previous runes in this aett,
we might be tempted to draw the conclusion that Nerthus is the
unnamed goddess who was the hypothetical mother of Tuisco and is
possibly identical with Berchta, the goddess of the Berkana rune.)
Mannaz is their son and Ingvio is one of the sons of Mannaz.

Ingvio, or Yngvi in Scandinavian tradition, is another name for
Frey, who is Freyja's twin brother. If Mannaz and Heimdal are one
and the same, it would explain the relationship between Freyja and
Heimdal. From Norse sources we know that Heimdal is Freyja's *leikur*
or guardian, a function which in Norse society was often taken up
by either the maternal uncle or the elder brother. This tradition goes
back to prehistoric times, when men were not aware of their role in
the procreative act and the maternal uncle was regarded as the

proven blood relative of the child and responsible for its welfare. This is some indication of the great antiquity of Northern mythology.

Laguz also has an Old Norse form: *logr* or *laukar*. This word means "sorcery," which is one of the rune's functions. Sorcery or seidr was, in particular, practiced in the Vanir cult; all the gods and goddesses mentioned above in relation to this rune, with the possible exception of Tuisco, are Vanir gods. It is Freyja who introduced sorcery to the Aesir, teaching it to Odin. Laguz' meaning of lake, water or sea, interpreted according to modern occult thinking, may reflect the astral substance. Water takes the shape of its container, and the astral or etheric matter can also be formed at will by visualization and concentration. The concentrated imagination forms the vessel in which the energy is contained.

Laguz can be inverted. It can also be reversed. When inverted, its meaning becomes negated. When reversed, it refers to the tide. An active Laguz rune Ⲅ symbolizes the flooding tide, and an inactive Laguz rune ˥ means the ebbing of the tide. In divination, this rune can be used to infer whether a particular project has been carried by a favorable tide.

Laguz is a powerful rune for occult work of a beneficial nature. Thus it differs from Hagalaz. Water, like the astral, is a transmitting agency or a mediating and conducting principle. Laguz can be used to influence others or to invade other people's dream-states. By projecting a Laguz rune between the eyes of an unsuspecting person, any reasonable request is more likely to elicit a positive response.

Laguz, according to some German writers, also means "love" or "life." There is some truth in this interpretation, for Laguz may well symbolize the waters of life; it also represents the forces of mutual attraction called "love." In fact the shape of Laguz is that of a half-Ehwaz, as has been already explained, and Ehwaz is the rune of partnerships and marriages.

Germanic name ♦ INGUZ

Anglo-Saxon name ♦ ING

Old Norse name ♦ none

Phonetic value ♦ NG

Traditional meaning ♦ the god Frey

The name of this rune refers primarily to the god Yngvi Frey. The position of the Inguz rune in the futhark ties in with the preceding runes. Just as Mannaz relates to Heimdal, and Laguz to Nerthus and Niord, so Inguz signifies Niord's children, Frey and Freyja. Frey is the son of Niord; "son of" is one of the meanings of this rune. In Anglo-Saxon and Friesian, patronomic names were formed by adding "-ing" after the father's forename; this is the usual significance of the "-ing" in names like Bunting and Hadding which are found in England and Holland. The old Swedish royal family was called the Ynglingar; they were supposedly descended from Yngvi Frey, just as the Anglo-Saxon royal families in England were said to be descended from Woden (according to the genealogies given by Bede). Inguz is also connected with the Ingaevones, described under the Mannaz rune. My personal belief is that the real significance of the name "England" is in fact "land of Ing," or "Ingland." The invading Germanic tribes, such as the Angles, Saxons, Friesians, Jutes, and later on the Vikings, were probably Ingaevones. In fact, most of the other Germanic countries appear to be associated with a specific patron god or goddess. Thus Holland could be identified with "Holda's land," Germany with "Tiw's land," Frisia could be matched with Frija, Austria (i.e., *Oesterreich*) might be seen as "Ostara's realm" (or *Reich*), and perhaps even Scandinavia is to be identified with the mountain giantess Skadi. Skadi may have also given her name to Scotland: the native Scottish goddess named Scathach has much in common with Skadi. Of course, these associations are not being put forth to explain the etymological derivation of specific countries' names, but rather to suggest their inner and more mystical significance.

Inguz is also a fertility rune. Frey, after whom this rune is named, is traditionally portrayed with a large erect phallus and can be regarded as the Northern equivalent of Pan. Nevertheless, I regard this rune as a symbol of *female* fertility, its shape being reminiscent of the female genitalia. There is an alternative shape of this rune used in some variants of the Scandinavian futhark: ᛜ. This would be the male form. If we take the Anglo-Saxon form of Inguz and duplicate it a few times: ᛜ, we can see that it has a remarkable similarity to a double helix, the shape of a DNA chain. This supports the preceding idea that Inguz is a rune of progeny, and it goes without saying that the phrase "son of" may be replaced equally well by the phrase "daughter of." Inguz is the carrier of genetic material and confers upon the individual inherited characteristics from ancestors. Reincarnation may be implied here as well, although we in the North interpret this concept in a slightly different way. It is a Northern belief that we are reincarnated into the same tribe or even the same family. This is connected with the spiritual idea of the evolution of the individual within the framework of a collective unit of which he or she is a part. In this context the Inguz rune represents the continuation of the tribal or family hamingja, and it was at one time considered possible to pass on the hamingja voluntarily to a chosen individual of the family before death had occurred by means of a magical practice which has now been lost. (A variant of this practice is known to have been preserved among people of African descent in Surinam and elsewhere.)

On a practical magical level, the Inguz rune can be used as an alternative form to a magical circle, for Inguz has the shape of a circle adapted to the use of carving on hard materials, and the four corners of the Inguz rune correspond to the four quarters in a normal magic circle. Within this circle, magical rune-work can be performed. Furthermore, the Inguz rune can be used in a spell or sigil to contain other runic energies within it, if the working is to be carried out over a longer period of time (for example, a gestation period). Magically, nine days would be an ideal period of gestation using Inguz.

The Inguz rune is an excellent rune to use for astral projection. This can be carried out in a way similar to the usual occult practice, by visualizing the Inguz rune on a door or curtain and then project- ing oneself through it. It would be even more magically effective to obtain or make a magical mirror in the shape of Inguz. This is one of the nine non-invertible runes, and it is associated with the world of Vanaheim and, to a certain extent, Alfheim. These worlds can be reached easily, as they are very close to the physical plane.

Inguz is closely related to Kenaz and Jera and can be seen as a progression of these runes. We can view Kenaz as either the male or female half of a polarity, depending on the gender of the person who is working with it. With Jera we see two similar shapes circling around each other; here we have both polarities, albeit still separate, like the two halves of a whole. In the shape of the Inguz rune we find both halves joined and integrated, symbolizing completion, totality and fulfillment. An interesting concept to think about from a Craft point of view when working with Kenaz, Jera, and Inguz is their use as a magical system symbolizing the three seasons of the agricultural year. (In olden days our ancestors knew only three sea- sons: spring, summer, and winter. The fourth season of autumn is a later addition.) Kenaz could be seen as the rune symbolizing sowing. Inguz is then the rune symbolizing the process of germination and growth, and Jera would be the rune symbolizing the reaping of the harvest. These correspondences tie-in very well with the other cor- respondences that relate to each of these three runes.

In runic divination, Inguz often denotes the completion of a sit- uation and the progression to the next stage of the querent's affairs, depending of course on the other runes in the reading. As such, Inguz can mean a transformation or even a dark night of the soul. It is one of the runes which can induce initiation, especially when one is working with the feminine mysteries. The Inguz rune is the rune to be employed for the practice of lunar magic, such as seidr or, in modern terms, witchcraft, fertility magic, and earth magic; in the worship of wells and trees; and in general the cult of the Vanir. At this stage of human development as seen through the cosmology, it denotes humankind's spiritual aspiration and the attempt of primitive humans to understand and manipulate the natural environment through the development of religion and magic.

Germanic name ♦ OTHILA

Anglo-Saxon name ♦ ETHEL

Old Norse name ♦ none

Phonetic value ♦ O

Traditional meaning ♦

inherited land

The oldest literal meaning of this rune passed down to us from the continental Germanic source is "noble." In this sense it is directly related to the Anglo-Saxon word *atheling,* meaning "prince" or "noble." The German word *adel* and the Dutch word *edel* also mean "noble." Both derive from the same root.

The god who is most obviously related to this rune is Odin. It is well established in literature from the Viking period that Odin was the god of the nobility, whereas the thralls had recourse to Thor. Personally, I cannot entirely accept this association of Odin with a particular class. It was a later introduction, instigated by the ruling classes, who misused this aspect of the religion to control the lower classes, as is usually done when a religion becomes powerfully established. In actual fact, Wodan originally was worshipped as a god of the people, as is emphasized in Chapter 5.

The shape of Othila is a combination of Inguz and Gebo, and Othila can be interpreted as the "gift of Ing," which probably explains why Othila has been related to the concept of inheritance by some modern commentators. By comparing the concept of inheritance to the Inguz rune, the previous rune in the futhark, it can be established that it is genetic material that is being inherited, at least on an occult level. On a material level, the meaning of Othila implies the inheritance of land and the rights to possession of that land. The right of "odal" is still a legal right in Norway and means that a person has the right to stay and live on an estate after the owner has died. Thus the right of "odal" stayed in that family until property was sold; even then it could be redeemed within a specific time, namely twenty years.

The mystery of blood and soil are also a part of this runic complex. Unfortunately, this mystery has been misrepresented by twentieth-century German politicians who had little knowledge of its real meaning. For the Anglo-Saxons, as for other nations in earlier times, the consecration of the soil by shedding blood in battle to conquer that territory ensured their willingness to defend it against subsequent would-be invaders. The mutual interdependence of the land with the people who worked the land, and who were thus prepared to die on and for it in defense of their community or tribe, was the means by which the land was secured for future generations. This is how villages, communities, and even nations are gradually built.

On a higher level of interpretation, the mystery of blood and soil refers to the sacrificed king. In the Germanic tribal system, the king was believed to be descended from the gods, usually from Odin but sometimes from Frey or Tyr. Furthermore, the king was seen as the bearer of the hamingja of his people. It was customary that when a king ran out of luck and could no longer guarantee prosperity and the power of fertility for the land, he was sacrificed. (This was also the custom in some of the Mediterranean countries.) The son became the next king if he was fit for the office; if not, another member of the royal family would succeed to the throne. Therefore the choice of the king's wife was considered especially important in light of the belief that the offspring would be the next to bear the hamingja of the people and would inherit the king's "luck" and vital abilities, such as courage and wisdom. In modern thought, this would of course be understood as the genetic inheritance referred to in the previous section on Inguz. We can thus conclude that it is of vital importance for the future of one's folk, and in consideration of one's responsibility towards one's ancestors, that any man or woman most carefully considers the choice of a spouse, who will be the father or mother of their children and who will pass on their hamingja to the next generation.

Of course, this theory by no means relates solely to the Northern European people; it holds equally true for all nations. Unfortunately it has been denied any validity and has been swept under the carpet. It re-emerged in a distorted form as racism or class division and as such manifested itself as the Jungian "shadow" in the collective unconscious. The Othila rune represents the virtue of loyalty towards one's family, tribe or village, and towards one's country. Loyalty, which is most aptly expressed in the Icelandic sagas, is one of the traditional values in the social structure of the Northern nations.

Magically, the Othila rune can be used to invoke Odin in his aspect of wanderer and teacher. Odin has three main aspects ascribed to him. These are Odin, Vili, and Ve; these names correspond to his aspects of warrior, shaman, and wanderer, respectively. Besides being one of Odin's names, Ve also means "sacred enclosure," which was that part of the hof or temple where only the officiating gothar had access. It was the place where the ritual regalia was kept. The Othila rune has been associated with an enclave by other rune-workers, and an enclave invokes images of safety and protection. It is mythologically comparable to the walls of Asgard, which were built as a protection against the giants.

Germanic name ◆ DAGAZ

Anglo-Saxon name ◆ DAEG

Old Norse name ◆ none

Phonetic value ◆ D

Traditional meaning ◆ day

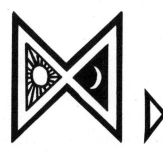

This rune has been accepted by most rune-workers as being the last rune in the futhark. Nevertheless, the oldest complete futhark, known from the Gotland stone in Sweden (425 C.E.), places Othila as the last rune. This is, in fact, the only case where two runes can alter position without drastically altering the esoteric meaning of the futhark sequence. Until now the whole futhark sequence has followed a coherent pattern, as we have seen, but for the moment we must examine the meaning of this rune and then discuss the question of whether to place Dagaz or Othila at the end of the futhark.

The meaning of the name of this rune is quite clear: *daeg, dag, Tag,* "day." All these words are derived from the name Dagaz. The associations of this rune are primarily with either the dawning of the new day or else with the midpoint of the day, when the Sun is at its zenith, at noon.

Dagaz can be considered the counterpart of Jera, since both runes refer to time. Jera relates to the division of the year and Dagaz relates to the division of the day. Dagaz is placed exactly opposite Jera in a futhark circle, and since Jera is especially connected with the Yuletide or midwinter and the return of the Sun, Dagaz is connected with midsummer, when the Sun is at its highest point and will begin to recede. In mythology this phenomenon is expressed as the death of Baldur, which instigates the Ragnarok.

Thus, like Jera, Dagaz is a rune of change. Jera, as mentioned previously, is a rune of gentle change, whereas Dagaz is the rune of cataclysmic change. Whenever energy reaches a saturation point, it is forcefully converted into its opposite nature. Whatever is fully positive will turn into a negative. The shape of the rune resembles a lemniscate, the symbol of infinity; it also resembles a Moebius strip, a symbol of timelessness and unlimited possibilities. A negative aspect of Dagaz is nuclear fission. The description of the Ragnarok does indeed correspond to what we now know would be the result of a nuclear war. Northern mythology mentions the Fimbulwinter, which will last three years; this describes exactly what present-day science knows to be a "nuclear winter."

Dagaz is a rune with many layers of kenning. It represents the end of an era and the beginning of the next cycle. It acts as a catalyst initiating change without changing its own nature. Therefore it is assigned to the controlling power of Loki and, to a certain extent, Heimdal, Loki's counterpart, and also to Surt, who is an agent of total destruction. Heimdal is the counterpart of Loki in the sense that he represents fire born out of water, whereas Loki represents wildfire. They are, however, adversaries who destroy each other at the Ragnarok. Dagaz is the rune of the rainbow bridge, the pathway to Asgard, which links the worlds of Midgard and Asgard. Heimdal is the guardian of this bridge and is there to act as the guardian on the threshold, a function common to other occult traditions. Heimdal is particularly associated with the evolution and progress of the human race. His domain is between the worlds, while Dagaz operates between light and darkness, mediating in both directions but partaking of neither. Dagaz synthesizes, transmutes, and dissolves all opposing polarities.

Dagaz is above and beyond all levels of being. It is both being and non-being and stands for the supreme mystery of existence. Magically, Dagaz can function internally as a rainbow bridge by connecting the right hemisphere of the brain with its left hemisphere. The left eye is controlled by the right hemisphere and the right eye by the left hemisphere. By visualizing a golden line of light, starting in the left eye, moving upwards to the left hemisphere and then downwards connecting with the right eye, and then continuing to visualize the line upwards to the right hemisphere and downwards to the left eye again, thereby closing the circuit, a Dagaz rune is traced. The result of a working of this kind can be a split second of total knowledge, or what is otherwise termed "cosmic consciousness." When connecting the hemispheres through the eyes, the crossover point located at the center of Dagaz is the mystical chakra corresponding to the pineal gland, known in traditional occultism as the "third eye." This rune can transform consciousness, and it is the most appropriate rune for the purpose of initiation.

On a practical magical level, Dagaz is used on the four- or eight-fold division of the quarters to designate the area outside time and space, or "between the worlds." For this purpose, Dagaz can be linked with Algiz in a bind-rune for extra protection. As we have seen, Algiz is also connected with Heimdal, and for situations requiring protection Heimdal is possibly the most powerful god that can be invoked.

On a very mundane level, Dagaz can be used to hide things from view. This can be exemplified by a personal anecdote. My colleague, Moonwulf, came to London and then discovered he had no padlock for his motorbike. So he simply enveloped it in Dagaz; when he came back after six hours, the bike was still there. In crime-ridden London that is an amazing piece of magic! Those who are well trained in visualization can envelop themselves in Dagaz and be "invisible"; in other words, they can remain unnoticed. Subsequent experience also proves that it can be used to make cars "invisible" to traffic wardens when out of need one has to park illegally!

It is my opinion that it is Dagaz, not Othila, which should be placed as the last rune in the futhark. All the runes have fixed positions in the futhark except these last two, which can be interchanged. I said earlier that Dagaz is opposite to Jera and complements Jera in its meaning, which would not be the case if we exchanged its position with Othila. The notion that Dagaz has a relationship with midsummer and by inference also with midwinter is also borne out by a Stone Age monument in Ireland known as New Grange. This monument contains an entrance on which are engraved eight Dagaz runes. Within the chamber of the monument is a stone altar which is illuminated, weather permitting, by the winter Sun at the winter solstice, this being exactly the opposite of the summer solstice in the calendar year. This proves that the ancient Irish knew the symbol which we now call the Dagaz rune and used it to denote a specific yearly phenomenon. Furthermore, we must bear in mind the association of Dagaz with the Ragnarok, which represents the end of one cycle before a new cycle starts again with Fehu. Both

Dagaz and Fehu are runes of the element of fire, Fehu operating as the creative aspect of fire, and Dagaz as its destructive aspect. At the end of a cycle Dagaz fuses with Fehu in a process of change. The futhark thus establishes an eternal cycle.

COSMOLOGY OF THE THIRD AETT

This last aett, the aett of Tyr, differs from the first two in a specific respect. Both the first and the second aett deal broadly with numinous beings. Whereas the first aett describes the gods and all other beings coming into existence, and the second aett describes the necessary antagonistic forces, the third aett gives an overview of the human condition. Although several runes are named after gods in the third aett, it nonetheless portrays the gods in their function as teachers and benefactors of humankind.

In this aett we examine the changes and development of human evolution under the guidance of the gods through the Ragnarok and beyond. This aett can therefore be thought of as the aett of transformation. This transformation represents a summary of the development of the human race which ultimately leads to the Ragnarok.

The Teiwaz rune symbolizes the Iron Age, during which tools and weapons for hunting and gathering were developed. Made of iron, they were more effective, so that warfare became a more organized occupation. (Human inventiveness, especially that of the Northern peoples, has always been applied to, among other things, producing more efficient means of killing.) The social concepts of rulership and justice were developed during this period.

Then comes the Berkana rune, the rune of birch, which is a symbol for the world of plants and trees. In the cosmological order it stands for the development of agriculture and the establishment of settled communities which superseded the hunting and gathering society. It also may represent the dominance of the matriarchal tradition, which was in turn succeeded by the domestication of animals as expressed by the third rune of this aett, Ehwaz. In the olden days, human's relationship with domesticated animals entailed mutual benefit. (In modern-day society, unfortunately, animals are abused and exploited.) With a civilized society firmly established, opportunities arose for humankind to explore higher levels of consciousness. Notions of law, the spirit, and the development of logic as an intellectual concept were developed. This progression is expressed by the Mannaz rune. At this point in history, the matriarchal tradition is superseded by patriarchy, the forerunner of the technological age. Simultaneously, the feminine tradition, deprived of political power, turns inward and paves the way for a new expansion in human consciousness, from which magic and emotional development arise. The rune expressing this is Laguz, which furthermore represents the development of the "feeling" side of human evolution, the emergence of a magical tradition, and spiritual awareness.

Further development occurs as humans realize the divine part in themselves and becomes aware of the gods or "invent" the gods, which is runically expressed by Inguz. This stage is accompanied by the seeds of destruction, as at this point society becomes stable and possesses constructed hierarchies of power and the corruption that these entail. However, the circle is drawing to a close, the seeds of destruction take root, and its flowers burst forth, marking disintegration. Society reaches a crisis point. All that was achieved in the past breaks down and the social structure disintegrates, leading to the Wolf Age of greed and the Axe Age of war.

Nothing is certain. Night becomes day. Day is indistinguishable from night. Confrontation, terror, and chaos rule Midgard. The fires of Muspelheim ravage the Earth, water engulfs the land. The old order passes. All of this is incorporated in the meaning of the Dagaz rune. However, this is not the end. The fires do not totally destroy, the waters do not submerge the Earth forever; both cleanse and purify the world in readiness for a new beginning. Many are destroyed in the Ragnarok, but the children of the gods survive and become the younger gods of a new age. Lif and Liftrasir come down from their hiding place in Yggdrasil and inherit their father's land made new. This is expressed through the meaning of the Othila rune as the last rune in the futhark, symbolizing the new and reborn homeland. (My preference is that Dagaz should be the last rune in the futhark for reasons given in the section on that rune. However, for the sake of balance, I present this alternative view, held by other rune-workers of which Michael Langford, a talented student of the runes, has contributed some of this most interesting interpretation.)

• 3 •

RUNIC DIVINATION

Theory of Runic Divination

Runes are the traditional symbols of the Northern peoples. They may have been developed from a much older system of related sigils, for example the North Italic or Etruscan alphabets. Alternatively, the runes could have been passed on by an older civilization such as that of Hyperborea. There are some interesting and quite convincing speculative theories along these lines.

Whatever their origin, the runes were initially not an alphabet but a series of sounds related to natural forces. Sound is vibration. It is energy. It is creative. Sound was a paralinguistic way of communicating. Gradually, particular sounds were connected with specific sigils and became concepts. Through the repeated use of these sigils the original concepts were deepened and expanded. Their use by successive generations invested the runes with special powers; consequently a large-storage memory bank was built up in the collective Northern unconscious.

Runic divination is one of the oldest divination systems in Northern Europe. Tacitus recorded in his writings that the Germanic tribes cut slips from a fruit-bearing tree and wrote certain sigils on them. They used these for divination. These sigils were most likely runes, although this has not been proven.

Each individual rune had a variety of meanings, ranging from the most profane level of understanding to the highest degree of eso-teric knowledge. Every rune-worker, by drawing upon the power of the runes, exchanges something of himself or herself in the process. Thus a mystic system evolved from the folk-soul of our people. Many ancient cultures have had mystery schools, as in Egypt and Greece; I believe that our ancients, long before the Viking Age, had a similar mystery school in which runic knowledge was passed in succession from one individual to the next. Owing to the establishment of Christianity, however, and its subsequent effacement of Northern lore, the exact manner in which runelore was taught is not known.

The runes make up a powerful key, providing access to the inner mysteries of Northern Europe. By using the runes to reestablish inner-plane contacts, we can regain much of our lost knowledge. Nothing is completely lost; it has all been preserved in the well of Mimir, or the collective unconscious, which in the Eastern world is known as the "Akashic records." The runes, like any other system of divination, require extensive knowledge and some inborn clairvoy-ant abilities. Simply learning the traditional meanings of the basic keywords ("wealth" for Fehu or "travel" for Rad, for example) is not enough. For true divination, a channel of communication must be established with the runes. They should be allowed to speak for themselves without interference from the analytical mind.

Runic divination is a kind of mediumship in which one has to mediate between the querent and the runes and interpret messages from the runic forces, of which the physical rune-stones or rune-staves are focal points or doorways. Divination is in origin a sacred act of taking counsel from the gods. The power controlling magic and the darker side of consciousness, of which divination forms a part, is in Northern European terms Odin. These powers in terms of past, present, and future time are identified with the three goddesses or Norns Urd, Verdandi, and Skuld—who weave the web of fate or orlog.

Thus the runes are sacred to our people and are closely inter-twined with Northern mythology, embodying our deepest spiritual values. To obtain the maximum benefit from the runes, it is neces-sary to possess knowledge and a profound understanding of the myths of the North and the various god-forms or archetypes. This is what divination was meant to be and is how it was practiced in olden days when our folk was young.

Clearly runic divination has nothing to do with the trivial fash-ion of fortune telling that has crept into our sacred mysteries in recent years. Although the runes were and are used for divination, they never were nor will be a mere fortune telling device. Predic-tions can be made using the runes, but are usually done in a more spontaneous manner that is not under the conscious control of the individual rune-worker. Predictions are not, in fact, very often suc-cessfully made, as is only to be expected—matters that are hidden in the future and predestined are mainly unavoidable major events forming part of a person's own wyrd. The more the individual is con-scious of the hidden side of Nature and of his or her own self, the more control the individual has over personal circumstances, in which case it is all the less likely that "predictions" will come true. Most so-called predictions by rune-readers consist of extrapolations from revealing conditions in the querent's present or past life which the rune-reader has discovered intuitively or through "leads" given by the querent. There is nothing wrong with this method, as long as the querent receives a sympathetic hearing and constructive advice.

Who can acquire the ability to work with the runes? Anyone with a genuine psychic gift can learn to divine up to a certain point, but to penetrate the deeper levels of rune knowledge, one has to be born into the Northern "group-soul." The ability to work with the runes is passed on through the psychic equivalent of genetic mem-ory, the group-soul called in our tradition, hamingja. People of other ethnic origins, especially those originating from a traditional tribal system bearing similarities to the traditional Germanic social struc-ture, can access the genetic memory and hamingja by marrying into our folk or by an oath of blood brother/sisterhood. Since writing this

book I have met two people of African origin who work with the
runes and are spritually integrated with our "tribe."

The Northern mysteries were developed from primitive ancestor-
worship, traces of which are found in various accounts of Anglo-
Saxon scholars such as Bede, who was aware that our people believed
themselves to be descended from the gods. This practice was by no
means limited to the Northern folk. Ancestor-worship was and is practiced by other cultures, such as the African, Chinese, and Japanese.

A parallel can be drawn between runic divination and a system
of divination and insight found in the Far East. Anybody can read
the I Ching (an ancient and very accurate Chinese divination system)
in English translation and derive some value from meditating on the
hexagrams, but only a Chinese person working with the I Ching in
his or her native language will manage to penetrate much more
deeply and correctly into its mysteries, through an understanding of
the subtleties and poetic expression of the Chinese language—which
is an expression of the person's own folk-soul.

The same applies to the runes. Language is an expression of
the soul of a nation, and the runes are indeed a language, one useful
for communicating at all levels, from straightforward written messages to focal points of concentration and communication with the
gods, who are the guardians of the evolution of the Northern
group-soul. Because the runes operate as a language, they communicate information about questions asked or readings done and allow
the rune-reader to make contact with the deeper layers of the querent's unconscious.

Through the runes an experienced rune-worker can tune in to the
individual's web of wyrd. The method I personally find most useful is
a general reading, using first the astrologically based twelve-house system of the zodiac which corresponds neatly to the twenty-four-rune
futhark. (Our forebears were no doubt aware of this method and might
have had their own names for the astrological signs. This theory is
developed further in Chapter 4.) A reading using the twelve houses
produces a correct printout of the recent past and the current situation,
by which one may explore the querent's present conditions and the

recent causes leading up to them. Afterwards, a more detailed reading would be carried out using more complicated systems, such as those discussed later in this chapter. These systems enable me to extrapolate the information received so far, and to successfully deduce likely near-future developments. Thus I can offer constructive help and advice.

Long-term forecasts, however, cannot be as detailed. They may contain contradictions as well, since before they are realized the individual concerned may make certain decisions or carry out various actions that will have changed the pattern of the web. There is no such thing as a fixed future; there is only the web that appears to us in time-bound and space-bound conditions as past, present, and future. In reality, the web is a complex whole and, when understood as such, can be utilized to exercise a degree of control over one's circumstances. By means of divination it is possible to gain information concerning a specific aspect of the web, for example the past. Because the web is an integral whole, it follows that any interference with one part of the web causes reverberations in other parts of it.

Once the information needed has been acquired, magic can be used. Magic is the act of interfering in one part of the web through operation of the will and thereby deliberately causing an effect in other parts of this web. Like a spider's web, the web of wyrd is fragile yet sturdy. It is constructed according to a geometric design and so delicately balanced that the gentlest tug at the periphery of the web transmits vibrations along all of its threads. This analogy can serve as an image to be kept in mind when working with the web.

A final aspect of the theory of runic divination is the distinction between reversible and invertible runes. An invertible rune is a rune which, when placed upside down, looks different from its positive or upright version.

Thus, for example, Ehwaz is M in its upright form, but inverted it looks like W. Ehwaz is therefore an invertible rune. However, Eihwaz, when placed upside down, looks the same: ∫. It is therefore a non-invertible rune. A reversible rune, on the other hand, is one that when reversed along its horizontal axis, looks different from its positive or upright position. For example, Kenaz normally looks like this: ⟨. Kenaz reversed looks like this: ⟩. A rune such as Ehwaz, when reversed, looks exactly the same as its normal upright form: M. Ehwaz is thus not a reversible rune.

Inversion of runes negates the meaning of those runes in their positive upright positions and consequently turns their meanings opposite. A very simple example would be Fehu. At its most basic level, it would normally mean "money." Inverted Fehu, however, would mean "lack of money." Now this is only true when runes actually can be turned upside down. The reversible runes act slightly differently; they act as mirror images of the runes in their normal positions. Here the rune is reversed along the horizontal axis and its meaning does not necessarily change into the opposite; rather, the meaning of the rune is inactive or introverted. To keep to the example given above, Kenaz inverted would mean roughly absence of light, rather than darkness.

The difference between reversed and inverted runes is very subtle. In divination it is not a paramount consideration. In magic, however, it is. Runes may change positions in different manners— either they change by being reversed along the horizontal axis or else inverted along the vertical axis. There are some runes that do not change at all in either way. These are Gebo, Isa, Inguz, and Dagaz. These runes are constant and are the most powerful in that they contain concentrated power. There are also nine runes which cannot be inverted: Gebo, Hagalaz, Nauthiz, Isa, Jera, Eihwaz, Sowulo, Inguz, and Dagaz. However, five out of these nine—Hagalaz, Nauthiz, Jera, Eihwaz, and Sowulo—can be reversed, and can only operate from left to right. The magical applications will be discussed in Chapter 4.

Divination Practice

The most authentic method of divination is described by Tacitus, the Roman historian, writing in 98 C.E. (*Germania,* Chapter X). His account describes how the priest or the head of a household would inscribe runes on strips of wood cut from a fruit-bearing tree, then close his or her eyes, turn north, invoke the gods, and cast the runes on a white cloth. From the runes cast on the cloth he or she would take three and interpret them in the light of the questions asked. Although this sounds like a simple way of divining, it is not, for it is necessary to be very intuitive to be accurate.

The best-known system of runic divination has been taken from astrology. This "twelve-house" system works well for those familiar with astrology. In fact, matching the twenty-four runes with the twelve signs of the zodiac can be a good exercise to gain familiarity with the runes. I shall not expand on this system, as sufficient material is already available in various books recently published on the runes.

One does not have to be familiar with astrology or any other non-runic branch of divination to work with the runes, however, as they are valid as a system of divination in their own right. There is a lot of hitherto unexplored information within the Northern mythology which can be used to build up a comparable divination system. I shall present some of these systems below, which I have developed from the available source material, mostly the Eddas. The psychological aspects of runic divination used below have principally been derived from C. G. Jung.

Yggdrasil Method

At the center of our mythological world is Yggdrasil, the sacred ash tree. Within the branches of this tree are situated the nine worlds, which can be divided into three levels or planes of being: the higher or super conscious, the normal waking conscious, and the sub- or unconscious. The nine worlds have specifically appointed places within this tree and can be equated with various psychological states of consciousness, which fits in very neatly with the psychological divisions formulated by C. G. Jung.

It is well known that most of the ancient shamanic world-views revolved around a tree. In modern occultism, it is the Cabbalistic Tree of Life that is mostly known and with which most workings are performed. The system of tree divination and traveling between the worlds, as presented in the magical section of this book (Chapter 4), is not a mere imitation of the Cabbalistic system. However, there are great similarities, which are only to be expected, since both tree-based systems go back to prehistory. One of the main differences is that the Cabbala divides its planes into four and its spheres into ten, whereas the Yggdrasil system is divided into three planes and nine worlds or sub-planes. The most important magical number in Northern mythology is nine, although three (which is the square root of nine) and eight are also of special significance.

I shall present the tree and its worlds first in a psychological context and explain how a reading can be done. I know this system inside and out and it is the most successful that I have ever used. In Chapter 4, I use the same model of this tree to explain its magical significance.

According to our cosmology, creation originates from two primal forces, fire and frost. The interaction of these forces results in the formation of the nine worlds. I have divided the nine worlds into three levels of consciousness, as illustrated on page 103.

The interpretation of a rune-reading is a reflection of the rune-reader's innate intuitive abilities. The rune-reader has to develop these skills and must study the runes and the nine worlds in great depth. Only experience can teach a rune-reader to "feel" the right combinations of the runes and the nine worlds. It would be pointless to attempt to describe the mechanism of divination in the style of an instruction manual or a cookbook. In a general sense, for example, Thurisaz in Hel would represent suppressed sexual feelings, but it must always be borne in mind that Thurisaz in Hel could have entirely different connotations for different querents.

The procedure for using the Yggdrasil-tree system of runic divination is as follows. Let the querent select nine runes unseen and

Asgard
Individuality
Highest plain
Higher self, Spirituality

Muspelheim
Intuition (Fire, Creative)

Vanaheim
Feeling (Water)

Midgard
The Personality,
Ego Consciousness
or Lower self

Swartalfheim
Sensation (Earth)
The Dark Elves are smiths,
like Volund, working with
minerals, taking base materials
from the earth and transmuting
them into higher materials

Lightalfheim
Thinking (Air)
Plants, elves, tree spirits
and birds are ruled over by
Frey, Lord of the Vanir

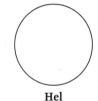

Jotunheim
Disruptive, raw masculine
forces of the unconscious;
the destructive male urge;
the chaotic part of the self

Hel
Destructive part of the
Feminine, hidden fourth aspect
of the moon; the devouring part
of the mother; the half-alive
half-dead daughter of Loki,
half black and half white

Nifelhel
The deepest part of the
shadow in the unconscious. Nifelhel of Nibelheim means literally "fog world."
Fog is an intangible, insidious state between water and air. All the rejects of the
conscious get deposited here. It is the place form which conflicts originate.

THE NINE WORLDS AND
THE THREE LEVELS OF CONSCIOUSNESS

lay them out as indicated in the diagram shown on page 103, which will form the basis of the interpretation. The reading may be started at the bottom of the tree with Nifelhel; from this place the root of the matter in question or the origins of the problem under consideration can be deduced. This position can and often does reveal the individual's background, either by elucidating the querent's childhood and its consequences for the present or else by providing information about the querent's previous existences and the wyrd accumulated, which may have many consequences bearing on the querent in the present life.

According to this system of divination, the next two worlds, Jotunheim and Hel, represent the animus and anima respectively, which is to say the opposing masculine and feminine principles. Usually parental influences will come to light through the meaning of the runes that occupy these positions. Moreover, these worlds also represent the male and female aspects of one's own self; any imbalance in the self will be indicated by certain runes turned up in these positions.

The three worlds described so far deal with various components of the unconscious. The following four worlds describe the four functions of feeling, thinking, intuition, and sensation, as defined by Jung.

Let us start with Lightalfheim and Swartalfheim, which again are displayed as a pair of complementary opposites. These worlds represent the opposing functions of thinking and sensation, respectively. As Jung taught, one of the four functions is usually overdeveloped to the detriment of one of the others. Often thinkers, for example, are impractical with down-to-earth matters. From the runes selected at these points the most prominent function at the time of the reading can be deduced. Should it appear that one of these functions is totally blocked by Isa, Nauthiz, or reversed Thurisaz, for example, magical exercises may be devised employing Raido or Sowulo to redress the imbalance. Divination is not just a matter of analyzing what is wrong but also a means of offering practical help to solve the problem. The runes are therefore an excellent tool to be used in psychotherapeutic counseling.

The next two worlds in the sequence are Muspelheim and Vanaheim. Muspelheim is the world of the element of fire, representing intuition, while Vanaheim is the world of water, representing feeling. It is important to look at the four worlds and their four functions as a whole and to question whether all of the selected runes are compatible with each of their respective worlds. It is necessary to examine the strengths and weaknesses revealed and how this disposition affects the world of Midgard, which is situated in the middle of the diagram and which represents the ego or outer personality. Midgard is to be seen as the center point of the reading, which all the influencing factors of each of the other eight worlds relate to.

Lastly, and on the top-most place in the diagram of the Yggdrasil system, is Asgard, which is in vertical alignment with both Midgard and Nifelhel and can be viewed as a higher version of these. Asgard therefore represents the higher spiritual reality, the realm of the gods, and from this realm guidance and inspiration can be received— which would be expressed by the rune occupying this position.

Fourfold Wheel

The Fourfold Wheel is a symbol common to both Celtic and Germanic mythology. It takes the form of a circle representing the universe, dissected by an upright, equal-armed cross. When this symbol is applied to divination, the horizontal line of its cross represents the line of time with the left-hand side showing the past and the right-hand side the future. The vertical line represents the line of space, intersecting the line of time and producing events in time and space.

A further refinement of the Yggdrasil method of divination involves the Fourfold Wheel. Any of the aforementioned runes representing the nine worlds may be selected in order to analyze a reading in even greater detail and especially to focus on problematic findings which the reading uncovered. Thus, if a deep-seated problem in the realm of Hel has been indicated in the reading and the querent cannot identify it, the problem may well be so deeply implanted in the unconscious that it is not accessible to the normal waking conscious. As this unconscious realm is ruled by the Hagalaz rune, Hagalaz should then be placed by the querent face up with four unseen runes placed around it crosswise, thus permitting a fourfold vision of the influences affecting the querent's problem. (See the Fourfold Wheel diagram below.) Of course, any other question can be investigated in a similar manner. For instance, if a querent wants to question the runes about finances, the Fehu rune would be selected and placed in the center of the wheel. In this way any matter one wishes to obtain information about can be identified by translating the subject matter into the concept of an appropriate rune. Incidentally, this is a good technique for acquiring working knowledge of the runes.

The wheel allows us to look at a problem from four angles. The horizontal line of time on the left shows the influences from the past—from what is already formed—which has possibly given rise to the present situation. Opposite it, on the right, is the future,

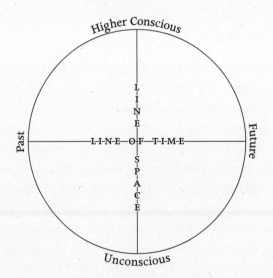

THE FOURFOLD WHEEL

which shows where you are going and what you can shape. There is an amount of flexibility in the web of wyrd and thus the future is not absolutely predestined. The vertical line represents space. The upper part of this line shows influences at work from the higher sources of consciousness, i.e., the gods or archetypes and that part of the self that is known as the higher self. Influences displayed here will provide help, advice, and inspiration. If a negative or inverted rune is found at this point it means that the querent is not in touch with the higher realms and therefore cannot expect any help. In most ordinary readings a neutral rune will be turned up in this position.

The lower part of the vertical line shows influences from the personal unconscious. These influences can be very obscure and in some cases may hinder the querent's personal and spiritual development. The rune in the middle represents the fundamental nature of the question or the person asking the question. A rune may be drawn unseen and placed in the center of the wheel in order to elucidate the querent's question and relate it to the other runes in the reading. Alternatively, analyze what the question is and translate this into the concept of runes. A question could, for example, be expressed in a bind-rune. This bind-rune is drawn on a piece of paper and placed in the center. The two runes at the top and bottom of the line of space, in combination with the rune on the left side of the line of time, point to the future outcome of the problem and will provide either a helpful answer or good advice. This should be confirmed by the rune on the right-hand side of the line of time.

Eightfold Wheel

For depth-psychological readings the Fourfold Wheel technique can be broken down into even further detail. By adding an X-shaped cross to the wheel, eight spokes are produced which can be defined in the following manner. The lines of time and space are now dissected by two additional lines which will mediate the forces of time and space and modify the reading, giving us the Eightfold Wheel—

eight sections representing fields of action and a ninth field of action in the middle representing the individual for whom the reading is performed (see diagram below). (The Eightfold Wheel is a key symbol in our religion and will be further explored in the section dealing with magic in Chapter 4. Here it will be studied as a means of divination.)

Between the points of higher conscious and the future there has now been inserted the active future. Any rune turned up in this position tells you what you practically can do for yourself and how you can handle the problem.

Diametrically opposite this line is the point of the passive or inactive past; it suggests unchangeable aspects from past experiences that just have to be tolerated; i.e., wyrd-related complications affecting the querent will be indicated at this point.

Between the points of higher conscious and past is the active past, which is any part of the past, such as a psychological complex, which still continues to affect the individual's life. More positively, the happier experiences of the querent's past and childhood will be

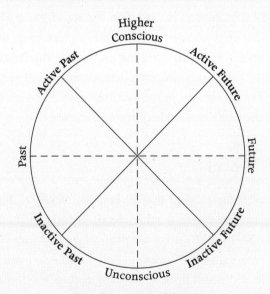

THE EIGHTFOLD WHEEL

indicated at this point as well. Any major influence of the individual's past, including traumas, initiations, occult experiences, and lessons learned from the recent or distant past, will appear in this position on the wheel. All these data have to be interpreted in the light of the subject matter of the reading. Furthermore, this part of the past can always be changed, as one's understanding of and emotional response to these aspects of the past can be actively interfered with by a variety of psychological techniques, or by the use of magic.

The diagonal line on the lower right-hand side of the wheel indicates the inactive future. The inactive future represents those forces in the unconscious that create aspects of your personal future which are predetermined and cannot be changed; in a word, your wyrd.

Thus by means of the four crossing lines and by finely tuning the reading to a deeper level, the energies can be modified in order to obtain more information. Any problem or question can be tackled by this eightfold division of the wheel to explain modifications of the four basic energies.

These four newly introduced additional points could be given designations more appropriate to depth-psychology (see diagram on page 110). The "active future" could equally be called the "extrovert conscious." In this part of the psyche resides all that is striving to emerge into consciousness in order to be dealt with. It describes one's behavior. The "inactive future" corresponds to the "extrovert unconscious," in which resides all the suppressed material, including dreams, premonitions, and anxieties, that invades consciousness; here the reasons for behavior patterns may be discovered. The "inactive past" corresponds to the "introvert conscious," referring to the hopes and expectations the individual is passively aware of, which he or she would like or is contemplating or gestating; those hopes and expectations which are in a process of ripening but have not yet been transferred to the plane of physical reality. The "active past" equates to the "introvert unconscious"; it is everything that you need to get rid of—those things which you need to release but that your lower self hangs on to (such as security, fears, or anxieties) because they are too difficult to confront. This method gives us an accurate psychological model with which to perform a purely subjective reading to gain knowledge of normally inaccessible parts of the psychic mind. This type of reading can be very subjective and therefore the rune-reader must be completely honest and objective with the interpretation.

By starting off with a tree-reading, and then extracting an aspect that is particularly difficult to understand, the ruling rune can be determined. However, there are no hard and fast rules. The ruling rune may not in all situations remain the same one. This is a very creative, growing, organic system in which runes drawn one day may well transmit a different current of consciousness from those that are drawn on another. This is not the kind of system found in "fortune telling" books in which, for example, a given rune in a given space means precisely such-and-such. In astrology, for instance, one would read "Mars conjunct Venus in Virgo means...."

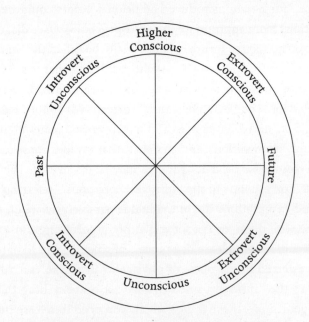

THE PSYCHE AND THE EIGHTFOLD WHEEL

With runes it does not work quite like that, because the runic system is creative and imaginative.

Although the runes do have certain key-word meanings with which they are always associated, they often trigger inner responses from the unconscious, calling something forth from within yourself. To gain a proper understanding of those feelings and responses from within, the reading must be translated into depth-psychological or intellectual concepts. It must be absorbed and fed through your personal "computer," to enable you to do something with it at a concrete, physical, and material level. Otherwise, the idea ends up merely floating in the air. It needs to be "brought down to earth" through your intellect. These vibrations are all extremely subtle, and it is the rune-reader's task to translate and interpret them.

The runes are divided into three aettir, or groups of eight; each aett can be used to cover a certain area of human experience. Thus by using the Eightfold Wheel method, a reading can be performed on a circular division of one of the aettir. In this application of the Eightfold Wheel it is the runes composing the aett that act as the indicators of the areas of the querent's life under investigation. The aett of Frey and Freyja is primarily related to practical and mundane matters. The second aett, the aett of Hagalaz, principally corresponds to emotional matters. The third aett may be used to inquire about esoteric matters.

This is a very rough-and-ready analysis, but it will serve to narrow down the area in which inquiries can be made and consequently make more accurate answers possible.

A useful technique for applying an Eightfold Wheel to a specific aett would be as follows. Make a cloth and paint on it two concentric circles. Divide them into eight and in each of the segments paint a rune, starting with the first rune in the aett. For those who are used to working with an astrological model it will be easiest to paint the first rune in the east and work progressively counterclockwise in the direction of the astrological houses, bearing in mind that there are only eight sections. The important thing is to retain the correct sequence of the aett, which must never be altered. Three cloths should be painted, one for each of the three aettir. Different colors may be used for the aettir. The choice of colors is a personal matter; however, my own suggestion would be yellow for the first aett, greenish blue for the second and red for the last aett.

The first aett deals with purely practical matters. Therefore the most basic and straightforward meanings of the runes in this aett should be assumed in order to fit its context. A more advanced reading with the same runes, projected at a more complicated level of depth-psychology, will not change their essential nature. The runes may change their "octave" but not their "ground-tone." For example, Fehu in the mundane sense means wealth and money prospects, whereas the same rune in a psychological reading means creative energies are available which allow the querent to improve life's circumstances. The more one meditates on and works with these creative variations within the runes, the more inner resonance one will develop; thereby a working relationship with the runes is established at a far more advanced level than that of mere fortune telling.

The basic meanings of the runes of the first aett to be applied in this type of divination are listed below.

Fehu ◆ Financial strength and prosperity of the present and near future.

Uruz ◆ Health matters.

Thurisaz ◆ Conflicts and complexities of an aggressive nature; psychological problems.

Ansuz ◆ Communications and transmissions; points things back to sources in the past.

Raido ◆ What is right or not right; what move to make; decisions; returns.

Kenaz ◆ Opening up of new ways; opportunities; information.

Gebo ◆ All matters of an exchanging nature; contracts; personal relationships.

Wunjo ◆ Gain; accomplishments; what is wished for.

These meanings are very simple and on the most basic level serve as the background for a straightforward reading, in which questions of a practical nature can be answered. As with other readings, one selects the runes unseen and places them in the area next to the runes already there. From the resulting combination one can deduce what is happening.

The second aett deals largely with the psychological conditions present within the individual. I have allocated psychological conditions to each rune of this aett by means of extrapolating their normally accepted meanings and projecting them to a more complex level in keeping with their original meanings.

Meanings of the runes of the second aett:

Hagalaz ◆ The uncontrolled forces in the unconscious, which are usually of a disruptive nature and which usually originate in the past.

Nauthiz ◆ Restrictive forces in the unconscious; fears; anxieties; feelings of guilt.

Isa ◆ Blocks; stultified conditions; grievances; anything that the individual is not prepared to let go of; the formation of the personality; conditioning.

Jera ◆ Hopes and expectations; turning points; gradual changes; results of earlier actions.

Eihwaz ◆ The driving forces in the unconscious; motivation; sense of purpose.

Pertho ◆ The deepest creative part of the unconscious; the hidden realm of higher material that is waiting to come to fruition and birth; hidden talents; occult or psychic abilities.

Algiz ◆ The strong, protective side in the unconscious; the influence that will protect you; religious aspirations.

Sowulo ◆ Position of the higher self in relation to the unconscious; the direction in which you will be guided by the higher self; the ability to establish contact between the higher self and the unconscious.

The third aett transcends the two others, in that it largely relates to relationships with other people, and also, to the sexual side of life. Whereas the first aett is largely concerned with the outer world, and the second mainly deals with the inner world, the third aett synthesizes both the inner and the outer world, and most of the runes in this aett contain a dual meaning involving both aspects. Their meanings for these purposes are as follows:

Teiwaz ◆ Creative energies in the martial sense; where your strengths lie; where to direct your energies in taking initiatives; honor and justice; leadership and authority.

Berkana ◆ Fertility; birth; rebirth; growth; maternity; family life; feminine Mysteries.

Ehwaz ◆ Adaptability; relationships with others; joint efforts; cooperation; sexuality.

Mannaz ◆ People at large; attitude towards others; other people's attitudes towards you; legal matters; friends and enemies; intellect.

Laguz ◆ Emotions; stability; imagination; psychic matters; affections.

Inguz ◆ Integration; gestation; expectations; progeny.

Othila ◆ Home life; country; spiritual heritage; experience; foundation; fundamental values; establishing.

Dagaz ◆ Transmission; opposites; position between light and darkness; initiation; balance between the worlds outside time and space; cosmic consciousness; change from one thing into its opposite; new beginnings.

The meanings given for the runes in this division of the aettir are very general. Eventually, the rune-reader has to accumulate a store of meanings based on personal experience. It is not necessary to keep rigidly to specific meanings for specific runes, as divination requires much more than book-learning. Only with hard work can one become proficient. In any event, divination is certainly not the most important use of the runes.

Psychological Profile-Readings

A further refinement of this technique that I have developed can be used to perform psychological profile-readings. Technically, this is not divination at all but more akin to counseling. One advantage of this technique is that anyone can do it for themselves and use the information gained for psychological growth.

The information gained through this reading will usually consist of a combination of long-standing psychological problems and some transient influences. The reading can be repeated frequently, as it is not time-related. Only if an inquiry is made about a specific period of time in the past could this technique be described as time-related, in which case it is necessary to concentrate mentally on the period of time in question. This method of counseling may be used to help clear up traumas from the past. Once the traumas have been identified, they can be worked out through means of psychology or magic. The runes are listed below in futhark sequence, and I have allocated psychological attributes to them that are extrapolated from their basic meanings and projected onto the level of human potential.

Fehu ◆ The individual's potential creative energies which can be used to create wealth.

Uruz ◆ The individual's physical strength, endurance, and assertiveness.

Thurisaz ◆ The strength of the individual's will and the opposing willpower from the environment.

Ansuz ◆ Higher sources of communications, from either within or outside the self.

Raido ◆ The individual's ability to relate and connect; the amount of control that the individual can exert in his or her life.

Kenaz ◆ The individual's knowledge and capacities.

Gebo ◆ The individual's attitude towards giving and receiving.

Wunjo ◆ The individual's potential for enjoyment and chances of being successful.

Hagalaz ◆ Disruptive forces creating change in consciousness.

Nauthiz ◆ Restrictive forces and unacknowledged needs; that which holds the individual back.

Isa ◆ Blockages, frustrations, and any hindrances.

Jera ◆ The time factor in the individual's development; returns.

Eihwaz ◆ The ability to achieve one's desires; tensions.

Pertho ◆ The ability of introspection and self-awareness.

Algiz ◆ The ability to defend oneself and protect whatever is nearest and dearest.

Sowulo ◆ The source within, which guides the individual on his or her path.

Teiwaz ◆ The ability of objective judgment and fairness; the potential for handling a conflict correctly; warrior attitudes and courage.

Berkana ◆ Creative abilities, nurturing and birth-processes in the self.

Ehwaz ◆ Emotional responses; adaptability; subjectivity; the anima.

Mannaz ◆ The mind and intellectual objectivity; the animus.

Laguz ◆ The intuitive faculties and the potential for sympathetic feelings.

Inguz ◆ The potential for individuation and integration.

Othila ◆ The relatedness to heritage and kin, and awareness of ethnic origins.

Dagaz ◆ The ultimate aim of transformation of the personal consciousness into whatever one envisages to be the greater whole.

The beginner may find it helpful if an example of a reading using this technique is given in detail. The following is a description of a profile-reading which was carried out as an experiment while I was testing my newly developed technique. It was the first reading done using the method described and was carried out in March 1985 for a female client, whom I shall refer to as L.

First of all, I drew a simple diagram with the twenty-four runes on it divided into the three aettir. This diagram can be drawn in a horizontal or vertical fashion. L was asked to select unseen a rune-stone and place it, face down, next to the Fehu rune drawn on the diagram. The rune-stone she picked up was Kenaz reversed. This process was repeated until she had placed runes face down along the whole futhark diagram. The twenty-four runes in futhark order were used as the background that the other runes were placed against, lending an insight into the area of life represented by the corresponding rune on the diagram. The Fehu rune represents "The individual's potential creative energies which can be used to create wealth." Kenaz reversed told me that at this moment there was not much chance of improvement in career terms, and that L's energies were not being applied to this matter. Indeed, she confirmed that she could not decide where to apply her energies. I asked L to later write comments about the reading, and give them to me to be included in my documentation, which she did in shorthand. I reproduced the notes here exactly as they were transcribed at this time.

As already stated, the first rune, Fehu, was in this reading paired with Kenaz reversed.

My comment: Career-wise, very much in a rut. Care must be taken not to force things too much. There does not seem to be much scope for improvement at the moment.

L's reaction: In relation to my present state of mind regarding my career at the moment, this is very true.

The second rune, Uruz, was paired with Teiwaz.

My comment: Abilities to assert oneself are good at the moment and energies are being directed in the right way.

L's reaction: I feel that my ability to assert myself when needed is quite good.

The third rune, Thurisaz, was paired with Ansuz inverted.

My comment: The ability to cope with conflict of any type is not very good. There is a tendency to avoid conflict through lack of communication.

L's reaction: This statement is so true. I have always had a tendency to clam up as soon as anything (emotional) or anybody becomes difficult.

The fourth rune, Ansuz, was paired with Raido inverted.

My comment: There is a difficulty with communication both with others and with the self.

L's reaction: This is also very true. I have never tried to do either, mainly because it is easier not to.

The fifth rune, Raido, was paired with Inguz.

My comment: The ability to relate and connect is present but is not being used to full potential.

L's reaction: I cannot remember the area this corresponds to as it took some time to write this reading down, and after a few days neither of us could remember some of the things discussed.

The sixth rune, Kenaz, was paired with Laguz inverted.

My comment: The conscious realization of gifts has not come about.

L's reaction: I have always felt inadequate in this area, but I feel this is due to my lack of confidence in my abilities.

The seventh rune, Gebo, was paired with Uruz inverted.

My comment: The ability to give is not balanced; able to give but not to receive.

L's reaction: Another point I feel is exactly right. I have always felt this.

The eighth rune, Wunjo, was paired with Pertho inverted.

My comment: The ability to experience joy is totally blocked.

L's reaction: This is correct in that I have never felt truly happy.

The ninth rune, Hagalaz, was paired with Gebo.

My comment: There is a reshuffling within the inner self causing a balancing out and development within.

L's reaction: I certainly feel more aware of my inner self and am coming more to terms with myself. This I am sure will lead to a certain development.

The tenth rune, Nauthiz, was paired with Isa.

My comment: Restricted due to emotional forces from the past.

L's reaction: I cannot remember what area this corresponds to. (Note: This was a difficult personal area to discuss and consequently L had not put this down.)

The eleventh rune, Isa, was paired with Sowulo.

My comment: You will be working to dissolve an emotional blockage, which in time will resolve itself, but only with a conscious effort. You must be aware of the problem and understand and deal with it.

L's reaction: I feel that this refers to many blockages which I am trying to resolve.

The twelfth rune, Jera, was paired with itself, Jera.

My comment: The previously discussed problems with the blockages will be sorted out with time, probably a year.

L's reaction: This is connected with the previous question and I feel it shows positive improvement and gives me hope.

The thirteenth rune, Eihwaz, was paired with Algiz.

My comment: Whatever is hoped to be achieved can be realized with work and development of the feminine side.

L's reaction: This seems to be a piece of advice, something that I will endeavor to work at.

The fourteenth rune, Pertho, was paired with Eihwaz.

My comment: The realization of your inner self is being worked on and in the right direction.

L's reaction: It is reassuring to know that my efforts are not in vain.

The fifteenth rune, Algiz, was paired with Mannaz.

My comment: When dealing with self-defense mechanisms more emphasis should be placed on thought rather than following the emotions, especially in dealings with men.

L's reaction: This is an obvious message, one that I need and must follow.

The sixteenth rune, Sowulo, was paired with Dagaz.

My comment: An experience will bring about a breakthrough in your self-development.

L's reaction: I hope that when this happens I will be able to learn from it.

The seventeenth rune, Teiwaz, was paired with Nauthiz.

My comment: The ability to judge a situation is restricted.

No feedback from L.

The eighteenth rune, Berkana, was paired with Thurisaz reversed.

My comment: There is a deliberate blocking of all creative abilities.

L's reaction: I think this is probably due to my fear of failure.

The nineteenth rune, Ehwaz, was paired with Fehu.

My comment: Abilities and energies are being directed on a humanistic level. Intuitions are being followed in this area.

L's reaction: This again I feel is very true.

The twentieth rune, Mannaz, was paired with Othila inverted.

My comment: There is a conflict on the mental level resulting in a feeling of not belonging. This is caused by a rejection of your heritage and is blocking your confidence.

L's reaction: This is partly true but the resulting feelings of not belonging and of rejection of my family are due to their rejection of me.

The twenty-first rune, Laguz, was paired with Berkana reversed.

My comment: Mental considerations rather than intuitive ones are being followed.

L's reaction: Another area that I am consciously trying to improve.

The twenty-second rune, Inguz, was paired with Ehwaz.

My comment: Movements within the self are leading towards a wholeness of self that can be realized.

L's reaction: This is what I am trying to achieve.

The twenty-third rune, Othila, was paired with Hagalaz.

My comment: There is a problem with your sense of belonging.

No feedback from L.

The twenty-fourth rune, Dagaz, was paired with Wunjo.

My comment: The problems you have will be solved by altering levels of consciousness. There is a positive transformation due.

No feedback.

L's overall reaction to the reading:

"I feel that this reading was very correct in all areas and will help me greatly to achieve what I want most of all. It has also given me positive advice and helped me to feel that all is not in vain."

Those who are interested in divination with runes and are still learning, I would advise to draw the pairs of runes mentioned above. Try to understand why I made my comment by comparing the meanings of these runes. Study them closely and try to see my reasoning. If you find you disagree with it, what would your comment have been? This reading was done without using any clairvoyant abilities; therefore everyone should be able to do readings in this manner. From the foregoing it can be seen that the meaning of the runes may be extrapolated and projected onto every area of life, and can be used to make prognostications or "predict" the development of situations.

Marriage and Relationship Counseling

The next technique I developed was for the use of relationship counseling. It works in a similar way to synastry astrology, although it is easier and faster. Each rune is interpreted to refer to a specific area of a relationship between people in keeping with the rune's basic meaning. For this technique to work, both partners must be present and each must have a set of runes. A cloth is made portraying all twenty-four runes, arranged either in a circle or in a straight line.

The following is an example. The first rune on the cloth is Fehu, which represents the financial prospects in the relationship and the attitude of both partners towards finance. Both partners select a rune unseen and place it on each side of Fehu. The rune-reader turns the runes over and interprets them in the light of the Fehu rune. If, for example, the first partner draws Gebo and the second Nauthiz, it could be deduced that the second partner regards the first one as having too generous or irresponsible an attitude towards money and security within the relationship, whereas the first partner may well take the view that the other is too restrictive with finance and too afraid to take risks. Clearly this could give rise to possible conflict. By being aware of potential problems, they can work together to reach a compromise in the matter. This is a very rough example of this counseling technique.

Below are listed the meanings of the runes adapted to the framework of personal relationships. I tried this technique when I was in Iceland in 1985 and found that it produced excellent results. It was accurate, and my clients found it very helpful.

Fehu ◆ The financial prospect in this relationship and the attitudes of the partners.

Uruz ◆ Endurance of the relationship.

Thurisaz ◆ General conflict area; battle of wills.

Ansuz ◆ Communication.

Raido ◆ The rights of the individuals within the relationship.

Kenaz ♦ Learning from each other.

Gebo ♦ Give and take.

Wunjo ♦ Enjoyment.

Hagalaz ♦ Unconscious influences operating within the relationship; past experiences in other relationships, including projections from parents.

Nauthiz ♦ Areas of restriction; possessiveness; mutual needs.

Isa ♦ Privacy; those areas in the relationship that are not shared.

Jera ♦ Long-term influences on each other.

Pertho ♦ Hidden aspects within the relationship.

Eihwaz ♦ Idealism; expectations.

Algiz ♦ Caring and protecting.

Sowulo ♦ Development of individuality within the relationship.

Teiwaz ♦ Combined strength; authority; who is the boss?

Berkana ♦ Fertility; children; parental projection of the self onto the children.

Ehwaz ♦ Sexuality; any joint efforts; adaptability.

Mannaz ♦ Intellectual compatibility and mutual understanding.

Lagaz ♦ Affection; emotion; flexibility.

Inguz ♦ Parenthood; integration; cooperation; unity.

Othila ♦ Domesticity; property; in-laws; social life.

Dagaz ♦ Contributions by one partner to the other's spiritual or psychological welfare.

These meanings are not hard and fast and they are offered only as a suggestion to help the beginner. As with all rune interpretations found in this work, they eventually need to be either corroborated or replaced in accordance with the dictates of the rune-reader's own experience.

A Case Study

Finally, I would like to record a recent reading I did to help a woman named Fee make a decision on whether to stay in London or move back to Devon. The actual subject of the reading was Fee's daughter, Freyja, a thirteen-month-old baby girl. Fee had moved to London from Devonshire after leaving the baby's father behind. Above all, Fee was concerned to do the best thing for Freyja.

Before we could even begin to do a reading, Freyja started "playing" with the rune-stones that had been laid out face down on the floor; three times she picked up the Berkana rune. Berkana's literal meaning is "birch," and Fee had told me that she had a strong feeling that her own personal runes should be made of birchwood. Next we attempted to gain insight into Fee's dilemma. The technique I used for this is very simple. If one is confronted by a choice of equally possible alternatives, the best way to pinpoint the results of different paths is to draw runes for each of the two directions, like a crossroads, and to extrapolate two hypothetical future courses of events, bearing in mind that there can be no such thing as a rigidly fixed future. In Fee's case two sets of three runes were drawn to indicate the option of either remaining in London or else returning to Devonshire.

The runes selected for the London option were Inguz and Pertho; before Fee could draw the third rune Freyja picked up Uruz. The interpretation I offered was as follows: Inguz means stability or a centering-down, and it also directly refers to Fee's child, Freyja. Pertho is an introspective rune, which would suggest that more time should be given to thinking matters over before making a decision. It also indicates the ability to work at occult levels. Uruz is strength; its application is short-term and it indicates an immediate strengthening.

Fee then asked what the outcome would be of going back to Devonshire. Fee added that her father would find her a place there, but that he would also try to exert control over her life. We next asked how it would affect Freyja if Fee were to go back. The first rune to be picked up was Raido inverted, meaning that going back would be the wrong thing to do (Note: This was in spite of what we logically felt would be the best thing to do). We then asked why it would be wrong. The runes selected here were: Ehwaz, Eihwaz, and Hagalaz. Ehwaz has to do with outward-going relationships. Ehwaz and Hagalaz were pulling Fee in two opposite directions, with Eihwaz in the middle representing the field of tension and the decision to be made.

I explained this as follows. If Fee went back she would be torn between the negative energies of the past (Hagalaz) and her own aspirations for the future (Ehwaz). If and when Fee were to go back to Devon, she had to be in a position of strength as a woman, not in a position of weakness or dependent on her father. Fee commented that everything said so far reflected what she had been considering and that the interpretation was in keeping with what she herself had been thinking. Fee then exclaimed that Freyja was showing her a rune. It was the Fehu rune. The power behind this rune is Frey and Freyja and it is linked with Berkana and Laguz. It occurred to me that the baby Freyja has occult abilities and that whatever happened Freyja would be in the goddess' keeping. However Fee was to determine their future, her daughter would be looked after. Fee then declared that she should leave the past and move forward. Fee's mind was made up.

• 4 •

RUNIC MAGIC

Definition of Magic

There are as many definitions of magic as there are practitioners; perhaps the best one is: "Magic is the art of causing coincidence." (I owe this definition to Chris McIntosh, a colleague of mine.) When we consider coincidence in terms of synchronicity, we are able to define the areas and methods by which magic operates. Aleister Crowley put it slightly differently: "Magick is the science and art of causing change to occur in accordance with will."

All magic originates from the will. The initial impulse to perform an act of magic originates from the desire of the operator. Corresponding forces are invoked and, when worked properly, the object of the working is realized. These forces are of a dual nature, partly originating in the mind of the operator and partly consisting of neutral cosmic energies given form by the will of the operator for a specific purpose. The laws of magic can be applied to causing change in one's consciousness as well as to causing change in the environment; usually change created at one level of consciousness will automatically have an effect on the other level(s).

One important consideration in magic, in particular the Northern European variety, is that nothing can exist in a vacuum, and thus energy invoked has to be compensated for. This is a simple fact of Nature and has nothing to do with the weak creed of reward and punishment. The law of compensation, which is named "karma" in the Eastern traditions, will in most cases operate automatically. If one is aware of this law and fully and willingly compensates during a working, most problems can be avoided.

There are two principal kinds of magic to be considered in relation to the Northern tradition: shamanic and ceremonial. We will discuss both in the following section.

Shamanic magic is an intuitive, spur-of-the-moment application. In shamanic magic, the catalyst is the magician's emotion, or deep-rooted feeling, or the emotion felt at a moment of pressure. In this type of magic, the magical energy comes from the immediacy of the feeling.

In defining shamanism, Joan Halifax in *Shamanic Voices* states that the word "shamanism" derives from the Vedic word *sram,* meaning "to heat oneself" or "to practice austerities." The Norse word *seidr* also means "heating" or "boiling." Therefore we can safely assume that seidr is a form of shamanism, albeit apparently practiced particularly by females and only very rarely by males. The only male mythological figure known to have practiced it is Odin, after having been taught by Freyja.

The main feature that distinguishes shamanism from more sophisticated forms of magic, such as hermetic magic and ritual magic taught in lodges, etc., is that shamanism is a system of magic that has to be experienced and developed individually through experiment.

There is no hard-and-fast system of teaching shamanism in the north of Europe. That the Northern religion is of shamanic origin is proven by the concept of the tree Yggdrasil, which is the focal point of the religion. All life, everything, depends on Yggdrasil. In Norse mythology Yggdrasil is the center of the universe and represents the universe itself. The type of magic practiced by the Northern peoples was for the most part shamanic. There were no schools of magic as such, the teaching being done either on a selective, personal, one-to-one basis or, as in modern times, by a shaman teaching oneself and learning from personal experience.

The magic is in the mind of the sorcerer, whatever kind of magic is used. Whatever energy is used has to be transmitted through two agencies. The energy is invoked, processed first through the subconscious mind and then processed mentally, before it is available for use. This is an act of will which creates change on three levels. In drawing energy from a given plane, a vacuum is created which has to be compensated for in turn. This is the magical working of the Gebo rune, the rune used in balancing. Life energy has to be exchanged for life energy; therefore the energy employed in magical work has to be compensated for with life energy from the Self. This results in:

1. A change in the unconscious of the individual.

2. A change in the personal web of the individual.

3. A change in the individual's conscious mind.

Shamanism relies heavily on the information received in altered states of consciousness, either in the dream state or during so-called "traveling." There are differences between these two states, and for the inexperienced it can be difficult to distinguish between the two. In dreams, things happen to the dreamer while in a passive mode, for it can be said that the dream state is a manifestation of the personal or, more rarely, the collective unconscious. In traveling or trances, however, the shaman remains in control of his or her state of consciousness, and actions continue to be determined by his or her own will.

The shaman is still able to make decisions, is aware of what is happening, and can intervene if so wishes. In these states the shaman is at a level which is deeper than the personal unconscious;

the shaman is on the level of the primal unconscious of the entire planet.

Each shaman will encounter different shamanic experiences. The shaman has to learn by experience how to distinguish between the various levels of reality and must clearly know what is real and what is fantasy, and to what extent he or she is acting under their own conscious will. The shaman must create his or her own system of working and not be enslaved by anyone else's. Shamanism is usually practiced alone or with only one or two apprentices.

Ceremonial magic is a disciplined, systematic, intellectual system based on hermetic philosophy and on the ability to establish correspondences and relationships between various objects and the purpose of the working. Ceremonial magic has the advantage of long-established tradition and expertise. This type of magic is practiced in Western Mystery lodges, Cabbalistic groups, and the Ordo Templi Orientis; it is largely derived from the Hermetic Order of the Golden Dawn in England and from the contributions of Eliphas Levi on the Continent. It is practiced in groups and usually subject to a hierarchical structure. There is no indication that this type of magic was practiced in the Northern tradition. That is not to say that it might not be developed in the future, as Norse mythology would be very worthwhile material to base rituals on.

Another tradition rooted in magic, but of a more religious nature, is Wicca. This system is a combination of shamanism and ceremony. It is a tradition comparable to the Northern Mysteries. However, in my personal experience, too much emphasis is placed on the physical aspects. The Northern Mysteries are more austere and make heavier demands on the individual's own strength and commitment.

In the main, magic can be used in a religious function to contact and relate to the gods and goddesses. Moreover, it can be used as a technique to realize and put into effect one's will. There has been a magical tradition in our past, one based on the runes. My task in this book is to reconstruct this magical system using traditional knowledge in synthesis with modern magical methods.

Magical Application of Runes

Firstly, the magical uses of the runes will be considered. For this purpose, and for the sake of convenience, the magical properties of the runes and their esoteric meanings are listed below. There is an unavoidable element of repetition, but it must be emphasized that the meanings of the runes, although always related to their primary and literal meanings, differ according to the purposes to which they are applied. The meanings attributable to the runes listed below are intended to stress their specific magical applications.

FEHU

Wealth, luck, responsibility, and creative energy are implied in Fehu. Its primary element is fire; its secondary element is earth (fire expressed through earth). The ruling gods are the Vanir, in particular Niord, Frey, and Freyja. The gender of this rune is female. The power of Fehu gives the practitioner the initial power to start a working. It contains the power of the creative and generative aspects of fire, as opposed to the destructive power of fire. It can be used to draw energy in for a given magical operation, and also as an energy to send, acting more or less as the moving force behind a working.

URUZ

Uruz means positive strength, determination, perseverance, courage, physical health, assertiveness. The god-force behind this rune is Thor. The Uruz power is used in healing workings. This rune is also linked with the element of fire, although there is a connection with ice as well. The gender of Uruz is male. It has a raw, unrefined power. The combination of Fehu and Uruz contains the potential creative energy of both: energy and form. The name of the rune is linked with the German and Dutch prefix *ur-*, meaning "original" or "primal," and with the name of one of the Norns, Urd. Uruz should be included in any healing.

THURISAZ

Conflicting energies are implied, as is the potential of the true will, although in an unrealized condition. In a negative aspect this rune is the shadow in the unconscious. The master god of this rune is also Thor, who is armed with his hammer to combat giants. Once again, the element of this rune is fire, this time in a more destructive form unless well mastered. In a curse it is the first and most important rune to be used. Like Fehu, it supplies energy to drive the curse, and in this aspect it channels an unmitigated destructive force as potent as a nuclear explosion. It is therefore exceedingly dangerous to work with and may backfire. It is a war-fetter which can cause panic or fear in one's opponent, and so is useful to combat any action. If Thurisaz is used against an opponent suspected of being powerful, use an Isa to cover yourself. In a positive mode, Thurisaz can be used to ensure protection. The basic energy contained in this rune is the higher will that drives an individual.

ANSUZ

Ansuz is the divine source in the self, part of the Odin consciousness. The power behind this rune is of an intellectual kind. The element is air, and the ruling god-force is the most powerful of the Aesir: Odin. This rune can be used to gain knowledge of Odin, the gods, our own ancestors and our ancestral heritage, giving the ability to go back to sources and discover our roots. In Northern European mysticism we consider ourselves to be descendants of the gods. The practical magical significance of this rune is of breath and correct breathing. There is an energy inherent in air which in the East is called "prana," and in the North is called "ond." It is reminiscent of the myth in which Odin, accompanied by Hoenir and Lodur, gives Ask and Embla ond, or breath.

RAIDO

Raido lends the ability to control and take initiatives. This rune contains the power to control a situation, to put things in order, and make them subject to one's will. It helps the practitioner to be boss of the situation at hand. It is linked with the Thelemic principle: "Every man and every woman is a star." Each follows his own path, motivated by will. In practical terms this rune can be used to move or remove things and to direct magical energies where needed. The ruling god of this rune is also Thor. The primary element is fire, the secondary element air; fire is expressed through air, and thus intuition and enthusiasm are expressed through the intellect and the will.

KENAZ

Kenaz means kinship, learning, and teaching—the quest for knowledge and the passing on of this knowledge through successive generations. The practical magical use of this rune is in gaining occult knowledge from other planes. Kenaz can thus be used for astral or shamanic travel, either to the higher astral worlds or to the shamanic underworld. The way the rune is used in this context is as a beacon to light the way and enable a safe return to everyday consciousness. Kenaz also is linked with the element of fire, in its most beneficial form. Gods associated with this rune are Baldur, Heimdal, and the goddess Freyja. Kenaz can be used to expose all that is hidden.

GEBO

Gebo is the art of giving and receiving, equilibrium, and the sacrifice of self to Self. The magical principle of Gebo is the balancing of all energies, in whatever form or manner. In magical workings it reconciles two opposed or complementary forces, such as male and female, which is known as "polarity magic." This rune can be used to bind and can also be employed to give a blessing or a curse. The element of this rune is air. The god who rules it is Odin.

WUNJO

Wunjo can be used to realize the true will and to act in accordance with it. One of the oldest concepts of this rune is wishing. Wunjo also expresses the will to win. The force of this rune is the power of exerting the will. It is a very magical rune, since all magic has to do with the operation and exertion of the will. It combines aptly with Raido, in that Raido operates as a means of controlling the will. The god ruling this rune is Odin, and one of Odin's aspects is named Willi or Vili.

HAGALAZ

Hagalaz signifies the realms of Hel or the underworld and one's personal unconscious. This rune can be successfully employed for negative magic of a feminine nature—the darker side of witchcraft. It can create confusion and disruption. It is a very strong help in astral attack or in invading someone else's dream state. The goddess ruling it is the goddess of death, Hella. A goddess secondarily associated with this rune is Urd. In a spell for vengeance, this rune can be used to turn someone's past against him or her, or to invoke someone's wyrd.

NAUTHIZ

The working of this rune is primarily defensive. It is used to restrict and constrain someone else in a magical attack. Like Thurisaz, it is a war-fetter and can be used in a combination to stop any incoming action. It is very direct and absolutely effective. The goddess controlling this rune is Skuld.

ISA

Isa is very similar to Nauthiz in that it is a rune used to defend; but in this case it acts to delay. Blocking is Isa's main function; with it, barriers can be placed in the path of any opponent or competitor. Goddesses associated with Isa are Verdandi, Skadi, and Rind. The negative forces that may be invoked through this rune are the frost giants.

JERA

This is a very beneficial rune, used to create a positive change in a situation. It works well in all matters involving time. In blessings or constructive spells, it will act to bend the web gently in order to help a person who is having difficulty working towards a specific end or in achieving a hard task. Unlike Dagaz, which is used to force a change and which is consequently not so durable in its effects, Jera can initiate a lasting change in the prevailing currents or in a person's consciousness.

EIHWAZ

Used for a situation that demands an outgoing, dynamic, go-out-and-get-it response, such as hunting or simply searching for a job or an apartment. There is another darker side to this rune: it can be used to "kill," as in shamanic hunting for a soul. Like Wunjo and Thurisaz, it is related to the will in the ability to impose one's will on someone else. Furthermore, this rune represents Yggdrasil and can be used in shamanic traveling to visit any of the nine worlds.

PERTHO

Like Kenaz, its power is related to knowledge. However, while Kenaz is more closely associated with intellectual knowledge, such as knowing the solution to a problem, Pertho relates to the recollection of hidden knowledge. It is excellent for use in regression work. It can help to put one in touch with the Norns, which is extremely helpful in divination, especially when any sort of "prediction" is required. It also represents the collective unconscious and contains the collective memory of our Northern folk, from which I gained my own rune knowledge.

ALGIZ

This rune is used to invoke divine protection. It is applied to the four quarters as a protective sigil in a manner similar to the pentagram in the Craft, except that its effect is more defensive. In particular it acts as a shielding device, especially in a working where the possibility of a backlash has to be considered.

SOWULO

Magically, Sowulo is often used for healing. It contributes strength to any healing spell. Its only specific function is to reinforce other runes with solar energy. It helps in centering and directing a working.

TEIWAZ

The magical use of this rune is primarily to gain justice. However, one has to have right on one's side to be able to use this rune successfully. It therefore cannot be used to pervert justice to one's own ends. The patron of this rune is Tyr, who, unlike Odin, represents unbiased, unequivocal justice. The combination in a bind-rune of Teiwaz and Raido can win a court case. Like Thurisaz, Teiwaz deals with conflicts, but mainly those of an intellectual nature.

BERKANA

This rune is very important for the feminine Mysteries. Its powers include the regenerating forces of Nature and the growth of vegetation. This rune also has very strong shamanic connections. Magically, Berkana is used to alleviate women's problems, such as difficult periods, pregnancy, and delivery. Berkana is a very soft, gentle rune which is linked with the Earth goddess, Berchta, who is the patron of children and who cares for mothers. It is one of the birth-runes referred to in the *Sigdrifumal*.

EHWAZ

This rune is used magically to create links between people or conversely, to split them up. Friendships and relationships can be magically manipulated for good or ill by a correct use of the Ehwaz rune. For instance, if two people are joining forces against you, Ehwaz is very useful to set them against each other. A bind-rune could be constructed using Thurisaz linked to the right-hand side of Ehwaz, with a reversed Thurisaz on the left-hand side of Ehwaz and both Thurisaz runes pointing away from each other: ᛗ. The gods associated with this rune are Frey and Freyja and any other twin divinities.

MANNAZ

This is a so-called "hugrune," one of the runes specifically dealing with the powers of the mind and intellect. This includes verbal communication, academic examinations, legal disputes, and the art of arguing one's case, all of which come under the influence of Mannaz. Combined in a sigil with Ansuz, it will give you an intellectual edge over your opponent in a debate. The powers of Mannaz can be used to arbitrate or mediate in a conflict. The god of this rune is Heimdal.

LAGUZ

Laguz is strongly connected with the occult. Its name is linked to *logr* or *laukar,* which are words for sorcery; and sorcery is the usual use of this rune. It is used to gain access to someone else's unconscious. If projected between the eyes of a person making a request, a positive reply will be more likely. Of course it would be nonsense to approach a bank manager with a request for a million dollars, for in practical magic one must work with what is reasonable and not to expect the impossible. This rune might work, however, in a request for a genuinely earned pay raise. Magically, Laguz also can be used to attract love.

INGUZ

The shape of the Inguz rune makes it a wonderful doorway to the astral; in this way it can be projected onto an imaginary door or curtain, as in a pathworking. Furthermore, the magical use of this rune is to integrate various components into a whole. A sigil composed of various runes placed in the middle of an Inguz rune will act as a vessel containing, integrating, and gestating the combined energies until they are needed. The Anglo-Saxon variant of Inguz is about the best shape on which to start building a sigil or bind-rune, for the function of this rune is to bind.

OTHILA

The magical principle behind Othila is establishing, centering, and "earthing" a working down to the physical plane. It is used ritually to invoke its master, Odin. Othila is beneficial in group-workings, as it creates a sense of belonging and togetherness. It is a powerful symbol to bind people together in a common aim and gives access to the group-soul of the Northern European people.

DAGAZ

Dagaz is mostly used to exclude or to render invisible. Magically, when used on the four quarters, it will place the working area "between the worlds." It is used to place something outside, or between light and dark. I have taught people to envelop themselves in this rune in order to go somewhere unnoticed. Another example would be to carry out the same experiment on a newly acquired object to see whether its presence is noticed.

A major point of rune-magic which must be emphasized is that the practitioner must make his or her own runes. It might be helpful to make a conscious choice of a suitable wood; various woods are suitable for different purposes. It is worth considering that Tacitus wrote that only the woods of a fruit-bearing tree were used in ancient times, and this guideline certainly holds true for divination. Wild apple and wild pear are native to the Northlands and are particularly suitable for women rune-diviners. For magical applications, hazel, willow, rowan, and birch are recommended. All these types of wood are especially suited to so-called Moon magic. Birch works well in fertility spells, willow for darker female magic; rowan is best for healing, and hazel is ideal in divination and witchcraft. Male workers may prefer ash or yew-ash for divination and other forms of magic, and yew for workings of a destructive nature (especially if the yew wood was gathered in a graveyard). There are many old graveyards containing yew trees, which is a legacy of pagan tradition.

The Twelve Palaces

Like the magical number nine, twelve also seems to have a special significance in Northern mythology. The *Grimnismal* tells of how King Geirrod tortured Odin by suspending him between two fires. A young boy named Agnar took pity on Odin and gave him a drink of water. Odin then told Agnar about the mysteries of Asgard, its twelve palaces, and the gods who dwell in each one. These twelve palaces can be superimposed on the twelve astrological houses. The twelve palaces are listed below with their respective gods and associated signs of the zodiac.

BILSKINIR

The name means "lightning." This is the dwelling of Thor, who roughly corresponds to Mars. Therefore I equate this palace with the sign of Aries.

THRYMHEIM

"Thunder-home," where Skadi, daughter of Thiazi, lives. This abode I equate with Taurus.

FOLKVANG

"Field of warriors," nine castles belonging to Freyja. Here Freyja gathers her share of the slain warriors. Freyja is one of a pair of twins. Therefore I assign this place to Gemini.

HIMMINBJORG

"Heaven hall," the abode of Heimdal, guardian of the Bifrost bridge. The corresponding sign is Cancer. Heimdal is known as the "Shining Ase" and for this can be classified as a solar god. He also is associated with the Dagaz rune and midsummer.

BREIABLIKK

"Broadview," the abode of glorious Baldur where no evil may enter. Baldur is the Sun god. Leo is the Sun sign, where everything is in its visible manifestation. This realm therefore corresponds to Leo.

SOKKVABEKK

The "stream of time and events," abode of Saga, the goddess of history. Saga and Odin drink every day in Sokkvabekk, and every day Saga sings of gods and heroes. Saga is equated with Frigga. This palace is thus linked with Virgo.

GLITNIR

"Hall of splendor," abode of Forseti, the god of justice. He always strives for a reasonable compromise. The corresponding sign is Libra.

GLADSHEIM

The "shining-home" belongs to Odin, the father of the gods. It contains Valhalla, the hall of the warriors slain in battle. The related sign is Scorpio.

YDALIR

The "valley of yews," the abode of Uller, the hunter god and divine bowman. I equate his home with Sagittarius.

LANDVIDI

The abode of Vidar, who is the avenger of Odin's death. Vidar is the silent one, who only speaks after he has avenged the Lord of Speech, Odin. Landvidi means "white land" or "broad land." Its sign is Capricorn.

VALASKJALF

The "halls of silver," the palace of Vali. Vali is the avenger of Baldur. He survives the Ragnarok and heralds the dawning of the "new age." His palace corresponds to Aquarius.

NOATUN

The "shipyard" abode of Niord, father of Frey and Freyja. Niord is the god of harbors and the sea. He is identified with Nerthus, the Great Goddess. This palace relates to Pisces.

When we consider that our ancestors possibly knew of the astrological or astronomical divisions of the zodiac under their Germanic names, might it also not have been possible that they knew about the existence of the nine planets (although it must be admitted that three of these planets were discovered only recently)? The nine planets, not counting the Sun and the Moon, correspond to the nine worlds. Midgard is obviously Earth. Allow me to speculate that Venus is Lightalfheim, Mercury is Vanaheim, Mars is Swartalfheim, Jupiter is Muspelheim, Saturn is Jotunheim, Uranus is Asgard, Neptune is Nifelheim, and Pluto is Hel. Those who are familiar with astrology will understand my reasoning behind these correspondences. However, as this is a book on runes I shall not expand on the astrological material.

The Nine Worlds

The subject of this section is the nine worlds and the runes which give access to each of them. Each of the nine worlds is associated with its own Guardian on the Threshold. There are nine runes associated with these nine worlds; they are non-invertible and do not change shape if turned upside down (see diagram on page 143). In the *Voluspa* the volva says, "Nine worlds I can count, nine roots of the Tree." In the *Havamal* Odin says, "Nine lays of power I learned from Bolthorn, Bestla's father." All this points to the fact that our Northern ancestors had a very well-thought-out system of correspondences between the worlds and the runes.

Let us begin with Asgard, which is the realm of the Aesir. Some of the Vanir took up their abode there after the war between the Aesir and the Vanir, when hostages were exchanged between them. Asgard is ruled by Odin. Its corresponding rune is Gebo, as Gebo indicates the action of exchanging hostages, and because a sacrifice is often required to gain access to this realm. The guardian to invoke and placate for admission is Heimdal, who functions in this respect as a dweller on the threshold and might challenge your right of entry.

Vanaheim is the home of the Vanir, and the deity to invoke in this case is Frey. Vanaheim is a pleasant realm, as the Vanir are the gods of peace and plenty. The Inguz rune is the key to Vanaheim. Inguz lends itself to functioning as an astral portal.

The proprietor of Lightalfheim or Alfheim is Frey, who was given it as a tooth-gift according to the sagas. Inhabited by elves, it is also the natural world of fertility and of plants and animals. Its guardian is an elf, Delling, who is associated with sunrise; for that reason the key-rune of this realm is Sowulo.

These three worlds are in the higher realms of the Yggdrasil; to travel there would entail astral traveling. There are three worlds in the underworld which can only be reached by shamanic traveling. The three higher realms are celestial, the three nether realms subterranean.

Midgard is the Earth, where humankind lives. Its guardian and defender is Thor, friend of farmers and workers. Jera is the rune most compatible to this world, since Jera's element is earth. Moreover, Earth is the only realm subject to time, which is another of Jera's attributes. Since we are living on Earth, it might well be asked why we should bother to include Midgard as a destination of magical traveling. The reason is that Midgard is the field of action where all the other worlds interact. It is also the place where the traveling starts, and the point of departure of both astral and shamanic traveling.

Midgard is flanked by two worlds: Muspelheim, the world of creative and destructive fire, and Nifelheim, the world of creative and destructive frost. Muspelheim is ruled by Surt, the destroyer at the

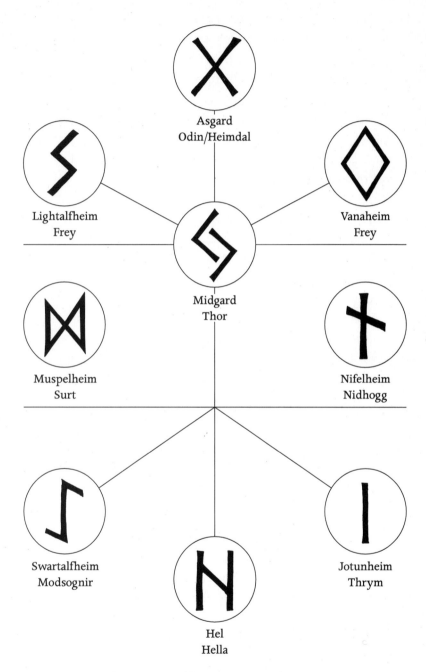

DIAGRAM OF NON-INVERTIBLE RUNES,
THEIR REALMS AND RULERS OR GUARDIANS

Ragnarok. It is inadvisable to try reaching this world. As this is also one of the realms responsible for both creation and destruction by fire, the appropriate rune is Dagaz.

Nifelheim is diametrically opposed to Muspelheim and is controlled by the dragon Nidhogg. It also has both a creative and a destructive function. It is from Nifelheim that the ship Naglfari, the ship of the dead, will sail with Loki at the helm at the Ragnarok. The rune allocated to this world is Nauthiz, which is a rune of constraint and therefore keeps the inhabitants of Nifelheim in their place until the appointed time. Nauthiz is also the fetter that binds Loki.

The last three of the nine worlds are all situated in the underworld. Swartalfheim, which literally means "home of the dark elves," is the world of the dwarves, or swartalfar, who are the counterparts of the lightalfar. They are useful beings, but not very friendly. They do not take very well to Aesir or humankind and it is only by inducements and threats that it is possible to come to any arrangement with them. They are greedy and treacherous and rule the treasures of the inner Earth, such as minerals and precious stones. Their ruler is Modsognir, and the rune allocated to this world is Eihwaz, although it must be admitted that my justification for allocating this rune is purely intuitive. I can only point out in favor of my choice of this rune that all the other non-invertible runes fit exactly to their allocated realms.

The world of Hel is ruled by Loki's daughter, Hella. It is the realm from which knowledge of the dead can be retrieved. It is here that Odin conjures up the dead volva. Hella, however, will demand her price! The rune to use is Hagalaz.

The ninth and last world, Jotunheim, is also hostile, as it is inhabited by the giants, who represent the forces of chaos. The ruler of the giants is Thrym, who is utterly hardhearted and an avowed enemy of Thor. Since the prevailing element in Jotunheim is ice, the Isa rune is associated with this world.

The Four Quarters

In most magical traditions guardians are appointed on the four quarters. Most often these guardians are not gods. They usually are representative of the elemental kingdoms. In the Western Mystery tradition they are archangels, and in Wicca they are named the "Mighty Ones," or sometimes "Lords of the Watchtowers." Hidden within the Northern mythology there are mentioned four elemental guardians who have the same functions. This is indicated in the *Havamal* in stanzas 134 and 135:

> *Runes you will find and readable staves,*
> *Very strong staves,*
> *Very stout staves,*
> *Staves that Bolthorn stained.*
> *Made by the mighty powers,*
> *Graven by the prophetic god.*

> *For the gods by Odin, for the elves by Dain,*
> *By Dvalin, too, for the dwarves,*
> *By Asvind for the hateful giants,*
> *And some I carved myself.*
> [TRANSLATED BY W. H. AUDEN AND PAUL B. TAYLOR]

These verses of the *Havamal* refer to various beings who are involved with runes. The dwarves are smiths and work with the element of fire. Therefore Dvalin is the guardian of the southern quarter. Asvind means "friend of the Aesir" and refers to Mimir. Mimir is a giant and is positioned in the North, as he represents the element of earth. Odin is placed in the East and represents the element of air. Dain is in the West, representing the element of water. Elves are nature spirits and closely related to the Vanir, who are traditionally associated with the western quarter.

In the futhark there are only four runes which can neither be reversed nor inverted. These four runes—Dagaz, Gebo, Inguz, and Isa—are each identified with one of the four quarters and, to borrow an astrological term, may be designated the "fixed runes." Isa is the element of ice and is linked with some of the goddesses and one of the Norns. Therefore it should be ascribed to the North. Inguz corresponds to the element of earth, fertility and the Vanir twins, Freyja and Frey. Therefore this rune goes in the West. Although Dagaz is matched with fire, it also relates very well to air; the name of the rune means "day" and we could place it in the East. Alternatively, Gebo also can be viewed as the rune of the element of air and of the gifts of the gods, particularly Odin; for this reason Gebo could equally well be placed in the East. In conventional magic the East is considered to be the quarter of light and intellect, which are both aspects of Odin. Likewise, Dagaz may feasibly be placed in the southern quarter, because it is connected with the element of fire, which may be interpreted as the fire of the Sun at midday. For magical purposes it makes more sense to place Gebo in the East and Dagaz in the South, although in this case it is really a question of personal preference.

The weapons to be stipulated for each quarter are: Odin's spear in the North, Tyr's sword in the East, Thor's hammer in the South, and Niord's axe in the West. The allocation of the weapons is applicable to a non-specific circle, such as is used at the full Moon. Tacitus provides evidence that the Germanic peoples did their workings at the full Moon, although the feminine and masculine traditions were kept separate and each had its own rites. Depending on the purpose of the ritual, it may be necessary to select different weapons in accordance with the gods invoked. An all-female circle could be constructed; the invocations made would be: to the Norns for the North, for they weave the web of wyrd and cords are the magical tools of this quarter; for the East, Frigg, whose magical implement is a distaff; for the South, Iduna, whose attribute is an apple; and finally for the West, Freyja, whose emblem is the Brisingamen necklace.

Use of Ritual Within the Northern Tradition

There is no extant evidence that the sort of ritual used in the present-day occult world was known in the North. Of course, as in any other agricultural society there were seasonal ceremonies and observances; but our information is sparse and usually derived from late Icelandic sources, and so not necessarily relevant to the rest of the Northlands. The rituals practiced at these festivals in late medieval Iceland were for the most part exoteric, in that the gothi would perform a "blot" or sacrificial ritual in the presence of the whole community. We know little about the more esoteric practices, but the principal subject matter of this chapter on magic is a result of a combination of my own research and inner communications. The latter of course I cannot prove; one has to experiment with the material for oneself to verify my statements.

What is the use of ritual? Its use is twofold. Firstly, it binds people together in a common purpose; secondly, it can generate group energy to achieve a specific purpose. This is done in all types of magic, and there is no reason to assume that this would not work in the Northern way of magic. One unfortunate trait of our Northern folk, however, is that we tend to be very individualistic, and for this reason it would be very difficult to construct and maintain a magical working group for long. It seems that by temperament we are more suited to the individualistic ways of the shaman.

Runic Ritual and the Pagan Year

Much of our information about festivals observed in Northern tradition is derived from Icelandic sources. The festivals mentioned in these sources, however, are largely of an exoteric nature and involved the whole community. Of these, there were three main festivals: Thorriblot at Yuletide; Siggiblot in spring, before they went "a-Viking"; and a harvest festival in which any surplus animals were sacrificed. Information from Germanic sources suggests that the festivals there were more in accordance with the English system, in which the solstices and equinoxes are celebrated. For this reason I have chosen to adhere to this system and have constructed a system of festivals in keeping with the well-known eight pagan festivals, which are combined with appropriate runes in futhark order and related to the Northern myths. This is then superimposed on the yearly calendar (see diagram below).

Starting with the third aett, which for this purpose can be regarded as the first aett, the first three runes (namely Teiwaz, Berkana and Ehwaz) correspond to the first pagan festival of spring, the spring equinox. This festival of birth corresponds to the runes when applied in the following manner: Teiwaz as the Skyfather, Berkana the Earthmother, and Ehwaz as the newborn life, like the foal, born in spring. A ritual could then be constructed along these lines.

The next festival is known in England as Beltane and in German tradition as Walpurgis night. Beltane or Walpurgis night was sacred

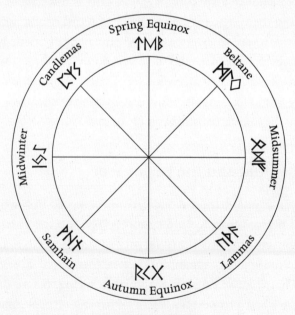

RUNIC CALENDAR

to Freyja, and the runes corresponding to it are Mannaz, Laguz, and Inguz; Mannaz represents the intellect, Laguz the intuition, and Inguz the integration of the two. Mannaz also means "men," whereas Inguz is female; Laguz then is the force of attraction between these two polarities. This can be symbolically enacted in a ritual featuring the sacred marriage between the God and the Goddess, or the Lord and the Lady within the framework of the Northern mythology. The oldest Germanic tradition used Wodan and Frija. Also, any pair of twins, like Niord and Nerthus or Frey and Freyja, are suitable for this sort of ritual.

The next festival is midsummer. The runes to use for this festival are Othila, Dagaz, and Fehu. Othila represents Odin. Fehu represents Freyja, given that in the oldest Germanic tradition Freyja is the same as Frigga, the oldest name for both being Frija. Dagaz, the rune of the summer solstice, represents the slaying of Baldur, the decline of the Sun, and the shortening of the days. A ritual employing these runes and constructed around the myth of Baldur's death can be devised in which Odin, Baldur and Frigga are all involved.

The next festival is Lammas or, in the Celtic language, *Lughnassad*. Lugh, after whom Lughnassad takes its name, is a Celtic solar god comparable to Odin. This is borne out by the circumstance that one of the runes for this festival is Ansuz, which represents Odin in his aspect of inspiration (inspiration being recognized as a solar attribute). The other two runes to be used are Uruz and Thurisaz, both of which are associated with Thor and which especially evoke a thunderstorm. Thor could therefore also be the god to be given priority in this ritual. The giants are also an aspect of Thurisaz. In this context they may well represent the unassimilated raw material of the human psyche.

It may be noticed that there is an element of confrontation here between two opposing forces, Odin and the giants, with Thor as the protective strength between them (we should bear in mind that Thor is part giant himself and thus takes the part both of Odin and of the giants). This ritual could be enacted as a "fight" between Thor and the giant, Hrungnir, to gain supremacy over solar power. Alternatively, a ritual could be enacted depicting the contest of wits between Odin and the giant Vafthrudnir. This series of runes could also be interpreted in a depth-psychological manner. Uruz would then stand for the raw, primitive, fiery urge; Ansuz would represent the higher function of the intellect; and Thurisaz would be the mediating field of conflict and interaction between the two.

The next festival is the autumn equinox; the runes associated with it are Kenaz, Raido, and Gebo. At the autumn equinox, the forces of light and darkness are balanced. At midsummer, the Sun is at its highest point, and at Yule at its darkest point; at the spring and autumn equinoxes the Sun is at a midway point. Since one of the meanings of Gebo is equilibrium and the balancing of opposing forces of equal strength, this rune is appropriate for the festival. Kenaz and Raido inform us about the nature of these forces, namely knowledge and consciousness. At this festival a ritual symbolizing Odin's initiation on Yggdrasil could be enacted, the meaning of which is the suspension of Odin between the realms of light and darkness in order that he could gain knowledge and achieve a higher state of consciousness.

Hallowe'en (Samhain) is the next festival. The month in which Hallowe'en falls is called *Blotmonath* in Anglo-Saxon, or "blood month." It was in this month that the ritual sacrifices were performed, and for a very practical reason. All the animals were slaughtered so that a supply of food was assured during the winter. Traditionally, Hallowe'en has been associated with the dead and the "thinning of the veil" between the realms of life and death, which facilitates communications between these realms. Hagalaz is the rune that provides access to the underworld of Hel, where the dead reside. In olden days in Holland and certain parts of Germany, boys used to wear masks to frighten the girls, and would make mischief like petty thefts. This was known as the "stealing right" or the "right to steal," and it derives from an old ritual in which the warriors of the tribe ceremonially enacted the part of the Einherjar or

heroes. The modern, reconstructed version of Einherjar's day is usually known as Remembrance Day and takes place on the eleventh
day of Blotmonath, or November. Both festivals, Hallowe'en and
Einherjar's day, concern the dead and their remembrance. For this
reason I correlate these festivals.

The associated runes are Wunjo, Hagalaz, and Nauthiz. Wunjo
represents Odin in his aspect of a shaman who consults the dead by
raising the volva; Hagalaz represents the volva, or *haegtessa*, and
Nauthiz represents Odin's state of dire need as he set out to find the
interpretation of Baldur's dream. A ritual symbolizing Odin traveling to the realm of Hel to consult the volva would be very appropriate, and a recital of the *Voluspa* by the priestess enacting the volva
would be a very powerful adjunct to the ritual. This ritual could be
adapted for the purpose of initiation. Nauthiz also represents the
approaching forces of winter, the frost giants and the need-fire.

The festival of Yule (midwinter) falls exactly half a year after
midsummer, and its runes are Isa, Jera, and Eihwaz. Isa represents
the frost giants. Jera is the turning point of the year, symbolizing
the return of the Sun or Baldur, and the lengthening of the days. The
Eihwaz rune represents Yggdrasil, the evergreen tree, which maintains the appearance of life throughout the winter. Incidentally, the
notion of the Christmas tree is a remnant of this belief; in olden days
it symbolized the life force in winter promising rebirth, its growth
perhaps suspended but not dead. At midwinter, in the easternmost
part of Holland, the midwinter horn was blown and a flaming wheel
rolled down a hill to celebrate the return of the Sun. The hailing of
the returning Sun could be symbolically enacted in a ritual involving the corresponding runes: Isa, Jera, and Eihwaz.

At Candlemas the appropriate runes are Pertho, Algiz, and
Sowulo. Pertho is the rune of the goddess Frigga, as well as of the
Norns. Frigga is the life-giving mother who gives birth to Baldur,
thus initiating the yearly cycle again; she is also the commander-in-
chief of the Valkyries. We can go back further and correlate Frigga
to Erda, who gave birth to the Valkyries. Algiz is the rune sacred to

the Valkyries. Sowulo represents the Sun gaining its strength, and the return of all life in Nature, to be manifested at the spring equinox and thus complete the year. A ritual kindling of the fire would be appropriate at this festival.

It is hoped that these ideas will inspire the reader to construct rituals for use in groups such as a coven, which in the old language was called a *hearg*. Modern English Asatru tradition accepts the term "hearth," which might be related to the older word.

The best way of making the right magical connections is through personal effort, meditation and experience. All information on ritual given in this book should be viewed as conclusions I have drawn and the lessons I have learned from my personal research and experimentation. These cannot be taken as the final, authoritative word on the subject; rather they are meant as building blocks to be used by the beginner in constructing his or her own individual system of rune-magic.

As in most magical traditions, work is carried out in a circle, although those with a Masonic or Rosicrucian background may be equally successful working in a square. The Inguz rune would also be suitable as a layout of the working space. There is some Continental evidence that the design of certain Masonic temples is based on an older runic system inherited from the Germanic Mannerbunde. It may well be that an all-male working group would be more suited to a square, whereas women may naturally feel more comfortable in a circle.

Runic Magic in the *Havamal*

In the *Havamal* and other Eddaic poems, references are made to rune-magic. The Icelandic original of stanza 144 of the *Havamal* is as follows:

> *Veistu hvé rísta skal? Veistu hvé raða skal?*
> *Veistu hvé fá skal? Veistu hvé freista skal?*

Veistu hvé biðja skal? Veistu hvé blóta skal?
Veistu hvé senda skal? Veistu hvé sóa skal?

The following translation of the Icelandic original, which I made for magical purposes, is a literal translation and runs as follows:

Do you know how one ought to cut, know how one ought to consult,
Do you know how one ought to color, know how one ought to test,
Do you know how one ought to ask, know how one ought to sacrifice,
Do you know how one ought to send, know how one ought to destroy?

This verse describes various magical actions that are required in working rune-magic. In the first line it says "to cut." This is not the act of cutting but rather what is being cut, i.e., runes. The Icelandic word *rísta*, meaning "cut," is exclusively used for the cutting of runes. The simple act of cutting runes into a material was considered an act of magic. It was done in a ritual manner and accompanied by concentration, invocations and rune-chantings of the rune that was being cut. Presumably there was a traditional way to cut each rune, which may be reconstructed by experimentation. It is advisable to try to feel the rune before cutting, and to sense the movement of the energies within the rune, in order to ascertain where to start the cutting.

In the first line's second question, Icelandic *raða* means to "consult" or to "counsel." It describes the abilities of divination.

In the second line, the word *fá* means "to color." It tells us that the runes are to be colored in certain ways. The coloring of runes goes further back to continental Germania, where the word used to describe coloring the runes was *redden*. There is an Anglo-Saxon phrase, *read teafor*, which means "to color red." The word *teafor* is possibly linked to the German word *Zauber* and the Dutch *tover*, meaning "sorcery." From this it may be assumed that it was a magical practice to color the runes red, in which case it is probable that a plant-based dye combined with blood was used. In the feminine Mysteries this would have been menstrual blood. The ninth stanza in the *Sigdrifumal* reads as follows:

Thought runes you should know,
If could be thought by all
The wisest of mortal men;
Hropt devised them, Hropt scratched them,
Hropt took them to heart
From the wise waters, the waters then run
From the head of Heidraupnir,
From the horn of Hoddrofnir.

[Translated by W. H. Auden and Paul B. Taylor]

The reference to thought-runes will be examined later. Our present concern is to examine the evidence for the theory that the runes were consecrated in menstrual blood and possibly male secretion. The "wise waters" is a kenning for menstrual blood; this expression is used even today in modern feminism. *Heidraupnir* is a combination of two words, *Heid* and *Draupnir*. Heid is the name of the volva in the *Voluspa* and as such has to be understood as a name of the goddess in her dark Moon aspect. Draupnir means "dripper." So Heidraupnir means "dripper of Heid." Thus the wise waters run from the "head" of Heidraupnir, where "head" is a kenning for the womb. "Horn" is a kenning for phallus. *Hoddrofnir* is also formed out of two words, *Hodd*, meaning "treasure," and *Drofnir*, meaning roughly the same as Draupnir. This verse therefore is making a reference to the two liquids employed in rune-magic.

However, the runes may have been painted in different colors for different purposes. Black, for example, would have been used for killing or cursing rune spells. Moreover, each rune has its own color.

In the second half of the second line of the *Havamal* stanza, *freista* can be translated as "to prove" or "to test." Here we are asked whether we know how to prove or test the runes. This is probably an obscure reference to an initiation practice. "Do you know how one ought to test?" may very well mean "Have you been tested?"

The third line of this stanza contains two words: *bidja*, which means "to pray" or "to ask," and *blóta*, which means "to sacrifice." We are asked here whether we know how to pray or ask properly in a magical context, in other words, whether we know how to invoke the power of the runes. From a magical viewpoint, blóta has associations with consecrations and dedications. In all magical traditions it is common practice to consecrate magical tools, which would in this case include the rune-staves used. After the runes were made they had to be imbued with the power to work in whatever manner was required, as each rune has a specific magical power and acts as a key to give access to this power. Each rune ought to be consecrated in its appropriate element or elements and dedicated to the god or goddess with whom it is associated. (A list of runes and their corresponding gods and goddesses is provided later in this chapter.) To consecrate the runes, a ritual should be devised for each rune in turn, in which all of its magical associations are deployed and the powers governing the rune are invoked. Once the rune has been consecrated and dedicated, an appropriate sacrafice should be given to the God or Goddess invoked in the ceremony—and this has to be done for each rune! For example, for Odin, a small glass of gin, whisky or vodka; for Thor, a can of beer; for Freya, a small glass of champagne or sweet liqueur—feel what is right for each. One must also state the exact purpose for which the rune is going to be used.

The last line of this stanza from the *Havamal* contains the word *senda,* meaning "to send." In the sagas we frequently find descriptions of a sending being carried out. My research suggests that this refers to an act of shape-shifting. All the runes are associated with specific gods and goddesses, and most gods and goddesses have their own totem animal such as, for instance, Odin's ravens. Runes can be used to create an ethnic animal from out of one's own psychic force-field. This creature can then be imbued with power, raised through emotion and will, and thus be activated and sent off to do some harm. The easiest way to attack an opponent is when the individual is in a dream state, as the dream state operates at a level very much akin to that at which the artificially created animal functions. In conventional occultism this level of operation is usually called the astral. After a working of this nature has been performed, it is vital to reabsorb the animal's remaining energies before assimilating and then banishing it.

The second verb in this last line is *sóa,* which is translated as "to destroy" and also means "to sacrifice." According to my interpretation, this means an act involving a sacrificial destruction, that is to say an act of killing someone after first dedicating the victim to Odin. This was the practice in the olden days, when it was customary to perform human sacrifices by hanging and stabbing while repeating the incantation, "Now I give thee to Odin." As we embraced so-called civilization, this custom became completely obsolete, but when necessary I do not see why this cannot be enacted on a symbolic level through sympathetic magic. These magical instructions hidden in this important stanza of the *Havamal* will repay serious study and research, for they provide information vital to the practice of runic magic.

Rune-Charms in the *Havamal*

There are eighteen rune-charms mentioned in the *Havamal.* Guido von List, a German scholar and one of the founders of the Armanen system of runelore, postulated that the magical futhark should consist of eighteen runes; given that nine is the magical number in the Northern tradition, this seems a reasonable assumption. Nevertheless, my studies of stanzas 133 to 155 in the *Havamal* made me realize that each rune-charm is associated with more than one rune.

My proposed interpretation of the *Havamal* charms assigns three runes for each charm. One of these runes must be non-invertible and represent the realm from which the power for the working is drawn. Some charms, however, use two non-invertible runes; in these cases only one of the two non-invertible runes represents the realm from which the power is drawn. The other non-invertible rune functions supportively to help attain the objective of the working.

The first charm is intended to give help to people in sorrow and distress. The following runes should be allocated: Fehu, Inguz, and Laguz. Fehu has been assigned to this charm by the Armanen tradition because of its connotation of wealth. Wealth will not solve all problems, but it certainly will alleviate many of them. The Fehu rune invokes the Vanir gods: Niord, Frey, and Freyja. Inguz is the rune of Vanaheim, the realm of the Vanir, the gods of peace and plenty. From this realm the power to gain wealth is drawn. Laguz is part of this combination as it is also associated with Niord and Nerthus. Furthermore, Laguz helps to regain emotional control.

The second charm is used for healing; the runes allocated to it are Uruz, Jera, and Sowulo. The realm from which healing power can be drawn is the Earth itself, Midgard, and the rune that provides access to the energy of this realm is Jera. The third rune in this combination is Sowulo, a strengthening rune and, like Uruz, appropriate for healing. The Uruz rune itself is the driving power of healing and resilience. In addition to this rune combination, it has been brought to my attention that Laguz was also known as a healing rune. The god to invoke for a healing working is Thor and/or the goddess Eir.

The third charm is used for the fettering of foes and can thus be described as a war-fetter, or in modern psychological terms, a means to constrain actions. The traditional runes to effect this action are Thurisaz, Isa, and Nauthiz. The Isa rune gives access to the power of the realm of Jotunheim, the realm of ice and of the frost giants. The Nauthiz rune is used as a backup that constrains. The Thurisaz rune in this case is used in a passive mode, that is to say, it is reversed. The god to invoke for this spell is Odin, as he traditionally possesses the ability to attach war-fetters. The Valkyries also share this power.

The fourth charm releases fetters. The runes to employ here are Ansuz, the traditional rune, in combination with Fehu and Inguz. Ansuz possesses the power to release fetters, by transcending them through magical techniques such as breathing and the use of the voice. In psychological terms, the concept of fetters may be equated with anxieties, frustrations, and inhibitions. Verbalizing one's personal fetters and analyzing them, or just plain primal screaming, are all connected with the attributes of Ansuz. Inguz again is the rune used to draw down the power from Vanaheim. The god traditionally associated with the releasing of fetters is Frey, who is represented in the spell by the Fehu rune, as he is the appropriate god whose aid is invoked in this spell.

The fifth charm provides the ability to stop a dart that has been set on course by means of fixing one's eye on it. Apart from its normal warrior connotations, this charm also refers to forms of magical attack. The "dart" then stands for any device, physical or otherwise, that a magical opponent may use to carry the ill-wishing spell. It certainly would be effective to counteract an elfshot. The runes for this working are Raido, Isa, and Kenaz. Kenaz is the rune of light, and thus is the rune which allows you to focus your attention on the object and on its intent. Isa is used to draw power from Jotunheim and slow the object down, while Raido can return it to its source. To accelerate its effect on the sender, Jera or Dagaz could be employed in addition to the aforementioned combination.

The sixth charm provides a similar defense in allowing a curse to be returned to its sender. The power to do this has to be drawn from the realm of Hel, and the rune to employ is Hagalaz. The accompanying runes are Jera, which turns a spell on itself, thus sending it back through time to the sender; and Raido, to direct it and ensure "karmic" consequences.

The seventh charm describes how to put out a fire blazing in a hall. The rune employed is Isa, which draws the power from the world of ice. The other two runes to use are Laguz and Nauthiz. Both Isa and Laguz are elements in opposition to fire, while Nauthiz is employed because of its restraining power.

The eighth charm confers the ability to bring about reconciliations. Gebo will help to draw in the power from Asgard, the realm of reason and intellect. Mannaz and Wunjo are combined with it, as both runes are associated with the idea of people as individuals and as part of a social establishment.

The ninth charm shows how to control the winds when at sea and how to avoid a shipwreck. Here also I would call in the power from Asgard using the Gebo rune in the center. Ansuz represents Odin's aspect as a god of winds, and Raido ensures a safe return journey.

The tenth charm mentions "witches" playing in the air, and how to confuse them and deprive them of their senses and shape. Not an easy task! However, Dagaz is certainly one of the runes to use, as it turns everything into its opposite very fast. Shape-shifting and sorcery are also indicated in this spell. Therefore the realm from which to draw power to counteract these actions is Muspelheim. The two runes to accompany Dagaz are Ehwaz, to confuse their shapes, and Laguz, to confuse their senses. All the above has to be interpreted in terms of an astral attack in the image of an animal. This may well be a rare occurrence, but these three runes will nevertheless help to combat it.

The eleventh charm deals with securing protection for friends in battle by means of the old Germanic practice of singing charms over the warriors' shields. For this I would call upon the protective power of the Vanir and use the Sowulo rune to draw down the power of Alfheim, the realm of the lightalfar. Other runes to combine with Sowulo are Algiz, to invoke the protection of the Valkyries, and Ansuz, to directly connect with the practice of singing charms. This latter rune is used to invoke the protection of Odin himself.

The twelfth charm concerns necromancy, or communicating with the dead. Hagalaz is the key rune here and is used to contact the realm of the dead, Hel, or even the realm governed by Nauthiz, Nifelhel, where one might well seek to contact the really evil entities that dwell there. The other runes to combine with Hagalaz are Teiwaz, which has been traditionally assigned to this type of working, and Kenaz, which functions as a beacon to guide you through the underworld and back.

The thirteenth charm instructs us in how to protect a young warrior by sprinkling him with water. The protective power is drawn from either Asgard by means of Gebo, or Vanaheim using Inguz. Protective runes that can be added are Laguz and Algiz. Berkana might also be considered helpful.

The fourteenth charm provides knowledge of all the gods and elves and the ability to distinguish between them.

The principle underlying this charm relates to magical knowledge, for which is required the ability to distinguish one god from another and to discern their individual functions and attributes. By this means it is possible to learn which god should be invoked for any particular purpose. The most important rune in helping us acquire this knowledge is Eihwaz, representing the realm of the swartalfar, the inner Earth. Eihwaz also corresponds to Yggdrasil. Because Yggdrasil contains all the realms within it, this rune grants access to the knowledge of all the gods. The accompanying runes would be two of the hugrunes: Ansuz and Mannaz. Hugrunes are runes of the mind and of intellectual abilities; these two represent communication and cognition, respectively.

The fifteenth charm, the one which Thjodrerrir chanted before Delling's door, gives power to the Aesir, prowess to the elves, and foresight to Odin. Thjodrerrir was a dwarf; his name literally means "setter in motion." Delling's door is the rising Sun, and we are told that Delling is an elf who acts as a watchman. "Before his door" means the time before the rising of the Sun. This charm can be interpreted as a spell specially designed to invoke and use pure solar power. As Delling is an elf, the world from which the power is drawn is Alfheim, and the principal rune to be employed is Sowulo. The rising and setting of the Sun is presided over by Delling and Billing, respectively. The charm gives power, prowess, and foresight, which are all abilities that the occult regards as solar. The two runes to be used jointly with Sowulo are Raido and Kenaz. Raido is used because of its associations with the solar cycle and Kenaz represents foresight in both its meanings: clairvoyance and the ability to look ahead.

The sixteenth charm is a charm to attract a lover. Runes to use for this are Kenaz, Jera, and Inguz. Jera relates to the realm of Midgard, from which the power is drawn for workings associated with love. It makes a difference whether the operator of this spell is male or female. If the operator is male and wishes to attract a female lover, the Inguz rune could be replaced by Thurisaz or Teiwaz, for both these runes have associations with male sexuality.

The seventeenth spell is very similar to the sixteenth, but differs in that it is a charm to maintain a long-lasting relationship such as marriage. Runes to use are Gebo, Inguz, and Ehwaz. Inguz is the predominant rune of the Vanir and of Vanaheim. It is used to invoke the blessings of the Vanir on the relationship. Gebo represents the process of mutual give-and-take in the relationship; Ehwaz has been traditionally accepted as a rune of marriage.

The eighteenth and final spell is very esoteric and may refer to the secret of "mystical union" or integration with one's "sister" or "brother." I interpret this to mean the union of the male with his anima or of the female with her animus, to use Jungian terms. The runes for this spell have to be discovered by each individual alone.

This material has been given as a practical alternative to the traditional Armanen system, without intending to imply that the traditional system is in any way invalid. However, my interpretation is more in keeping with the modern occult school of thought.

To put the *Havamal* spells into practice, a circle should be cast. The first requirement in casting a circle, as those of other magical traditions will agree, is to establish the correct correspondences and to define the precise aim of the working. Firstly, therefore, choose an appropriate day to perform the working. A healing, for example, would be done on a Sunday or a Thursday; the gods corresponding to these days are Baldur and Thor, respectively. Cursings are best done on a Wednesday or a Saturday; these days are under the influence of Odin and Loki, respectively. Protective and love-workings are to be performed on a Friday, while Tuesday is best suited to a working designed to achieve justice. Personally, I do not like working on a Monday, but there is no binding reason that certain workings cannot be done on that day. Perhaps Monday workings are good for ensuring success with new beginnings, for instance when starting a job or a course. As ever, one has to experiment for oneself.

After establishing the appropriate day, meditate on the gods and decide who is most appropriate to the objective of the working. In a fertility working invoke the Vanir—Frey and Freyja—on a Friday. Frigga and Thor should also be invoked, as all four of these gods have fertility attributes. Invoke them by their individual respective runes. For example, for Frigga, invoke Pertho; for Frey, Inguz; for Freyja, Fehu; and for Thor, Thurisaz.

Each of these four gods can be allocated to one of the four quarters. For example, Frey is associated with the Sun and his weapon is a sword. Therefore invoke him from the East, although normally, in a general-purpose circle, he would be placed in the West. In this specific example, Freyja would be located in the western quarter, for she represents the aspect of the maiden and the element of water. Thor belongs to the South, his normal quarter, and Frigga, as the elder goddess, belongs in the North because she is magically related to the Norns. Before casting a circle, a cleansing ritual can be performed with water, salt, a torch of fire, and, if required, incense, although I have not found any evidence for incense being used in Northern magic. The torch of fire is used to claim the working space and it only needs to be done on the first occasion in order to consecrate and dedicate the place where one expects to perform regular workings in the future. After the circle has been opened, construct a talisman, such as a rune-stave, and carve the selected runes on the stave. In this example, a fertility charm would consist of Pertho, Inguz, Thurisaz, and Fehu. Use the same runes that were used to invoke the gods, and chant the runes while carving them. For the purposes of increasing fertility it is advisable to stain the runes with appropriate liquids.

Power Sigils

Certain sigils that do not form part of the traditional twenty-four-rune elder futhark are sacred to specific gods. These sigils are, strictly speaking, not runes as such, but are related and form part of the same magical tradition. The most important of these sigils are the Swastika, the Valknut, and the Shieldknot. I myself attach a specific value to the Valknut, because it is the symbol of Odin. This sign is profoundly magical; however, it is not widely used because, as my colleague Peter Seymour suggests, the Valknut is essentially the

symbol of sacrifice made to Odin. The Valknut implies that its bearer is one of the einherjar who has freely dedicated his life to Odin
and who accepts that Odin is entitled to claim the life thus consecrated to his service whenever Odin deems fit. The Valknut is depicted on the Gotland Stone in Sweden, which portrays a scene
suggestive of a sacrificial death. Hence the darker connotations of
the Valknut. It is fair to say that when I started wearing this sign I
was not aware of its darker meaning, but now that I have discovered
its esoteric significance I am fully committed to accepting the consequences. The shape of the Valknut is that of three interlaced trian-
gles, symbolizing the triple nature of Odin. The nine angles of the
Valknut symbolize the nine realms. Visualization of the Valknut is a
difficult exercise, but once mastered it can be used to invoke Odin
with great effect.

DEOSIL SWASTIKA   WIDDERSHINS SWASTIKA

VALKNUT   SHIELDKNOT

POWER SIGILS

The Swastika, or Fylfot, is more widely known and has been used by a variety of cultures as wide ranging as the Tibetan, Native American, Japanese and Greek, to name but a few. Unfortunately it was misused in Nazi Germany. It has always been viewed as a symbol of the Sun. In the Northern tradition it is the sign sacred to Thor. The Swastika is one of the most potent signs in the collective human experience, and it is high time that this sign regained its rightful place and was redeemed from its negative implications. It lends itself well to magical workings and can be used in its two principal forms. The deosil or sun-wise form is employed to attract forces; the widdershins form is used to expel forces. The Swastika's shape lends itself to combinations with runes (see examples on page 163).

The Shieldknot is a protective symbol. It also is sacred to Thor, although its elemental value is earth. A flat disk on which this symbol has been depicted would function well in a circle-working as a replacement for the more widely known pentacle. It can be used successfully on the four quarters as a shielding device. All this information can be applied to magical practices current in modern-day occultism.

Shamanic Drumming and Chanting

My initial training in various schools of the Hermetic system led me into experiments in shamanism. Most of my shamanic experiences, including out-of-the-body experiences, were involuntary. In explaining my own views of shamanic practices, the reader should bear in mind that the issue of shamanism is an essentially subjective field. Therefore the reader is encouraged to verify any of my own stated views for themselves. Whereas the magical techniques described before are safe and sound and well tested, shamanism is a highly personal and experimental system. Therefore I can only give an outline of the various principles involved as they relate to the Northern Mysteries.

In shamanism one of the most valued techniques is the use of sound, whereas in other occult systems the emphasis is largely placed on the ability to visualize. There are two main techniques: chanting, and drumming, which is combined with breath control and synchronized with the heartbeat. The main reason for employing these techniques is to achieve an altered state of consciousness or trance. There are, in my experience at least, two different kinds of trance states. One is exhilarating and leads to a tremendous amount of energy. In this state, magical acts can be performed usually on the spur of the moment, regardless of whether it is the correct day or whether the right gods or forces have been invoked. With this sort of trance the emotion is intensified as the working is carried out spontaneously and without forethought. I once reached this state involuntarily through an excessive use of alcohol; in that condition I cursed someone who had threatened my life. The curse was effective. The second kind of trance is an almost somnolent state in which the mind is turned totally inward. This is used for divination or mediation. This ability is inborn with me and is not the result of any shamanic training. For this reason I cannot explain how to achieve this form of trance through shamanic practices. I do not advocate the use of drugs, as they can distort experiences and have the great disadvantage of distorting the memory of what happened during the trance. This may also be the case with alcohol.

Runes form relationships with each other, and by exploring the runes in various ways we find certain runes, like Kenaz, Jera, and Inguz, sharing a common theme (as described elsewhere in this book). Runes can be looked upon as being either complementary to each other or in opposition to each other. Here are some examples: Fehu and Uruz are complementary, both dealing with bovine livestock. Thurisaz and Ansuz are opposing forces as giants and Aesir. It is very useful to explore the runes in this way for practical magic. Another example of a purely sexual combination of runes is Thurisaz and Inguz. Thurisaz is also the opposing force of Isa; when one combines both runes in a working, such as in a chanting or a power-raising working involving two people, each invoking and channeling the power of one of these two runes, one can raise a great deal of power for whatever purpose. Another such combination, although of a gentler nature, is the combination of the opposing forces of fire, Kenaz, and water, Laguz. A ritual torch, symbolizing Kenaz, could be ritually extinguished after use in a cauldron of water, representing Laguz.

One of the better-known practices in runecraft is the use of bind-runes. A bind-rune consists of two or more runes superimposed on one another tautalogically in order to fuse their energies and create a magical effect. This is widely used to create sigils and talismans. Information on bind-runes can be obtained in most books written on the runes in recent years. A very good idea is to construct a bind-rune using the runes that spell out one's given name or magical name, and to use this as a sigil for one's own personal use.

In order to practice shamanic drumming, a drum has to be obtained which resonates in harmony with the individual's unique ground-tone or magical frequency. (Tibetan tradition teaches that each person has his or her own unique magical sound to which he or she responds, and which is in harmony with their psychic force-field.) This magical ground-tone can be found through experimentation. For drumming I recommend the *bohran,* which is a round Irish drum. Start by just playing with the drum to establish a rapport with it. Various rhythms will be suitable for different individuals. It is necessary to experiment to find one's frequency. Drumming can create altered states of consciousness very easily. One of the signs of a good result being achieved is hearing a secondary drumbeat far away. Some of my apprentices were engaged in practicing shamanic drumming and heard a chorus of female voices joining in with the drum.

Shamanic chanting is another useful technique. There are accounts from Icelandic sources that songs or chants were used in seidr workings. These chants unfortunately have not survived; but I have reconstructed some of them with the help and inspiration of the goddess Freyja. Whether the chants I have composed bear any resemblance to the originals is impossible to verify, but I can assure the reader that they do work, according to the following principles. Each rune has its own particular frequency on which it vibrates. However, this may differ slightly for different individuals and there must certainly be great differences between the appropriate notes used by the female and the male voice. The only way to master this technique is by practice and hard work. Through chanting the runes, one can express the meaning of that rune. Powerful examples of this Galdr technique are found on the compact disc I made, *Songs of Yggdrasil*.

On the disc it can be clearly understood how the runes Thurisaz and Hagalaz sound doom-laden and menacing. Thurisaz, if chanted correctly, sounds aggressive and Hagalaz sounds vicious or dark. Inguz, on the other hand, has a light sound at a higher pitch and displays a degree of elfin feeling. It is very worthwhile to develop an ability to chant the runes, as it gives great power. One example of how chanting could be used is in charging a runic talisman or spell. By chanting runes and hitting the right frequency, a slight vibration will be felt in the area of the throat where the throat chakra or thyroid gland is situated. Chanting runes while visualizing them is a strong magical method which makes contact with the runic forces. During chanting it is also important to regulate one's breath; exercises for breath control can be found in most occult books.

Advanced Shamanic Techniques and Shape-Shifting

Advanced shamanic techniques include shape-shifting and the use of "power-animals." Most occultists are familiar with the principle of assuming god-forms in a ritual enactment. The same technique can be applied to adopt an animal's shape. Study the chosen animal carefully and make yourself familiar with its attributes. Choose an animal you have some affection for and you are familiar with. When invoking the animal's spirit, dress in its skin if possible and imitate the noises it makes. This is done to integrate the animal's nature within oneself. In olden days initiation practices were performed in which the warrior was symbolically adopted in a cult sacred to the animal. Thus the "berserkers" were dedicated to the cult of the bear. Two other less well-known cults practiced in the Northlands include the Ulfhednar, whose totem animal was the wolf, and the Chatti, who worshipped cats.

What is known as shape-shifting covers more than one technique. For instance, the easiest and most practical way is to assume an animal's shape, imagining that you actually look like the animal. A sensitive person will actually perceive you as that animal, at least on the unconscious level. I once chased off a would-be rapist who was following me by suddenly turning around and feeling myself to be a sharp-beaked hawk. I could positively feel the beak and managed to chase him all the way back down the road.

There is a more advanced form of shape-shifting which involves a total astral projection. My understanding of this technique is as follows. Astral material, or *hamr*, as it is called in the Northern tradition, can be externalized in a form created by the mind or *hugr*. This will be visible to some sensitive people and to most animals, especially to dogs and cats.

A successful shape-shift consists of three components: the material, the imagination, and the intent or will. Firstly, the etheric body of the requisite animal is created. The image-making facility shapes the material into a thought-form. The next step is to associate and identify with the animal's soul or attributes to "load" or "charge" the created shape. Then one projects one's consciousness into it. One of the ways of doing this is to try to see through its eyes and look back at one's own body, which by this time should be sitting or lying down unconscious. By this means one can move about and visit other places.

I once assumed the shape of an Alsatian and chased an unwanted tenant out of my house. Of course, when I launched this attack, it was done on an etheric or astral level. It is obviously not possible to assume an animal's shape and attack someone on the physical plane. Animals can also be created for a specific role, such as that of guardian. Because the experiment takes place on a different level of reality, it may be difficult to remember the experience afterwards; on returning to normal consciousness, all the energies used in the shape-shifting must be reabsorbed.

It must be borne in mind that every shamanic act is very personal and each person seems to develop his or her own technique. There is no technique available which would suit everybody. The principal feature of shamanism is that it is necessary to learn by experimentation. Shamanic experience is very subjective, and although results produced will have similarities all over the world, the techniques applied vary from one individual to the next. There also seems to be a more advanced technique involving the creation of an animal's form outside the self, like an artificial elemental which will more or less act independently, carrying out its instructions automatically. Such beings were often created as guardians, for example, to protect the sanctity of a burial place. Also there are reports from Icelandic sources that animals were created and sent off to harm an enemy. This was called a "sending." Animals were used in this way to plant a curse or an ill wish on the receiving party.

Magic to Complement Divination

In Chapter 3, I outlined how to investigate the balance of the forces involving the individual. Suppose that in a specific reading a situation is portrayed which indicates that an individual has an imbalance in his or her elements, with an excessive preponderance of air, or thinking, and a totally blocked aspect of water, or feeling. It is first of all necessary to establish whether this is a temporary condition triggered by specific problems, or whether it results from a magically unsound condition in the individual's persona. If it is a temporary condition, it might be left alone to fade away when the underlying cause is resolved. On the other hand, if it is an entrenched condition, limiting the person's growth or magical expansion, techniques can be devised to redress the balance. Runes, of course, are the medium to be used, accompanied by some ritual.

To examine the given example further, let us assume that a tree reading has been carried out and that an Isa rune occupies the area designated as the element of water and feeling. This might be interpreted as meaning that the feeling side of the individual is blocked. The rune to use to redress the balance is Sowulo, to melt the ice influence, or Kenaz if it is necessary to obtain information concerning the causes of this blockage and to establish when and why it has been erected. A talisman involving one or both runes can be made as an aid for concentration and invocations. The rune or runes have to be visualized several times a day, especially in the morning and before falling asleep. The person for which the work is carried out has to immerse him- or herself in these runes, and try to chant them to feel his or her energies loosening up the blockage. At the same time, the individual should try to express feelings outwardly, either towards a much-loved person or inwardly, for example, by writing about his or her feelings. By means such as these, runes can be used as complementary or opposing energies. This technique can be applied for most life situations, such as lack of communication, lack of confidence, fear of failure, and whatever other psychological weaknesses may exist. The runes therefore can be applied to all sorts of personal, emotional, and psychological problems, relieving blockages, stresses, and inhibitions and thereby improving the quality of the individual's life.

Table of Runic Correspondences

Each of the runes has a relationship with at least one god or goddess, and sometimes with more than one. Furthermore, each rune has a primary element and sometimes also a secondary element. Although the runes are normally colored red, it might be useful for some magical purposes, such as in making a talisman, to color each rune in a shade corresponding to its respective deities and elements.

The following system of correspondences is by no means rigidly fixed, and it may be altered and improved as long as it appears justified (see table on page 172). The reasons for the correspondences of the gods, polarities, colors, and elements have already been explained in previous sections of this book.

Rune	God-form	Polarity	Color	Element(s)
⍓	Frey/Freyja	Feminine	Fiery red	Fire/Earth
∩	Thor	Masculine	Red	Earth
Þ	Thor	Masculine	Red	Fire
ᚠ	Odin	Masculine	Indigo	Air
ᚱ	Thor	Masculine	Red	Air
ᚲ	Heimdal/Freyja	Feminine	Red/orange	Fire
ᚷ	Odin	Neutral/both	Blue/gold	Air
ᚹ	Odin	Masculine	Golden	Earth
ᚺ	Hella/Holda	Feminine	Gray	Water (hail)
ᚾ	Skuld	Feminine	Black	Fire
ᛁ	Verdandi/Skadi Rind/Frostgiants	Feminine	White	Water (ice)
ᛃ	Frey/Freyja Baldur/Hodur	Both	Green	Earth
ᛇ	Skadi/ Uller/Odin	Masculine	Green	All
ᛈ	Nerthus/Mimir Frigg	Feminine	Silver	Water
ᛉ	Heimdal/Valkyries	Either	Rainbow	Air
ᛋ	Baldur	Masculine	Gold	Air
↑	Tyr	Masculine	Red	Air
ᛒ	Berta/Holda	Feminine	Green	Earth
ᛗ	Frey/Freyja	Both	Green	Earth
ᛘ	Heimdal	Masculine	Blue	Air
ᛚ	Nerthus	Feminine	Sea	Water
◇	Frey/Freyja	Both	Green	Water/earth
ᛟ	Odin	Masculine	Red	Earth
ᛙ	Heimdal/Loki	Masculine	Red	Fire/air

· 5 ·

GOD-PROFILES

What Are Gods?

The Northern tradition is very distinctive and has a unique magical structure, with its own elements and numerology. The Nordic gods cannot be equated with, for example, the Greek gods. There are similarities between the two pantheons but not exact correspondences. In fact, there are a lot more similarities between the Nordic Gods and the Loas of the Voodoo religion; this also applies to the Orishas in their most natural form, when stripped of Catholic overlays. Nevertheless, I shall try, where necessary, to describe the attributes of the Nordic gods in comparison with those of the Greek gods.

Let us suppose that at a certain point in time and space, consciousness evolved from energy, and creation was initiated. Out of this consciousness, differentiation occurred in accordance with cosmic laws. At some stage, various types of beings came into existence, such as gods, nature spirits, humans, and probably other life-forms unknown to us. How did the gods, in general, develop from within their relative environment?

All organic religions are born from the folk-consciousness and begin with two principles, an Earthmother and a Skyfather. Both of these gradually develop subsidiary personalities which eventually become more or less independent entities and are treated as such. In this way, a pantheon is formed which originates from two primal forces of Nature and is credited with personal attributes symbolizing natural phenomena such as thunder or rain. These two primal forces, which initially were simple energy, gradually develop more personal traits and adopt distinct characters.

How does this come about? Let us assume for the moment that these energies are cosmic forces, with no attributes other than those of being and of expanding. Who or what gives form to these energy patterns? It is human consciousness and the human mind which gives them form and eventually their names. Large groups of people of similar origin, sharing the same environment, will develop a shared idea of gods or demons, or whatever it is that they wish to personify. All life-forms in Creation are extensions of those energies, differentiated at various levels of consciousness. The gods are higher forms of those energies, operating through the human mind; in return they become "humanized," and are endowed with human personalities, human caprice, and human failings. They are imagined as looking and acting like human beings.

Although more powerful than humans, the gods are not necessarily more perfect than we are. They need us as much as we need them. The concept of perfection has no place in an organic, evolving religion. As human consciousness grew in its understanding of the world around it, these god-images became more and more complex as the various human species developed in their diverse geographical circumstances and, accordingly, created different god-forms. "Forms," mind you, not "essence." The essence of cosmic energy is universal, but its interpretation will be colored by environment, which is only natural. The concept of one universal male god-form has caused a lot of destruction among our own folk, and among other traditional peoples all over the world.

So what we call "the gods" are those forces which created us and we, in return, created. This is not to say that the gods are not real, or that they are just creations of the human imagination. In fact the reverse might be equally true. Who, then, imagined whom? It is a case of a reciprocal symbiosis of consciousness. I strongly believe that the gods are real on a different level of reality from ours, and that they have the intelligence and the power to make decisions independently of the human mind and certainly of the individual human mind. It is hypothetically possible that they are more or less the executors of the will of the collective human mind, operating within the limits of the particular environment which shaped them. For the most part, the gods direct the collective will, but they also carry out the decisions made by that will. So there is a two-way process. Although they can probably make decisions independently of the individual human mind, they may well not be able to take a decision that is contrary to the interests of the collective will of the people involved. This is equally true for all gods, all over the world, including those of the monotheistic religions. It is nonsense to insist that only one's own god exists. The gods created us and we created them, in a self-perpetuating process of exchanging energy. We can thus conclude that a god ceases to exist when there is not a single individual left who believes in that god. When this occurs, the energy of the god will return to its source, and from this other god-forms can be built up.

This theory sheds light on our understanding of the myth of the Ragnarok. Real as the gods are, they should not be regarded as static stereotypes. As the consciousness of a people develops and progresses to a greater understanding of the world around it, so its god-form evolves simultaneously; over a long period of time, changes occur in the god-form which reflect the changes in the consciousness of the people.

An improved image or set of ideas is then projected onto the god and the god responds accordingly, improving the consciousness of the people in a mutual support system with two-way feedback. Thus the gods develop in symbiosis with their people. I will attempt to illustrate this by giving as an example the origins and development of the most interesting and complicated character, that of the god Odin.

Odin is the highest god in the Northern pantheon. There is a great deal of evidence to suggest that Odin was originally a minor god who worked his way up the scale. However, any examination of the development of Odin's character will reveal that this god, who is known by various names, also has widely different aspects and characteristics in various countries of the North, so much so that some people are of the opinion that the various names indicate different gods altogether. However, the majority of scholars and religious thinkers believe that in essence we are talking about one and the same god or archetype. His names, beginning with the oldest, are:

Wodanaz in primitive Germanic

Wodan in Dutch

Woden in English

Odin in Norse

Wotan in German

These are the main names by which our god has been known in the North for the last 2,000 years. The name Wodanaz is the oldest form and is of similar date to the god-names Thurisaz and Teiwaz, which are related to Thor and Tyr respectively, and appear in the futhark as names of the runes associated with those gods. We see from this that there are five different names for Wodan (as I prefer to call him in my own rituals, according to the tradition in my own country), and associations with some of these five names indicate immediately some of his different characteristics. If someone mentions the name "Odin," an image springs to mind of the Viking god of war. When "Wotan" is spoken of, the reaction is "Oh, yes!—*The Ring*—Wagner." How many people are aware that Wotan is actually the same god as Odin, and that the story of "The Ring" has been largely borrowed from the Icelandic *Volsung Saga*?

For the sake of clarity, I will refer to the gods by their Scandinavian names, as most of the various literary sources quoted throughout this book are Scandinavian. It can be imperative in certain occult work to be very precise when using names of power. The names "Wodan," "Woden," and "Wotan" might differ in sound, but never in meaning. The name "Odin," however, is another matter. Although he is the same deity as Wodan, he displays different aspects. It could be said that Odin is Wodan when he is in a bad mood!

Although we are speaking of the same deity when referring to Wodan or Odin, their different aspects should be borne in mind since, in a magical working, it can make all the difference to the result of that working if one is aware of the differences and remains conscious throughout the working of who, or rather which aspect, is to be invoked. Odin's distinctive attributes were developed mostly during the Viking Age. To my mind, there has since been a slight shift in the elements, or rather in the relationship of the elements.

In any occult tradition, some of the first things to explore are the elements corresponding to the god with whom one wishes to work. One of the purposes of this is to align the god with one of the four quarters. This is an easier task with some gods than with others. For example, if I were to suggest putting Thor in the South, I doubt whether there is one occultist who would disagree with me. But where Odin is concerned, it is not so simple. He has so many aspects that it is necessary in a working to narrow it down to whichever aspect of Odin is to be invoked, applied, employed, or concentrated on.

Wodan or Odin are both chiefly concerned with the element of air, but with Wodan there is a stronger link with the element of water and some connection with the element of earth. In the Continental parts of Northern Europe Wodan has, of old, been associated with the weather and the harvest. (At the end of the harvest, it was a folklore custom to leave the last sheaf of corn on the field as a thanksgiving for the harvest and as food for Sleipnir, Wodan's horse.) However, with Odin there exists, in addition to the element of air, a strong element of fire, which causes him to be much more aggressive than the old Wodan. With Odin, the element of fire is second only to that of air, the influences of earth and water being so negligible as to be virtually indiscernible. I have thought about this and tried to grasp the principles behind it. My understanding is as follows.

Although they stay essentially the same, gods change slightly over a long period of time. Like people, they are not perfect and, as we have seen, they evolve along with their worshippers. The people who worshipped Wodan two thousand years ago are not the same as those who worship him today. Therefore Wodan has changed as well. Gods either change and grow with the growth of the consciousness of the people, or they become outdated and die. We can see, for example, that the first concept of Wodan was of a storm giant or demon called Wode, which roughly translated means "rage." He gradually developed the very complicated and sophisticated characteristics of the intellectual magician-god, Wodan/Odin, but the raging storm aspect is still there, and has only been overshadowed by later aspects and abilities attributed to him.

There are two main forms of religion: monotheism and polytheism. Paganism, or heathenism as we in the North prefer to call it, is polytheistic. Out of the Middle East, three major religions have developed. All are monotheistic, and two out of the three are positively aggressive in their attitudes towards each other, as well as towards the rest of the world, which chooses to think differently. Why? We shall see.

Suppose that, at a certain point in the evolution of consciousness, two opposing currents evolved, one directed towards differentiation, and the other one opposing differentiation. The latter current, working towards homogenization and the dissolution of differences in both gods and humans, has been very strong over the last two thousand years—until now, that is—when we are experiencing a renaissance in a variety of heathen traditions. It seems that the end result of the concept of "one god for all" is the limiting of the creative faculties of the human mind.

Why, in any case, is there a need for gods? The human mind is not capable of relating to the cosmic intelligence directly. It therefore invents mediating images. Our observation of the human race, and of the differences between individuals as well as between groups, leads us logically to conclude that each person finds a god or goddess with whom he or she can identify, a deity who acts as a model on which the individual's aspiration and higher self can be projected.

In a monotheistic religion, however, there is no variety. There is only one possible choice: a male authoritarian figure who imposes upon his followers a list of dos and don'ts, keeping them in submission by threats and promises based on such philosophically unrealistic ideas as absolute good and absolute evil.

There is an occult axiom which says, "All gods are one god, all goddesses are one goddess; there is but one initiatrix/tor."

Monotheism went wrong not so much in tracing the gods back to their original, more or less abstract principles, but doing so in an unbalanced manner.

The historical figure who started monotheism was an Egyptian pharaoh from the Eighteenth Dynasty named Achnaton, or Amenhotep IV, who in his time was confronted with a corrupt hierarchy of greedy priests. Reacting against this hierarchy, he instituted, in a more or less violent revolutionary manner, a religion with only one god, Aton. By this act, the original mistake of monotheism was made. No acknowledgment was made of the feminine part of divinity. This new monotheism was totally male-dominated. If Achnaton had gone one step further and recognized that what he envisaged as being a single deity was of equally balanced polarity, or else was something of a completely neutral nature with no concept of gender at all, then a great deal of suffering would have been avoided. From this concept of monotheism were created Judaism, Christianity, and Islam, the latter two developing as heresies from the Judaic tradition which was originally a development, via Moses, of the Aton cult. Thus it can be seen that Achnaton started monotheism and in the process made possibly the most disastrous error in the history of human thought—the ousting of the feminine principle from Nature. By so doing he created a split between the female and male halves of the human being. All of us are partly male and partly female and so, too, are the gods, even Odin and Thor. Achnaton himself seems to have been complex-ridden in regard to female sexuality. He came down through history depicted in Greek mythology as Oedipus, and eventually ended up on Freud's couch!

In heathenism, we have been spared any of this nonsense. Each of our gods is like each of us, a mixture of good and evil, although on a grander scale, for good and evil are themselves relative notions which reflect the norms prevalent at a particular time in a particular society, or in more advanced cases, in the minds of individuals.

Before dealing with the magical considerations of specific god-forms and giving detailed profiles of the gods, we must first of all make a clear distinction between the Aesir, the Vanir, and the giants. The giants in Northern mythology, such as the frost giants, the mountain giants, and the fire giants, represent the raw forces of Nature in their primitive form. The people or race that preceded the present inhabitants of Northern Europe were primitives with an animistic outlook. Anything they did not understand was either worshipped, or feared and placated. It is most probable that the giants were once the gods of these people, and that when a new concept of religion developed, centered on the Earth and its fertility, these gods who had been seen as threatening natural forces became the giants. The gods whose cult was then introduced in the Northland were the Vanir, who became the major objects of devotion and worship. Worship of the Vanir must have started around the time that the first hunters and gatherers began to develop an agricultural way of life. The Vanir, therefore, are the gods of water and earth. The Aesir are the gods of fire and air. They may have originated at a later date than the Vanir and in a different area. The war between the Aesir and the Vanir may well be a folk-memory of the invading tribes, who were first and foremost warriors. Unpleasant as war may be, it usually results in technological developments. Thus it could be that the giants were the gods of the Stone Age, the Vanir the gods of the Bronze Age and the Aesir the gods of the Iron Age.

Let us now consider the gods in magical terms and for what purposes particular gods would be invoked, together with their associated weapons or tools, colors, elements, animals, runes, and quarters. The goddesses are separately described in Chapter 6, "Feminine Mysteries."

Each individual that relates to a god invokes a certain response, but the response will only display that aspect of the god that is invoked. What any god does is to project back and magnify the initial input, provided that whatever is invoked is in keeping with the character of that god (it would be absurd, for example, to invoke Mars for peace or Venus for war). Let us begin with Odin.

Odin

Names ♦	Odin (Norse), Woden (English), Wodan (Dutch), Wotan (German)
Main element ♦	air
Secondary element ♦	water
Colors ♦	indigo, dark blue, woad
Numbers ♦	nine, three
Totem animals ♦	horse, raven, wolf, eagle, snake
Personal sigils ♦	Valknut, Tridiskil
Aspects ♦	Odin, Vili, and Ve; warrior, shaman, wanderer
Magical items ♦	spear, wand, arm-ring
Invoked for ♦	wisdom, occult knowledge and power, guile, invisibility, war, healing, revenge, cursing
Runes to use ♦	Ansuz, Gebo, Wunjo, Eihwaz, Othila, Dagaz

Odin would normally be invoked from the North, although there are specific workings in which Odin could be invoked from one of the other quarters.

The origins of Odin are surprisingly humble. In his most ancient manifestation, he appeared in Continental Germanic beliefs as a raging storm giant named Wode and endowed with the function of assembling the souls of the dead. Although greatly feared, he was not a widely worshipped divinity in this guise. This, his oldest aspect, survived in the legends of the wild hunter. From being god of the dead he later became associated with magic, secrets, sorcery, and runes. It appears that he ousted Tyr from his position as Sky-father and absorbed some of his aspects. Tyr was the original god of war and Wodan was the god of those matters that we now term "occult." Even in the later Viking Age, Odin was still associated with the dead. His classical appearance, at least in Holland (my country of origin), is as a wise old man, the archetypal magician in the mold of Tolkien's Gandalf. Only later did he become increasingly associated with war and battle. This is a reflection of social changes in Northern society. Odin was adopted by kings and chieftains as their patron, but originally he was a god of the people. Until the last century, in the Dutch province of Groningen, a corn man used to be made at harvest time and was left in the field in honor of the "old man," as he was affectionately known. After he was adopted by the ruling classes, Odin became tainted with their corruption and treachery; this is reflected in various narratives in the mythology. Hence his reputation of untrustworthiness in later times.

Let us examine two instances in which it is implied that Odin is an oath-breaker. In the story of the building of the walls of Asgard, Odin promises a miraculous builder the Sun and the Moon, and the goddess Freyja, if he succeeds in building Asgard's wall within a year. When Odin realizes that the builder is on the point of keeping his part of the contract, Odin tricks the builder and fails to honor his original promise. A great deal has been said about Odin being an oath-breaker, but what is often forgotten is that the builder was a giant who tricked Odin into believing he was a mere man, who would not therefore have been expected to complete the task of constructing the walls. Thus Odin was cheated first, and it is only right and natural that he avenged himself. Likewise, in the story of King Vikar, Vikar made an agreement with Odin to secure fair winds in exchange for the sacrifice of one of his crew. The lots were drawn three times, and each draw indicated, to the king's dismay, that it was himself who was to be the sacrificial victim. Vikar tried to extricate himself by substituting calf's gut for the rope, a sapling for the tree, and a reed for the spear, which was in those days used to dispatch hanged men more quickly. Thus he intended to cheat Odin by carrying out a mock sacrifice. The story relates how Odin transformed the reed into a spear, the sapling into a tree, and the calf gut into a rope, rightfully claiming his due. Most of the stories suggestive of Odin's treacherous nature can be seen, on closer examination, to prove a different point altogether, namely that Odin's reaction is perfectly reasonable.

The element usually associated with Odin is air, but he is so complicated and rich in character that he can be invoked from more than one of the quarters for different purposes. He can be invoked from the East for wisdom and healing, and from the South for victory in battle. The North is the quarter from which he is normally invoked and from this point he can be called upon for occult power, sorcery, revenge workings, and cursing. His main weapon is the spear, Gungnir. It never misses its target and on the shaft are written the runes that uphold the law. The runes are themselves Odin's magical acquisitions, as is the ring, Draupnir, a symbol of fertility which replicates itself nine times every ninth day. Magical animals associated with Odin include Sleipnir the horse, the ravens Huginn and Muninn, the wolves Geri and Freki, and also both the snake and the eagle. In the myth that deals with the recovery of Odrorir, the sacred mead, Odin changes himself first into a snake and later into an eagle. We will come back to this subject in the section dealing with feminine Mysteries.

Odin's magical number is nine, which is especially sacred in Northern mythology; although nine has been mostly associated with Odin, it also has wider associations. Nine is the number of nights and days that he endured initiation on Yggdrasil in his quest for knowledge. This number of days clearly indicates a symbolic birth process, as nine is also the number of months in the gestation period of a child in the womb. For this reason nine is usually seen in other magical traditions as a lunar number, and quite rightly so, especially considering that the Moon is regarded as male in Northern mythology.

Nine is also the number of Heimdal's mothers, the nine sea-maidens who are daughters of Aegir and Ran. Although the father of Heimdal is not specified in any written sources, we can be sure it is Odin. (What else would move the waves of the sea if not the wind?) Some sources state that there are nine Valkyries, who are the daughters of Odin. Because the Norse sources are not very clear in specifying who their mother is, we can look to Wagner, where we find mentioned a goddess named Erda, whom I equate with Odin's earlier consort, Jord, and who is apparently Frigga's elder sister.

Almost as sacred is the number three. Odin appears in a three-fold form, as Odin, Vili, and Ve. This threefold division represents the three aspects of Odin as warrior, shaman, and wanderer. When we express this principle in runes we use Ansuz, Wunjo, and Othila, respectively. These three runes themselves represent three stages of initiation. The first of these stages figures Odin as the conquering warrior, as described in the *Heimskringla Saga*. Reference to Odin the warrior occurs also in the Gylfaginning (or Beguiling of Gylfi) section of the *Prose Edda*. (Both works are by Snorri Sturluson. However, I prefer to work from the *Voluspa* as my main source of reference.)

Let us examine the sequence of events leading up to the transition of Odin from warrior to shaman. After the establishment of order in the universe, the appearance of Gullveig initiates the war between the Aesir and the Vanir. Odin's decision to burn Gullveig had far-reaching consequences, as Gullveig represents another aspect of the Goddess. Gullveig is often equated with Freyja, who is virtually synonymous with Frigg in the older Continental sources. We could interpret this action as a patriarchal ousting of the feminine principle.

Although Gullveig no doubt represents a negative aspect of the Goddess, Odin's action in burning her three times gives rise to the creation of the Norns. Thereupon a sequence of irreversible events is set in motion. Odin at that stage had not yet acquired his all-knowing, all-seeing abilities. He acquired these by means of his sacrificial act on Yggdrasil, which transformed him into a shaman. As in most shamanic traditions, he received a wound by sacrificing his eye in the well of Mimir. Firstly he received knowledge of the runes by hanging nine days on the tree, Yggdrasil. Then he was taught by Mimir how to use them. These are the nine lays of power Odin learned from Bolthorn, Bestla's father. Bestla is Odin's mother, so Bolthorn is Odin's maternal grandfather. It is commonly accepted that Bolthorn is none other than Mimir. Odin exchanged an eye for the knowledge of past, present, and future. The sacrifice of Odin on the tree precedes Odin's manifestation as the wild hunter and conductor of the dead.

It is on the tree that Odin transcends death and by doing so gains the ability to traverse between the realms of life and death. This sequence of events brings us to the question of which eye Odin sacrificed. Nowhere do the Eddas state which of his two eyes it was. For some reason modern writers insist that it was the left eye, but I beg to differ. I want to argue in favor of the right eye. Is the suggestion of the left eye logically in keeping with modern occult teaching? Whoever it was who first suggested the left eye had probably been influenced by Christian thinking. In Christian superstition the left is sinister and belongs to the devil. On the Continent until very recently, left-handed children were forced to learn to write with their right hand. From a modern occult perspective we can understand why the left has been regarded by Christians as betokening evil. The left hemisphere of the brain deals with one's analytical ability, while the right hemisphere is concerned with the intuitive ability. However, there is a crossover: the right side of the body is controlled by the left hemisphere, while the left side of the body is controlled by the right hemisphere. Following this line of thought, it seems logical to conclude that if Odin had to sacrifice an eye and its corresponding ability (that is, if he had to make a choice between the analytical ability and the intuitive ability), then he would have sacrificed his right eye. Therefore he must have retained his left eye, for this eye is connected to the intuitive ability, which as a result would be greatly developed.

Odin at this point became the wounded healer. The most important spell that mentions Wotan as a healer is the second Merseberg charm. This is a healing charm and particularly depicts Wotan as a healer of animals. The third phase of Odin's transition changed him into the wanderer. After he had gained all knowledge he realized that he could not change *orlog;* so he rejected all power and became the wanderer and teacher who, although he would not be able to survive the Ragnarok, would ensure the survival of others. He thus became Odin the psychopomp; but instead of guiding people through a personal death, he guided them through a major shift in consciousness. Odin's main function in modern times is primarily that of a magician, instructing his folk in occult matters, guiding them through the Ragnarok. In other words, he is the instigator and guiding principle leading his folk towards the next stage of evolution. For the Northern people he is the greatest initiator.

So far we have discussed Odin in terms of the myths as they have been passed on to us, without considering that the mythology that reached us through Icelandic sources has probably been altered by the Christian scribes, especially in the descriptions of the Ragnarok. In this story of the last battle, we can detect a vague similarity to the ancient pagan Greek legend of the battle between the gods and the Titans, in which the Titans lost and were bound. In the Greek story, however, there is no mention of total destruction, which is peculiar to the Northern mythology. Since both Greek and Northern myths derive from the original Indo-European mythology, it would not be unreasonable to suggest that the detail of the total consummation of the world recorded in the Icelandic Eddas is a late addition, possibly influenced by the Christian myth of the Last Judgment. Thus the Ragnarok myth would originally have been closer to its Greek counterpart.

According to the Eddaic Ragnarok myth, hardly any of the participants in the final battle survive. Niord is the only god mentioned who will return to the Vanir, and we can assume that the goddesses survive. At the Ragnarok, the gods are paired up to fight in single combat with their particular enemy. Thor's enemy is Jormungand, the Midgardsorm or Midgard serpent. They had already confronted each other once before, when Thor went on a fishing expedition. Thor on that occasion captured the Midgardsorm and struck it on the head with a mighty blow from his hammer. No wonder then that when the Midgardsorm is unleashed at the Ragnarok it immediately seeks out Thor. Similarly, Heimdal and Loki, as sworn enemies, are paired up as adversaries on various occasions, such as when they fight for the possession of Freyja's necklace Brisingamen. Frey is pitted against Surt who is in possession of Frey's sword—the only sword that could have withstood the giants and which Frey surrendered as a marriage gift to Gerd's father, who is the kinsman of Surt. Odin, according to the myth, fights the Fenris wolf and is devoured by it. Odin, however, is not the chief enemy of Fenris. That is Tyr, who betrayed the wolf's trust when the gods bound it. If the wolf were to be released at the Ragnarok, would it not be logical that he would seek out Tyr as his principal adversary?

Tyr, however, is described in the Ragnarok myth as fighting against a dog called Garm. This is illogical, since Garm is the watchdog at Gnipahellir and barks the alarm when Fenris breaks his fetters. Garm therefore is in the service of the Aesir and has no reason to attack any of them. I think that in the original myth, Tyr was the adversary of Fenris and would die in the last battle, whereas Odin, who had already transcended death during his ordeal on Yggdrasil, could not die twice since he is himself the conductor of the dead.

Tyr

Names ♦	Tyr (Norse), Tiw (English), Zio (Dutch), Ziu (German)
Main element ♦	fire
Secondary element ♦	air
Colors ♦	purple, dark red
Numbers ♦	one

Personal sigils ♦ Teiwaz rune
Magical items ♦ shield, helmet, sword
Invoked for ♦ arbitration, battle, justice, swearing oaths
Runes to use ♦ Teiwaz, Raido, Dagaz, Sowulo, Mannaz

Tyr's existence as a god goes back to the dawn of Indo-European history. The oldest name by which he was known in the Common Germanic period was Teiwaz, a name which still appears in the futhark. There are two other god-names going back to the same proto-Germanic period: Wodanaz and Thurisaz. All these names end in -*az*. One could argue that the suffix -*az* is in fact an older form of *ass* or, in Anglo-Saxon, *oss*. The word ass means "a god," or "deity." Comparing this information with other god-names, we have, firstly, Wodanaz. *Wuot* is the oldest form and it means "rage" or "storm-rage." So Wodenaz literally means "storm-raging god." *Thurs* means "giant," even in modern Icelandic. Since -*az* means "god," Thurisaz means "giant god," an apt description of Thor. Tei or Ziu derives from its oldest form *djevs,* and means "sky" or "light." Teiwaz then means "sky god." Hence his association with solar power and daylight.

Tyr was the original Allfather or sky god. He was called Saxnot by the East Saxons and was ancestor of the kings of Essex. The aconite plant used to be called "Tyr's helmet." Tyr's quarter is the East, and his principal rune is Teiwaz. Tyr is invoked for justice, combat, legal disputes, and law and order.

He is also invoked when swearing oaths. In war, Tyr is invoked for bravery, courage, valor and victory. More appropriate in modern magical practice is to invoke Tyr for court cases and legal disputes. In the Icelandic tradition, Tyr appears to be single and has no consort. There is, however, one obscure reference to Angrboda in the Eddaic poem *Lokasenna,* where Loki says, "Enough, Tyr! You know that your wife mothered a son by me." The son referred to is supposedly Fenris. However, in the older Germanic tradition, a goddess Zisa is named as his consort.

Interestingly enough, there is some evidence that the original concept of Tyr was double-sexed and that like many of the Germanic gods he had a feminine counterpart named Zisa. Tyr himself in this context was named Zio. We also find this twin divinity concept with the combinations of Frey and Freyja and Niord and Nerthus. The mythology is not always clear about the exact nature of these relationships. Sometimes the pairs are represented as twins, sometimes as husbands and wives.

Tiw was as important to the early Saxons as Odin was to the Norse people. The Romans equated Tiw with Mars, but this is not entirely correct. Whereas Mars is the god of soldiers, Tiw would be more a god of judges and lawyers. The name Tiw is linguistically related to Zeus; both were the heads of their respective pantheons. Tiw is first and foremost the law-giver, the establisher of law and order, and only within that context operates as a warrior-god when law and order have broken down. He is not a mindless butcher. Later developments among our people endowed the gods with far more inhumane aspects than they originally had. A prime example is the change of the magical woodland god, Wodan, to the bloodthirsty Viking equivalent, Odin. We can assume that a similar change befell Tyr. Nevertheless, we can distinguish Tyr's noble character in the story where he, alone of all the Aesir, had the courage to put his hand in the mouth of Fenris as a pledge of good faith. Here we see Tyr as the patron of law, honesty, truth, and justice being the first one to commit perjury by swearing a false oath to the wolf, who is led to believe that he will be released. The price Tyr pays for this is the loss of his right hand. Paradoxically, it is the god of truth who is placed in the position of having to swear a false oath and sacrifice a hand. Odin does submit to the loss of an eye and sacrifices himself on Yggdrasil; but whereas Odin does this to gain knowledge and power in a somewhat selfish way, Tyr's sacrifice is completely altruistic. Nevertheless, he was the first oath-breaker.

Tyr is classified as a solar god. It has been established beyond any doubt that Tyr was the original Allfather of the majority of the

Germanic peoples. Under the name Tuisco, he is mentioned by Tacitus as having sprung from the Earthmother Nerthus, who in a later
context is seen as his consort. She is probably identical to Zisa, which
could be a local name. Legend also informs us that Tuisco had a son,
Mannaz. He in turn had three sons, Ingvio, Irmio, and Istvio. These
gave their names to the Germanic tribes from which all the subsequent tribes descended. In Frisia there was a cult of a local god,
known as Forseti, who is also mentioned in the Eddas. He taught the
Friesians law, and he gave them rules to govern themselves. The first
law book in Germania was the *Asegabook*. I believe that this god is
another variant of Tiw. The Vikings also knew about him and made
him a son of Baldur.

The first rune of the last aett is the Teiwaz rune. This rune is
immediately followed by Berkana, which is associated with the goddess Berchta; together they can be interpreted as Skyfather and
Earthmother. The next two runes are Ehwaz, meaning "horse," and
Mannaz, meaning "man." From this we can deduce that Tyr and
Berkana are the joint creators of both the animal kingdom and the
human race. Tyr is also directly related to the sky and is associated
with various stars. The name of Sirius in Old Persian was Tir. The
word *tir* means "arrow" in Persian and we can see that the Teiwaz
rune is shaped like an arrow. Usually Tyr is seen as a sword-god, but
then how long have swords been known in the North? Bows and
arrows were in use well before swords. Therefore the oldest weapon
of Tyr may have been an arrow.

In the *Anglo-Saxon Rune-Poem* we find this reference to Tyr:

Tyr is a special sign. With princes it keeps faith well.
It is ever on course over the night's dark:
It never fails.

This verse refers to the Pole Star, used by the Northern people for
navigation. Metaphorically, we can interpret this verse as meaning
that Tyr is the leading "star," or that if the Teiwaz rune occurs in a
reading it may signify the need to remain on course.

Thor

Names ♦	Thor (Norse), Thunor (English), Donar (Dutch), Donner (German)
Main element ♦	fire
Secondary element ♦	earth
Color ♦	red
Number ♦	four
Totem animals ♦	goat, bull
Personal sigils ♦	Swastika, Sunwheel, Shieldknot
Magical items ♦	hammer, belt, gloves, chariot, thunderbolts, oath ring
Invoked for ♦	defense agricultural fertility, pleasant weather, strength
Runes to use ♦	Uruz, Thurisaz, Raido, Sowulo

The quarter from which to invoke Thor is the South. He is especially invoked when taking an oath. His consorts are Jarnsaxa and Sif.

At first sight Thor would seem to correspond to Mars or, as Aleister Crowley states in his 777, Ares and Hades. Crowley's suggestion of Hades is erroneous, however, since if anybody from the North corresponds to Hades, it would be either Odin or Hella, Loki's daughter. It is understandable that Crowley would suggest a correspondence between Thor and Ares or Mars, since the element of fire is common to all three. However, there are some irreconcilable differences. In particular, the planet Mars, which of course corresponds to Ares, does not correspond to Thor, because Thor is a son of the Earth goddess, Jord, and Thor's title is "Son of Earth." For this reason Thor has much to do with the growth of vegetation, and Thor is the special patron of those who work the land, the farmers and peasants. Thor's planet, therefore, is the Earth. In essence, Thor is a fertility god. Thor's hammer symbolizes the male power of fertilizing and generating life in the Earth.

There is another matter in which Thor and Ares differ greatly. Ares is an attacker, the archetypal military man. Although like Ares, Thor is a tough fighter, he is the defender of Asgard and Midgard, not an aggressor. Basically peace-loving and acting only in defense, Thor is a friendly, big, softhearted character who is known to lose his temper only when danger threatens those in his care. He is a friend of man.

In most of the literature, Thor is described as a rather simplistic character. This is somewhat misleading. One of the myths about Thor contains quite a profound mystery, when viewed from a modern occult standpoint. It concerns the well-known myth about Thor's loss of his hammer; this myth forms part of the Lay of Thrym in the Eddas. Thor awoke to find his hammer gone. It had been stolen and hidden by Thrym the giant, who promised to return it only on condition that he would be given Freyja as his bride. Heimdal devised a scheme to win back the hammer by dressing Thor in Freyja's garments, using her veil to cover his face and beard. Thor traveled to Giantland in the company of Loki and found the opportunity to kill Thrym and regain possession of his hammer.

What does this myth mean? Thor stands out among the gods as the most masculine warrior and a typical soldier, whereas Tyr more resembles a general and Odin a statesman. Thor also is the god of fertility and fruitfulness, which is an attribute he shares with Frey. Thor's hammer, as we discussed in the section on Thurisaz in Chapter 2, represents his masculinity. This is the attribute that is stolen by the giant. The Thurisaz rune also has a strong connection with the giants. In fact, it could be said that this particular giant, Thrym, is Thor's shadow. The only way possible for Thor to retrieve his hammer is to disguise himself as a woman, and not just any woman, but the goddess of love herself, Freyja. In Jungian terms Thor has to integrate himself with his female aspect, or anima, in order to regain his fertility.

There is a class difference between Odin and Thor. Odin was regarded in the Viking Age as the god of the ruling classes. Thor is the patron of the working classes, the yeomen as well as the thralls. His hammer has been taken by the Socialists as a symbol of the workers. Thor's wife, Sif, is the Northern corn-goddess. Her golden hair is the symbol of the yellow corn at harvest time. She might therefore be associated with a sickle. It is to Thor that the thralls go after death. Thor is protector of the hard-working ordinary fellow. His function is to protect the underdog. Even the slaves came under Thor's protection. No wonder that Thor was the most popular of the Northern gods and was far more widely worshipped than Odin. Thor cares for the land and the people. Conservationists would do well to invoke his aid in their struggle against the exploitation and pollution of the Earth.

Frey

Names ♦	Frey (Norse), Frea (English), Froh (German), Frodi (Danish), Fricco (Swedish)
Primary element ♦	earth
Secondary elements ♦	water, air
Color ♦	russet
Totem animals ♦	boar, horse, honey bee
Aspects ♦	the "horned god"
Magical item ♦	sword, antlers, ship Skidbladnir
Invoked for ♦	peace and plenty, releasing of fetters
Runes to use ♦	Fehu, Jera, Ehwaz, Inguz, Ansuz

Frey is the ruler of Alfheim, the world of lightelves who are responsible for the growth of vegetation. Frey is the Northern equivalent of the "horned god," patron of fertility, and his main characteristic is a large erect phallus. He is invoked for peace and plenty. His quarter is the West. The Ansuz rune is included among Frey's runes because it is used traditionally to unfetter—and Frey is the god invoked to release fetters. Frey would be invoked from the Western quarter, usually together with his twin sister, Freyja. Frey is the god of summer sunshine and is the noblest of all the brave gods. His sword, however, is the only protection against Surt, who has been portrayed as a fire-demon. Surt is the kinsman of Loki; he is black and comes from the South. Frey's sword is a magical flaming sword which fights of its own accord. Frey surrenders it to the father of Gerd as a dowry, and through Gerd's father it ends up in the possession of Surt, who wields it at the Ragnarok and destroys the nine worlds. This sword, which Frey surrenders to the enemy, may well represent fertility. At the Ragnarok, Frey fights Surt with a set of antlers. Of all the Northern gods, Frey is most closely comparable to the gods Pan and Cernunnos, who are worshipped in the Wiccan traditions.

Niord

Names ♦	Niord
Main element ♦	water
Colors ♦	blue, gray, green
Magical item ♦	axe
Invoked for ♦	prosperity
Runes to use ♦	Fehu, Laguz

Niord, like Frey, would also be invoked from the Western quarter. Niord's element is water, for he is god of the sea. His colors are the colors of the sea. Niord is also identified with Nerthus, who is said to be either his wife or his sister. Niord is one of the Vanir and the father of Frey and Freyja. He is the patron of the sea; fishermen used to invoke him for a rich catch. Niord, furthermore, is the patron god of all riches. Niord's esoteric title is "blameless ruler of men." One of his functions is to reconcile people with one another. Nevertheless, during the war between the Aesir and the Vanir, the Vanir were victorious and it was Niord who sank his axe into the door of Asgard. Thus Niord's weapon is an axe.

Heimdal

Names ♦	Heimdal, Rig (Edda)
Main element ♦	water
Secondary element ♦	fire
Color ♦	brilliant white
Totem animals ♦	ram, seal
Magical item ♦	horn
Invoked for ♦	protection, teaching
Runes to use ♦	Kenaz, Mannaz, Dagaz

Heimdal I believe is one of the Vanir group of gods, because he is connected to Freyja and consequently to Niord. His title is "the shining Ase." Heimdal's magical tool is his horn, the Gjallarhorn. This is the horn that Heimdal is said to blow at the onset of the Ragnarok, summoning the Aesir and the Einherjar to battle. Heimdal has acute hearing, for he can hear the grass grow and even the wool growing on a sheep's back. The myths relate that Heimdal's horn is hidden below Yggdrasil. I wonder whether it isn't actually Heimdal's hearing that is hidden below Yggdrasil, as this would be in keeping with the other two sacrificing gods, Odin and Tyr. I suggest that Heimdal also committed a sacrificial act which cost him an ear, in a similar manner as Odin sacrificed an eye and Tyr a hand. The myth concerning this is lost, but it would explain how Heimdal acquired his acute hearing, just as Odin is said to have become all-seeing after the sacrifice of one of his eyes.

Heimdal's function is to mediate between Asgard and Midgard; he can be invoked for protection and to assist in the teaching of the runes. Heimdal is the guardian of the rainbow bridge. The rune Kenaz is used in this context to invoke Heimdal for the acquisition of knowledge. Moreover, Heimdal as the shining Ase is invoked to shed light upon any hidden matter, such as hidden motives. Mannaz can be used when Heimdal is invoked as teacher, since it is Heimdal who teaches the runes to man. Dagaz is appropriate when attempting a "journey" to the realm of Asgard, and it would help to facilitate travel between the worlds. Heimdal, as one of the solar gods specifically associated with the dawn of the new day, is invoked from the Eastern quarter.

Uller

> *Names* ♦ Uller (Norse), Wulder (English)
> *Main element* ♦ snow
> *Aspects* ♦ Aurora Borealis
> *Magical items* ♦ bow, glory-twigs (wuldortanas), oath-ring
> *Invoked for* ♦ hunting, oathtaking, duels
> *Runes to use* ♦ Eihwaz, Wunjo

Not much is known about this ancient god, but he has found some favor in the eyes of people active in the Asatru religion. Thus I will include a description of him. Uller is the stepson of Thor, from a previous union between Sif and Orvandil, a star hero. This puts Uller among the Vanir. Uller, like Orvandil, is probably much older than the Aesir or even the Vanir and has been identified as a very archaic god of death in Norway, where a number of localities have been named after him. Uller's name means "the brilliant one," and in Scandinavia he is connected with the Aurora Borealis. It seems that at some time in history Uller was held to be just as important as Odin, and in winter time he was considered to be the ruler in Asgard.

Uller is the winter god and moves about on snowshoes. His weapon is a bow. His consort is Skadi, whose name means shadow. She was also a local archaic goddess of death. Other authorities state that Uller had a female counterpart named Ullin, his twin sister. Ullin appears to have been the Scandinavian equivalent of Holda, the goddess of snow. This is in keeping with the general system of twin divinities appearing throughout the Northern mythology.

Uller would be invoked from the North; his rune is primarily Eihwaz and, secondarily, Wunjo, either of which could be used to invoke his favor. The best combination to use in invoking Uller is a bind-rune of both these runes. Uller was invoked in duels, and he was also one of those gods called upon to witness an oath. Uller thus had an oath-ring placed upon his altar. The Anglo-Saxons knew him by the name Wuldor, which means "splendor," "glory."

Loki

Names ♦	Loki (Norse), Loge (German)
Main element ♦	wild-fire
Color ♦	red
Totem animals ♦	salmon, seal, fox
Invoked for ♦	trickery, destruction
Runes to use ♦	Dagaz

Loki is one of the most mysterious figures among the gods. He seems to be very ancient, predating the Aesir and Vanir. He might even go back as far as the Stone Age as the original god of fire. If that were the case, the originally beneficial Loki would have been of giant stock. This idea has been preserved in the Northern myths, in which his parents are named as Laufey and Farbauti, both giants. Loki was credited in later times with more evil characteristics; this happened to most of the giants who were once the elder gods. Loki seems to be related to two other elemental giants or gods: Kari, whose element is air, and Hler, who has been identified as Aegir, another giant ruling the sea with his wife Ran. The element relating to Hler is of course water. All of these figures go back to the oldest Northern tradition. Loki has been credited with much evil. However, although he is a trickster and a catalyst, I consider his evil aspects to be a Christian development. When the Christians turned Baldur into a Northern equivalent of a "weeping Jesus" figure, and saddled Odin with the characteristics of Jehova, they also needed a "devil." Thus the much-maligned Loki was cast in this role.

By careful study of the myths it is possible to discern some positive values in Loki's character. For instance, during his exploits with the swartalfar, when he brought back as gifts Thor's hammer, Odin's spear, and Frey's magical ship, it is clear that his actions are praiseworthy, as he does not keep any of the gifts for himself but instead hands them to the Aesir. Thus he is not attached to anything; he is a catalyst who induces change without himself being affected by it. Nevertheless, I do not encourage the practice of invoking Loki, although similar warnings have been given about invoking Odin which never deterred me.

Loki fathers the three monsters Fenris, Jormungand, and Hella. Hella seems to be a corrupted version of Holda. On the other hand, Loki also is the parent of Sleipnir, Odin's steed. Sleipnir is the only horse that can traverse between the nine worlds. Incidentally, when Loki gives birth to Sleipnir he adopts the shape of a mare and so acts out a mother's role. His other offspring were engendered through his union with Angrboda, a giantess, and in this he took the male role. He is a therefore a shapeshifter and a sex-changer. In his later, evil form Loki is the instigator of Baldur's death and through this act initiates the Ragnarok. Again, it is possible that the gloomy Norse version of the Ragnarok, with its tale of total destruction, is a relatively late development, and that the original story had it that it was the giants who were bound. This is precisely what is said to have happened to Loki. He was captured and bound to a rock, where a poisonous snake continuously spat its venom into his eyes.

Loki's element is fire in its uncontrolled state. His color is bright red. In modern terms, Loki represents nuclear energy. In psychological terms Loki is the impulsive, destructive, immature aspect in human nature. Loki has been said to have sworn blood-brotherhood with Odin, and we can view Loki as the "shadow" side of Odin. Both are considered to be tricky characters.

• 6 •

FEMININE MYSTERIES

The Feminine Principle in the North

In 1987, 1 wrote that the modern-day revival of the Northern religious tradition had been largely the work of men, perhaps partly due to the exaggerated masculine image of the elder faith inherited from the Viking Age. Since then, there has been a virtual revolution in Asatru, and women are more and more involving themselves in a significant way. In the Ring of Troth (ROT) Europe we actually have more or less equal numbers. The fact that the leadership of the ROT Europe includes women may be a contributory factor, but cannot be seen as the sole reason for this development. Perhaps this book too has had an influence. With this in mind, I have updated and extended this chapter, exploring the matriarchal aspects and feminine Mysteries which deserve to be given much greater prominence in the Northern religion. I shall draw largely on older Germanic sources, however, where appropriate, I shall correlate the traditional information within a modern context. After all, our religion hasn't stood still.

From the original body of lore, wisdom, and intuition our folk wisdom has developed and mutated into a variety of modern forms, spiritual and philosophical as well as scientific. The literature bequeathed to us from the Viking Age contains detailed information on the gods but, with the exception of the goddess Freyja, there is not sufficient information available concerning the other goddesses who are also of central importance. In addition to the goddesses, there are other female beings in the Northern system, such as the Disir, Valkyries, and Norns. Rather than being part of either the Aesir or the Vanir, two of these, namely Disir and Valkyries, are usually regarded as closer to the human race and often interface with the human race on behalf of the High Gods. The Norns, however, are more impersonal, but all three are involved with fate or wyrd; the Valkyries and Disir are often involved with the individual or the individual family, whereas Norns are involved more on a collective level of fate or *orlog*. Orlog means *oerlagen* or in English "primal layers," i.e., the conditions of existence, unalterable by any individual. Changes in orlog are wrought by the collective mind and take place whenever critical mass is reached. A prime example is the condition on the planet Erda (Earth). The original state was pristine, healthy, and abundant with life—with, of course, the occurrence of natural disasters built into the equation. Now, we find that the conditions have been changed by humans, and the orlog is changed to the effect that unnatural disasters are occurring and will occur more and more, as a result of our bad stewardship. Each individual will be more or less affected by this, the rich less and the poor more and this is tied down with individual wyrd. Of course, this is not fair, but life is difficult! Wyrd is more flexible in the sense that it is almost like a fractal version orlog tailored to an individual and their family. Wyrd can be changed, either by working hard to change one's circumstances or by the practice of magic and personal growth.

As often happens in religious development, the older matriarchal tradition was usurped, or rather absorbed, into the late-developing patriarchal tradition; as a result, these females play a mediating role between the world of the gods and the world of men. A curiosity is that the most famous of the Valkyries, namely Sigdrifa (better known as Brunnhilde in Wagner's *Ring*), actually wouldn't be one, since she disobeyed Odin and was downgraded to a mortal woman, albeit a mortal woman with extraordinary might. She is referred to in some of the poetry as a Dis, and here we see clearly that there is an overlap between the two states of being. Though Brunnhilde loses her immortal status as a Valkyrie, she was motivated by compassion and thus became a Dis. She is also referred to as shieldmaiden in the *Volsung Saga*. The function of both shieldmaiden and Dis seem to have much more in common than either of these with Valkyries. From being a slayer of men she became a protectress thereof. Whether this is a promotion or a demotion depends on one's point of view.

Female practitioners of magic in the Northern Mysteries were described in various ways in different areas. In Old Norse the name for a female magician was *volva,* which means "sibyl" or "prophetess." Her main function was to practice divination; there is a correspondence with the role of a *seidkona,* who was a woman practicing seidr. In Old English the name for these women was *haegtessa.* This term dates from pre-migration Northern Germany. A similar word exists in Dutch: *hagedisse.* Incidentally, the name of the Dutch capital city, The Hague, is a remnant of this association, for the area was renowned as a center of female magic. *Hagedis* is the Dutch word for "lizard," and I venture the hypothesis that the name *hagedisse* originated in a time when our people had totem animals and when the lizard would have been associated with female magic and witchcraft. As members of the reptile family, lizards suggest snakes, which symbolize hidden feminine wisdom, as corroborated in other shamanic practices such as that of the Australian aborigines. On the other hand, the same word, *hagedis,* may have been applied to lizard-like creatures such as salamanders and newts, which can live in more than one element (in water and on land). Likewise, a haegtessa, like a shaman, can move in more than one element. In occult terms this means the astral plane, the upper world or the underworld, or in more modern terminology, they have multidimensional access.

In olden days a haegtessa was often consulted on tribal issues of importance and arbitrated in disputes. Moreover, she had a voice in councils of war and her judgment was highly valued, as the Germanic people set great store on women's natural psychic abilities. The Romans report that a haegtessa predicted that Drusus would die if he were to cross the Rhine. Needless to say, this prediction was accurate. Attila the Hun had a similar experience when he tried to cross the river Lek in modern-day Holland. The most famous of these early Germanic seeresses is undoubtedly Valeda, whose name may very well have been a title, with some resemblance to the Norse word *volva*. She is mentioned in Tacitus as having been actively involved with the Batavi Rebellion. She was considered so "holy" that she herself had no contact with the outside world; she lived in a high tower and only communicated via intermediaries. It seems logical that these intermediaries where female relatives, perhaps in training for succession.

Valeda ended up being taken prisoner by the Romans. She became a priestess in a Temple of Vesta, and must have been held in some esteem by the Romans as she was more or less treated with honor and remained a priestess rather than being sold off as slave as was often the case with Roman prisoners of war. Valeda's reputation and the respect accorded to her was the result of her paranormal abilities, not necessarily because she was devoted to any particular god.

As these women were priestesses dedicated to the gods, they did not usually belong to a man, which is not to say that they were virgins in the modern sense of the word. However, the aforementioned Valeda definitely was a virgin as such she was mentioned by name in a Greek satirical poem. A further insight is provided by a well-known present-day British shamaness who informs me that the power of the female shaman, seithkona, or volva is contained in the womb. We know that the pagan Romans, even before the Roman Church, had virgins attending the fires of Vesta. Now I have not come across any evidence for this to be part of the Germanic pagan tradition, which in itself does not mean that there wasn't such a tradition; after all, absence of evidence does not constitute evidence of absence. We do know, however, from modern parapsychological findings that girls by the onset of puberty often display paranormal abilities, most often in the form of poltergeists. There is an obscure reference somewhere in the Arthurian collection that Guinevere was indeed a psychically gifted girl and that to preserve her psychic abilities after her marriage she was given "the black draught" which would prevent conception from ever occurring. This now ties in with the information I obtained in private conversation with the aforementioned shamaness (who incidentally, does not work in the Northern tradition) that on the etheric level there is a power source or gateway within the womb, and giving birth would damage that gateway forever.

Now, I know married women who have given birth who have nevertheless regained their native abilities, usually when they are through menopause. Today, the word "spinster" sometimes has a pejorative meaning, suggesting an old maid. Mythologically, it refers to the three Norns who spin the web of fate.

The Norns are indeed single, hence their connotation of unmarried women. Weaving and spinning the threads of the web is an old magical tradition which survived in Wicca as cord magic. In some magical traditions it is customary to use a thread of wool to take someone's measurements. Weaving and spinning are in themselves magical workings. Women often spun and wove special garments, enforced with incantations, runic or otherwise, for their men going into battle.

A haegtessa or volva uses divination to gain insight into someone's individual "web of wyrd," and magic to create changes if at all possible. The patron goddesses of the haegtessa are Freyja, the Norns, and Frigga. The latter is associated with spinning; her magical weapon is a distaff. The expression in modern English "the distaff side" is still used to denote the line of female descent. Frigga then also is the main patroness of the Disir as well as Freyja.

The Disir were perhaps the most important cult figures in Germania, where they were known as the Matronae. This word most likely stems from the Roman period when this cult was very important, but statues and artifacts are found dating well into the Bronze Age. They may, in fact, not only pre-date the Aesir but the Vanir as well; however, there is evidence of a merging between various female deities of different periods in history. For example, the Nerthus cult was very big in Germania, but no equivalent goddess to Freyja was known. Frija of course is the equivalent of Frigga. The Scandinavian tradition has some evidence of Disir worship and they even had their own festival involving the whole community as well as more female-only rituals. The cult of the Matronae, or "the mothers," is not exclusively of Germanic origin, as at least half of the names known are of Celtic origin. Most of the votive stones portray the matrons in groups of three. They were often named after tribes, people or places, for example: *Matribus Suebis*, meaning "Suebian Mothers" and *Matribus Frisiavis paternis*, the "paternal Friesian mothers." They also give their name to rivers and springs, such as the Waal and the Niers. Some of these goddesses have been invoked for a specific purpose, such as healing or justice. For example, there are two Friesian goddesses, Beda and Fimmilena, corresponding to the Scandinavian Vor and Var. These two are known as the Alaisaigae and are mentioned alongside "Mars Thingus" or Tyr on house steads on Hadrian's Wall. They all are connected with justice. Two other goddesses are also named Baudihillia and Friagabis, although they may be the same goddesses.

In these women's Mysteries, there was a support system in which a strong emphasis was placed on the female ancestral line. The Disir, called Idises in Germany, were originally deified female ancestors. They were a remnant of an earlier matriarchal religion practiced in these areas, which dates from well before the religion of the Aesir, which it became intertwined with. The leader of the Disir is Freyja; one of her titles is Vanadis, or Dis of the Vanir. From all the available evidence, it seems that the religion of the Vanir predates that of the Aesir.

The function of the Disir is closely interconnected with that of the Valkyries and Norns. Like the Norns, the Disir and Valkyries were also involved in dispensing fate or wyrd. One of their activities is the protection and guidance of the tribe or the individual leader of that tribe. In this capacity they could be very hostile indeed, and like the Valkyries, they seemed to have had the power to fetter enemies and frighten them. They were also regarded as intermediaries between the people and the high gods. Furthermore, they were greatly involved with divination and witchcraft and were thus helpers of the volvas. They have the ability to bind and check, or in other words to impose war-fetters. They also have the ability to release fetters. In the Icelandic sagas the Disir appear dressed in either white or black, signifying, respectively, helping or hindering aspects. This, of course, is from the point of view of the opposing parties. The Disir were important enough to have their own festival called the "Disablot," which was celebrated at different dates in different countries of the Norse/Germanic area. This festival was known as Modraniht or "Mothers' night" in Anglo-Saxon England where it was celebrated on December 21/22. In Norway the date was mid-October, coinciding with and perhaps part of the Winternights celebrations. In Sweden the date was the beginning of February. In later days, this festival was frowned upon by the strongly entrenched Christian establishment. There was a more primitive peasant variety of the Disablot, in which the object of veneration was a dried horse phallus.

These festivals did not sit well with Christians, and Olaf Tryggvason, who forcibly introduced Christianity in Norway, burned female practitioners of magic whenever he had the chance. Various accounts of persecutions have been recorded from this period which predate the more widely known and recorded "witch" persecutions in the later Middle Ages. Even in the later sagas, such as the *Eyrbiggja Saga* (which is partly placed in the pagan period), female practitioners were put to death for sorcery, and those who were responsible for this were not Christians, but patriarchal pagans.

In tenth-century Norway, under the reign of Olaf Tryggvason, a group of women holding a Disablot were burned to death in their house when they refused to convert to Christianity. The Disir, however, were important enough to have had their own Temple at Uppsala, the Disarsalr or hall of the Disir.

One form of Dis was a *spae-dis*. She is understood to be a personal Dis with Valkyrie attributes, attached to a single individual hero usually from birth. She can appear in dreams and foretell the future or give warnings, seeming to operate in this respect almost as a personal Norn, and perhaps may be compared to Crowley's concept of the Holy Guardian Angel. The spae-dis (feminine) or *spae-alf* (masculine) can be seen as the Germanic equivalent of the HGA or Higher Self—the interface between the human consciousness and the god or goddess, and the embodiment of one's own wyrd. This wight is usually spoken of in terms of a lover where the human's goal is to wed (that is, become one with), as is the case in the Helgi poems of the Elder Edda and the tale of Sigurdr and Brynhildr. The traditional examples are all of men with spae-dises, but obviously women have Higher Selves as well, for which we have thus taken the term spae-alf. The *spae-wight* is the ideal lover of the soul: it is thus likely that gay people will experience this wight as being of their own gender. In the literature, the spae-dis is usually described in connection with a hero. Nowadays, of course, the concept of hero has expanded somewhat and is not necessarily confined to the warrior class, but may include poets, magicians, artists, and indeed, everyone who is involved with spiritual or secular progress.

As I rewrote this chapter, the news was reported of the death of Diana, Princess of Wales, in a car crash on August 31, 1997. If ever a Dis was born, it was in the week following her death. The amount of grief experienced by ordinary people all over the world and especially in the UK was exceptional; it can only be compared with the American bereavement experience following the assassination of President John F. Kennedy. Millions of people lined the roads, strewn with flowers all the way from London to Northamptonshire where she was buried on an island in a lake; may Nerthus enfold her. Diana Spencer, like the family she married into, descended from the Anglo/Saxon Wodening line. In the days and weeks after the event, over ten million people gathered at Kensington palace to lay wreaths and sign books of condolence. Here in Scotland, extra trains and coaches were made available to cope with the demand. I am well known for being hard-nosed and have no time for pompous "crap," royal or otherwise, but this display of genuine emotion, in my opinion as an occultist, has shifted the collective wyrd of this nation and perhaps far beyond as well. I expect some people will keep photos, with flowers and candles in front, as they did in 1963 for Kennedy. Most people who will be doing this are, of course, not of our religion but nevertheless this is how Disir are born. Perhaps some of the Matronae started off in a similar way, honored and remembered initially by their kinfolk after their death for remarkable deeds.

Seith

Some of the magical practices of the women in the Heathen period were reputedly of a dubious nature, especially when they took the form of magic known as Seith, defined in the dictionary as "spell" or "enchantment," referring mostly to magic and sorcery of a predominantly darker nature. The literal meaning of the word *Seith* is obscure, but it may be related to "seething" or "boiling." Boiling has a metaphorical meaning referring to a state of fierce or enraged emotion; in magical practice intoxicating substances, such as certain herbs and mushrooms, are often boiled in order to induce trance states. Trances played a major part in performing seidr. Trances were used in the conventional sense for communicating with other entities, such as dead ancestors or helping or hindering nature spirits known as alfar or elves. Trance was also used as a means of traveling in a vision-quest to explore other realms of consciousness.

In the later sagas, the kind of seidr practiced has more in common with spiritualistic trance mediumship. Seidr was predominantly performed by women; in the later Icelandic sagas it was frowned upon, partly owing to the Christian bias of the writers, and partly to the dominating patriarchal outlook prevalent in the Viking Age. Odin is the only male god known to have practiced seidr, after being taught by Freyja. My personal view is that Odin's practice of seidr may derive from a late Viking interpretation of an older magical discipline, for Swedish sources suggest that if a man did practice seidr, he was required to dress up as a woman in a sort of ritual transvestism. This practice has also been observed by anthropologists among some Native American tribes. There are occult reasons for this custom, which does not necessarily imply homosexual practices, however, it does not exclude these either. Modern Seithmen are for the most part gay and they are the best I've ever worked with. Ritual transvestism was a remnant of a very ancient tradition going back in history to the time when only women were allowed to practice shamanism. It was thought that a man had to change himself spiritually into a woman to be able to serve the Goddess. Perhaps this too is a practice that could be revived within the context of a male Vanic mystery cult. Seidr certainly included a form of what is nowadays called sex magic. Shape-shifting, "sending," cursing, healing, and the use of spirit animals were all part of the curriculum. Women who practiced seidr did so seated on a platform, while younger women or junior priestesses sang certain songs or Galdr to enable the seid-kona to enter a trance. These songs were known as *Vardlokkur,* or "spirit tempters," and that was the magical purpose of these songs: to entice spirits to cooperate. A very similar song is known as *Seithleati,* meaning "magic tune." This had something of a similar nature to the shamanic powersongs. In fact, these disciplines—Galdr as well as Seith—may have had their origin in a prehistoric form of shamanism. The shamanic form of singing known as *Joiking,* still practiced today in Saame (Lapp) culture, may be related to Galdr, as both involve the magical use of the voice for chanting. Also, especially relevant to Galdr, repetitive poetry is used to induce altered states of consciousness. Galdr involves the magical use of the voice in the "singing" of runes. The appropriate training in modern Galdr entails the vibrating of the sounds and names to call upon the powers represented by the runes, either individual runes or a combination of syllables derived from runes to create a vocal bind-rune especially when secrecy would be required.

Despite the criticisms leveled against the practice, seidr magic is a valid and useful part of the Northern tradition which can have positive personal and social benefits. It is the role of Northern womanhood to restore this and all other aspects of the feminine Mysteries, and to give them their due prominence in the Northern tradition. Since the first edition of this book has come out, this restoration has indeed come about, mainly thanks to efforts of Asatru Gythia, Volva, and famous author, Diana Paxson.

Spae Craft

One particular aspect of Seith, more properly identified as *Spae,* according to Kveldulfr Gundarsson, is by now a thriving spiritual force all over the U. S. and Europe as well. As I understand it, Diana Paxson and her group Hrafnar reconstructed the ancient ritual in a modern format, and freely shared their knowledge and experience with the rest of the Asatru community. Many readers will be familiar with the relevant episode in *Eirik's Saga,* therefore I shall keep this very short. The story is set is Greenland. A volva or spae-kona visits the village, which has been beset by problems. She has a ritual meal containing the hearts of all wild creatures and the next day sits on a platform, and through the singing of a Vardlokkur song goes into a trance and prophesies and communicates with ancestors. This ritual has been updated to serve modern Spae-folk. It's based on a group pathworking through the worlds of Yggdrasil, ending up in front of Hella's gate. One person designated beforehand enters the gate to Hella's realm, and at this point the spae-person climbs on the High Seat and a song is sung which allows the seer to alter his or her state of consciousness. A dialogue is kept with the guide and questions can be answered. This technique can be used to obtain rede from the other worlds. It also can be used for far seeing; the past as well as the (probable) future can be accessed. I have been on the High Seat myself and although I haven't had the spectacular results of others more suited to this work, I have had results and answered questions from people whom I did not recognize when they asked the question. It feels a bit like being partly asleep. This of course will be different for each individual trying this technique. The pitfalls are the same as in spiritualism; care must be taken when acting on rede thus obtained, and a second opinion via a reading by other means is often desirable.

A different kind of priestess is known from Icelandic sources. The officiating priest or gothi was usually a man, but by no means always. The name given to a female gothi was a gythia. This function was largely secular, and these officials presided at rituals or "blots" in which, as with other pagan festivals, the whole community took part. In the latest heathen period in Iceland around 1000 C.E., this function became more and more secular. In fact, gothar, to use the plural term, were usually involved in law-speaking, and can be considered as the forerunners of modern-day lawyers. The function of arbitration and law-speaking was, in the older continental Germanic tradition, the privilege of women.

Odin and the Feminine Mysteries

A significant aspect of the Northern tradition which has not been sufficiently explored is the extent to which Odin is dependent on the goddesses. When Odin is in a tight corner, for example, he consults female divinities. Freyja is the one who teaches him seidr, and he asks Frigga's counsel before setting out for a contest of wits with Vafthrudnir the giant. Most noticeably, Odin is subject to the decrees of the Norns, like everyone else. Even one of his ravens, Muninn, may be female, as Muninn means memory and memory in occult terms is regarded as a female function. Odin is the Skyfather. In this capacity it is understandable that he is described in the mythology as polygamous. As the Skyfather, his function is to impregnate and fertilize the Earthmother, the source of life, who is portrayed in various aspects by Jord and Frigga, and Erda.

Norse mythology includes various stories about Odin and his involvement with the fair sex. We know that his first wife was Jord, a giantess who represents the primitive Earth and who is the mother of Thor (thus Thor is half-giant and is equally matched against giants in combat). Frigga is Odin's second wife and normally functions as his consort in Valhalla. Frigga is the daughter of Night or Fiorgin, who is probably identical to Jord; she is the mother of Baldur, Hodur, and Hermod. These two goddesses are Odin's wives in the proper sense of the word. The other goddesses and women with whom he consorted were more like mistresses; but like everything in mythology, this surface feature has a deeper meaning. In the case of two of these female partners, namely Gunlodd and Rind, Odin had a valid reason to get involved. Both women served a specific purpose.

In Gunlodd's case Odin's intention was to recapture Odrorir, the sacred mead. The story of the sacred mead takes place after the war between the Aesir and the Vanir. As part of the terms of a truce, hostages were exchanged and a new god-form was created by mingling the Aesir's and the Vanir's spittle in a vessel. From this brew the wisest of all beings, Kvasir, was born. His great wisdom was the result of the combination of attributes contributed by all the Aesir and the Vanir. (It is known from other mythologies that spittle has been used for its fermenting properties, but within the context of the feminine Mysteries we may surmise that whatever was deposited in the vessel was not spittle, but substances creating life.) Kvasir was then killed by two dwarves, who mixed his blood with honey to make mead. These dwarves were, in turn, captured by giants and ransomed themselves by handing over the mead. Odin learned about this and set out to obtain the mead. After various adventures he finally found out that the mead had been hidden in a mountain guarded by a giantess, Gunlodd.

Odin now had to get inside the mountain. He solved this problem by persuading one of the giants to drill a hole in the mountain.

Odin then changed his shape into that of a snake and crawled in. Once inside, he transformed himself back to his original form and seduced Gunlodd. He obtained her permission to take three draughts of the mead, and he drank the lot. He then escaped to Asgard in the form of an eagle and left Gunlodd pregnant. She later gave birth to Bragi, the god of poetry. This part of the myth is rife with sexual symbolism. The mountain can be viewed as the womb of the Goddess, the mead she guarded as menstrual blood; Odin's transformation into a snake and his method of entering the mountain also have sexual symbolism. Incidentally, both the snake and the eagle are symbols of Scorpio in astrology. When I attempted to compare the Northern gods to the astrological concepts, it was Odin more than any other who fitted the characteristics of that sign. Runes that may be connected with Gunlodd are Laguz and Berkana.

Rind was the goddess who gave birth to Vali, the avenger of Baldur. She needed some persuasion to consent to this; again Odin had to resort to trickery. After failing to win her favour by using various disguises, he finally cast a spell over her by which she lost consciousness. Then he changed himself into an old woman and offered to heal her. Once he had gained access to her room, he forced her to accept him. This myth has a seasonal significance. Rind is the goddess whom Odin depends on to give him a son, according to advice given to Odin by a sorceress. Baldur is slain by Hodur at midsummer, and Rind represents the frozen earth in early winter, which is reluctant to yield to the Sun, or Odin. Vali has to be born in order to slay Hoder and thereby facilitate Baldur's return at Yuletide. Runic correspondences to the myth of Rind are Isa and Jera.

Valkyries

The Valkyries are said to be either nine or thirteen in number. Both suggestions make sense. Nine is the most magical number in Northern mythology, and thirteen is especially sacred to the feminine Mysteries, as it symbolizes the thirteen lunar months in a solar year. The Valkyries are armed with spears and helmets. Their task is to conduct the dead heroes to Valhalla. Sometimes they have the power to decide the outcome of a battle; on other occasions they carry out Odin's wishes. Mythologically, the Valkyries are the daughters of Odin. In the Icelandic myths there is no reference to whom their mother was. German tradition has it that their mother was Erda or the Vala, another aspect of the Earthmother. There is a different tradition relating to the Valkyries, in which they are not represented as beings of divine origin but as human daughters of kings. It seems that some Valkyries have different functions, as can be seen when we examine their names. One Valkyrie is named Mist. Her function is to envelop the battlefield in a mist when needed. Others have more warlike names such as Skogul and Hildr, meaning "rager" and "warrior," respectively. Most interestingly, there are two Valkyries who are especially associated with the binding and bettering of enemies. Their names are Hlok, which may mean "lock," and Herfjotter, which means "war-fetter." These Valkyries could be called upon for a magical working to bind an enemy.

The most famous of the Valkyries is Brunnhilde, mostly known from the *Nibelungen Saga* and especially from Richard Wagner's operas. Brunnhilde appears in the *Volsung Saga* under her Icelandic name Sigdrifa. Let us examine the Wagnerian version of this theme first. Part of Wagner's drama centers on the tragic figure of Brunnhilde. Like all Valkyries, she was considered to be an aspect of Wotan's will. Wotan commands her to give victory to an undeserving party called Hunding. Brunnhilde disobeys him and protects Siegmund instead. At that moment, she makes her own decision and becomes a person in her own right; previously she was merely an emanation of Wotan's will. When she took an independent decision, she disengaged herself from Wotan and created her own individuality, her own wyrd, and this wyrd cannot be manipulated. All that Wotan can do is put her to sleep for twenty-five years, to wait for Siegfried, Siegmund's son, to grow into manhood. Wotan is in one sense very pleased that she did what she did, for he was forced into a decision and shifted the onus of the decision to her. Both Siegmund and Sieglinde were destined to die. In one instance this would have come about through Wotan's decision to destroy the Volsung lineage in accordance with a promise he made to Frigga (or else Sieglinde would have been drowned, which was the traditional fate of married women who did not remain faithful to their husbands). Looking aside from the mythology both Siegfried and Brunnhilde seem to have been real historical figures minus the legends overlaid onto them. They appear in the Burgundian records. Siegfried and Brunnhilde had a female child named Aslaug, who appears to have been a real person too and an ancestor of mine, so I am told.

The Icelandic version of the story of Brunnhilde has been handed down in the *Volsung Saga*. The *Sigdrifumal* is one of the poems in the Eddas which contain a treasure of rune-magic directly related to the feminine Mysteries. There follows a magical interpretation of the *Sigdrifumal*. The part of this poem that is relevant here is the section in which the Valkyrie Sigdrifa gives Sigurd magical knowledge of the runes and practical counsel for everyday life. This legend suggests therefore that it was the wise woman's function to teach magical practices to men, as well as to advise them in ethical matters. In this respect there is a similarity to the older Continental tradition in which women arbitrated in legal disputes and gave advice in councils of war. The *Sigdrifumal* is well worth studying, but it is too lengthy to be reproduced in its entirety; therefore I only include the relevant verses. This translation is by Kveldulfr Gundarsson.

SIGDRIFUMAL

Sigurðr rode up on Hind's Fell and turned south towards Frankland. On the Fell he saw a great light, as if fire burned and lit up to heaven. But when he came there, there stood a shield-burg with a banner above it. Sigurðr went into the shield-burg and saw that a person lay there and slept with all battle-weapons. He took first the helm off the head. Then he saw that it was a woman. The byrnie was fast as if it were grown into the flesh. Then he cut with Gram from the byrnie's neck opening downwards, and so out in the direction of both sleeves. Then he took the byrnie off her. She awakened and sat up and saw Sigurðr and spoke:

1. *"What bit byrnie? how broke I sleep?*
   how fell the pale fetters from me?"
   He answered:
   "Sigmunðr's bairn!—a short time ago
   raven tore corpse-flesh—Sigurðr's blade!"

2. *"I slept long, I was asleep long—*
   long are sorrows to folk!
   it was Óðinn ruled that I might not
   brandish staves of sleep."

Sigurðr sat down and asked her name. She took a horn full of mead and gave him a memory-draught.

3. *"Hail day! Hail day's sons!*
   hail night and daughter!
   with unwrathful eyes look upon us,
   and give victory to the sitting ones!

4. *"Hail the Æsir! Hail the Ásynjur!*
   hail the much-giving earth!
   Words and human wit give to we two well-famed ones
   and leeches' hands during life!"

She named herself and was a Valkyrie. She said that two kings did battle: one hight Helm-Gunnarr, he was then old and the greatest army-man, and Óðinn had promised him victory, but "the other hight Agnarr, brother of Auða, whom no wight wished to protect."

Sigrðrifa felled Helm-Gunnarr in the battle. But Óðinn stuck her with a sleep-thorn to revenge this and said that she should never afterwards bring victory in battle and said that she should be given in marriage.

"But I said to him that I had sworn an oath there in answer, never to be given to a man who knew fear." He spoke and asked of her to know her wisdom, because she knew tidings from all the worlds. Sigrðrifa said,

5. *"Beer I bring thee, byrnie-Thing's apple!*
   blended with main and main-glory;
   it is full of songs and liking-staves,
   good galdrs and pleasure-runes.

6. *"You shall ken victory-runes if you will have victory,*
   and rist on the hilt of the blade,
   some on the guard, some on the grip,
   and name Týr twice.

7. *"You shall ken ale-runes if you wish that another's woman,*
   not betray your trust, if you trust.
   They shall be risted on horn and on hand's back,
   and mark Need (ᚾ) on your nail.

8. *"You shall sign the cup, and this against fear,*
   and cast a leek in the liquid.
   Then you know that never will be for you
   mead blended with ill.

9. *"You shall know protection-runes if you would protect,*
   and loose children from women;
   they shall be risted on palms and over the limbs' span,
   and bid then the disir aid.

10. *"You shall make brine-runes if you will have protected*
    sail-mares on the sound;
    on mast-stave shall be risted and on the rudder's blade
    and lay fire on the oar:
    then high waves fall not, nor so the blue waves,
    but you come whole to the harbor.

11. *"Limb-runes shall you ken, if you will be a leech,*
and know how to deal with wounds.
They shall be risted on bark and on the leaf of a tree,
from which the limbs bend eastward.

12. *"You shall ken speech-runes, if you will that no man*
pay you back for injury with hate-deeds.
Wind them around, weave them around,
set them all together
at that Thing where folk shall fare
in full judgment.

13. *"Soul-runes shall you take if you wish to be*
the most sharply understanding one of all.
Hroptr (Óðinn, "Maligned One") fully reded them,
fully risted them, fully understood them,
from that liquid which had leaked
from the skull of Heiðdraupnir,
and from the horn of Hoðdrofnir.

14. *"On the berg (he) stood with the edges of (the sword) Brimir,*
he had helm on head,
then spoke Mummer's head
wisely the first word,
and said truthful staves.

15. *"(He) said they were risted on the shield which stands before*
the shining god,
on Arvakr's ear and on Alsviðr's hoof,
on the wheel that turns under Hrungnir's wain
on Sleipnir's teeth and on the sledge straps,

16. *"on bear's paw and on Bragi's tongue,*
on wolf's claw and on eagle's beak,
on bloodied wings and on bridge's end,
on loosening palm and on healing spoor,

17. *"on glass and on gold and on men's luck,*
   in wine and in wort and on the will's seat,
   on Gungnir's point and on Grani's breast,
   on norn's nail and on owl's beak.

18. *"All were scraped off that were risted on,*
   and cast into the holy mead,
   and sent on wide ways;
   they are with the Æsir, they are with elves,
   some with wise Vanir,
   some have human men;

19. *"those are beech-runes, those are protection-runes,*
   and all ale-runes,
   and mighty main-runes,
   who knows them unconfused and undestroyed
   has them for himself as good luck,
   gain, if you take them,
   until the doom of the gods!

Runes in the *Sigdrifumal*

The *Sigdrifumal* mentions various sorts of runes, such as birth-runes, ale-runes, and victory-runes. The first runes mentioned are victory-runes, which are to be used in combination with Teiwaz to invoke Tyr. The fact that they are called victory-runes (plural) indicates that there is more than one rune to be used in a charm for victory. I suggest that, besides Teiwaz, these runes include Wunjo and Othila. Wunjo is associated with the will, and no one should engage in a battle without the will to win. Wunjo also binds warriors together in a bond of comraderie. Othila is associated with the homeland either the land one has to defend or the new land to be conquered— for gaining new land was often the reason for battle. Moreover, Othila is Odin's rune, and it was customary before a battle to dedicate the enemy symbolically to Odin in sacrifice by throwing a spear over the enemies' heads and shouting, "Odin has you all," or words to that effect.

Ale-runes are also mentioned in the *Sigdrifumal;* the formula for this is Ansuz, Laguz, and Uruz. These runes form the magical word "ALU," which is traditionally regarded as a protective device. The stanza mentions the ale-runes that one needs to know in order that another's wife, whom you trust, shall not betray you. "Write them on the back of your hands, on your horn scratch them and inscribe "Need" on the nails." This is a naughty spell, the purpose of which is to avoid discovery in an affair with someone else's wife. "Write them on the back of your hands" is clear enough, but to write them on your "horn" could be interpreted as a sexual reference. And "Need" (Nauthiz) is written on the nails to prevent discovery.

The third charm in the *Sigdrifumal* gives protection against poison. "Thou shouldst bless the horn (before drinking) and cast a leek in the cup." This charm is related in *Egil's Saga*, where the hero receives a horn containing a poisoned drink. He carves runes on it and bloods it; the horn cracks, spilling the drink onto the floor. To bless the horn, make the sign of the hammer over it and invoke Thor. To "cast a 'leek' in the cup" is a kenning for the Laguz rune, this being one of the ale-runes which, as we have seen, has a protective function. In Old Norse, Laguz is also called logr or laukar, which means both "leek" and "sorcery," as has been explained in the section on Laguz in Chapter 2. Therefore, it is reasonable to assume that the sign of the hammer was made over the horn, a Thurisaz rune was scratched on the rim of the horn and stained with blood, and the Laguz rune was made in the horn itself by dipping a finger into the drink.

Birth-runes can be used to relieve a woman in labor. The runes I suggest for this are Fehu, Berkana, and Pertho. Fehu has already been mentioned as a help-rune in the *Havamal*. Berkana is the real birth-rune and Peorth is Berkana turned outwards in a position of release, suggesting the process of giving birth. These three runes are also associated with the goddesses Freyja, Berchta, and Frigga. They are cut on the palms of the hands of the woman and in a circle around the joints of the wrists; a firm hold is taken on the wrists and the elves are invoked. In modern practice, it might be better to draw or paint the runes, rather than to carve them.

Sea runes are used to control the elements. The runes I suggest for this are Ehwaz, Laguz, and Raido. Ehwaz means "horse," and "steed of the waves" is a kenning for ship. Laguz is the element of water and here represents the sea, whereas Raido is used to control the direction of movement and to sail a ship safely into harbor. Sowulo and Teiwaz may also be applicable to this charm, for the Sun is used for navigation during the day and the pole star at night. The combination of Ehwaz, Laguz, and Raido can also be interpreted psychologically. The sea represents any emotionally disturbing life situation, as water is the element linked with the emotional side of life. To steer oneself safely into harbor in this context means to regain emotional control.

The healing runes named in the *Sigdrifumal* are primarily Uruz and Sowulo, as stated in the section on these runes in Chapter 2. Teiwaz can be added for extra energy, and Ehwaz representing among other things the physical body. Speech-runes are used in any situation involving verbal conflicts, such as court cases. To ensure that an argument is won, these runes can be threaded and woven together in a pattern at meetings where people gather to settle disputes. The first and foremost rune for this purpose is Ansuz, because Ansuz represents communication. It is used in combination with Teiwaz, Wunjo, and Raido. Teiwaz is a rune directly related to justice and the god of justice, Tyr. Court cases were held on a Tuesday for this reason. Wunjo again is used to ensure success in winning the case, and Raido to enforce one's rights. The reference to threading and weaving is an instruction to combine these runes into a blind-rune, which can be worn as an amulet.

The thought-runes or hugrunes, which "one should know if one wishes to be thought of as the wisest of all," are runes of the mind. I suggest Kenaz, Mannaz, Algiz, and Ansuz. Kenaz is the rune of knowledge, Mannaz the rune of mental ability and memory; Algiz invokes divine aid, while Ansuz invokes inspiration. "To be the wisest of all" means to have wisdom on more than one level. It does not just refer to knowledge of an intellectual kind but also to the divine guidance of inspiration. The relevant verse in the *Sigdrifumal* continues to describe that Hropt (or Odin) read, cut, and thought out these runes with the help of the wise waters of Heidraupnir's head and Hoddrofnir's horn. (This reference is explained in Chapter 4.) The verses that describe how Sigdrifa revealed to Sigurd the objects on which runes were cut are still very obscure, and a lot of research and meditation has yet to be done to decode the significance of these objects. I shall give an example of how this could be done. The first object mentioned is "the shield that stands before the shining god." I take the shield to be the Sun and the shining god to be Heimdal. The runes that would be written there are Sowulo and Mannaz. Verse 18 states that the runes that were first scratched on the shield were then scraped off, steeped in the holy mead and cast far and wide, some to the Aesir, some to the Vanir, some to the elves and some to man. These runes had been initially scratched onto sacred objects by Odin; they then acquired the inner properties of the objects. Thus they became "runes," and apparently each race of beings has its own set of runes. Humankind received the twenty-four-rune futhark in which all cosmic mysteries are concealed, waiting for us to discover them.

Norns

The Norns are usually three in number. They represent the three aspects of time: past, present, and future. Their names are Urd, Verdandi, and Skuld, respectively. They shape the fates of all beings, acting according to the decrees of orlog, or the immutable cosmic law, to which even Odin himself is subject.

Urd is the eldest Norn. She rules the past. Verdandi is the second Norn and controls the present. Skuld is the youngest of the Norns and rules the future. On occasion, Skuld accompanies the Valkyries to the battlefields to choose the slain. The magical implements of the Norns are threads or cords and a knife. Although the Norns shape the fate of men, they do not necessarily create it. Fate or wyrd is created by each individual throughout his or her life. The concept of the three Norns is evidently very old and dates from the matriarchal period. Corresponding female beings, known as the Fates, are called Clotho, Lachesis, and Atropos and are to be found in Greek mythology. In the Anglo-Saxon tradition the Norns are known as the wyrd sisters. In this form they appear in Shakespeare's *Macbeth*. The name wyrd is related both to Urd, which means "origins," and to Verdandi, which means "becoming." And since all that exists originated in the past, the eldest Norn must be the first cause, or origin of existence. Her name, Urd, also relates to Erda, meaning "Earth," and this immediately identifies her as the Earth goddess. Verdandi's name is etymologically cognate with the Dutch verb *worden* and the German *werden,* which mean "to become." The third Norn, Skuld, is the dispenser of death. She is particularly associated with witchcraft and in this respect resembles the goddess of death, Hella.

Of all the Norns, Urd seems to be the most prominent, and the two others can be seen as aspects of her. Wiccans may well consider that then Norns represent a triple goddess: Urd is the grandmother, who has all the experience and wisdom of old age and in the matriarchal structure is the most powerful; Verdandi is the mother, who symbolizes fertility; and Skuld is the maiden, albeit in her aspect of destroyer, since it is she who cuts the thread of life and also participates in the death-dealing activities of the Valkyries. Urd is the Norn who possesses all knowledge. She is the guardian of the well named after her, the well of Urd, which is esoterically interpreted as the well of origin and collective memory. My view is that the well of Urd should be identified with the well of Mimir, and that Urd and Mimir are probably aspects of one and the same spirit, for both are described as being of giant stock. Mimir's name means "memory" and Urd is the Norn of the past. It is from the past that all memories are recalled. The myths have it that each day the gods meet in council at the well of Urd.

In addition to the three Norns we also find accounts of thirteen Norns, which reflects the concept of the thirteen moons. The Norns are perhaps the most underestimated figures in modern Northern heathenism. Nevertheless, they can be considered as the most powerful of all beings, because they control fate and dispense wyrd. For divination and magic, one is well advised to call on their assistance. They can be magically represented by three cords: white, red, and black. Although they operate as aspects of time, they are beyond time itself. Moreover, it has been considered that each individual has his or her own personal Norn, who is responsible for their fate. This concept could be interpreted as one's own conscience.

Since writing this, I have been given a different understanding of time and therefore, of the Norns. It seems that the Germanic people did not perceive time as linear, but held the view that "that which is," i.e., what exists right now, is Wyrd or Urd. This is the immediate moment in which one exists. The past is already included in this as "that which is" is the result of all things past. The future is a probability, in the process of being shaped by Wyrd. Time, then, seems to be non-linear as the so-called past and the future are equally distant from the immediate present or the current moment. Kvedulfr Gundarsson in *Our Troth* explains this concept of time in the Germanic world view as follows, speaking about the three Norns:

> They are the great ones, who shape the wyrd of the worlds; but the greatest of them is Wyrd, for it is by her might that the other two work. Superficial text often explain the Norns as "past, present and future," but that is not correct: the Germanic time-sense is not triple, like that of the Greeks and Romans (from whom contemporary western culture inherited it) but dual. For our forebears, there was only the great structure of "that which is," in which the eldest and the youngest layers were at the same time and the one was just as close and real as the other; and

the current moment, "that which is becoming." There was no sense of future as such: spae-sayings, that told of what "should" happen, were literally statements of Wyrd—that what is, seen with the wisdom that knows what must then arise as the effect of an existing cause.

Magically, if one considers the past as part of the present, one can then with a retrospective magical action alter the past subjectively and therefore shape one's future. By altering a certain emotional resonance in the past, one sets up a current which will shape a corresponding future.

Frigga

Names ♦	Frigg (Norse), Fricg (English), Frigga (Dutch), Fricka (German)
Main element ♦	air
Secondary element ♦	water
Colors ♦	silvery gray
Totem animals ♦	falcon, ram, spider
Magical items ♦	distaff
Invoked for ♦	marital fidelity, childbirth
Runes to use ♦	Fehu, Pertho, Berkana

Frigga is the first of various goddesses whose role in the Northern mysteries we shall now consider. In modern-day Odinism, the goddesses are not given sufficient prominence because very little has been written about them in the Icelandic sources, from which most of our knowledge about the Northern tradition derives. These sources, however, are of a later provenance and are greatly influenced by the male-oriented Viking Age and by the Christian views of the scribes who recorded the Eddas. The legal position of women in the society of either medieval Scandinavia or Anglo-Saxon England was not unfavorable compared with contemporary Mediterranean culture, although their traditional status of independence became much curtailed during the feudal period, which in England was heralded by the Norman Conquest. In fact, Tacitus observed that among the Germanic tribes, women were considered to have twice the value of men, for the wergild for the killing of a woman was twice the amount for a man in a similar position, and it was the women, usually the mother or the grandmother, who presented the young warrior with his first shield. In the *Prose Edda,* Odin (Just-as-High) says, "The goddesses are no less sacred and no less powerful."

First and foremost of the goddesses is Frigga, Odin's consort. Frigga is very powerful but renowned for her silence. She has total knowledge of the fates of all men, including that of her own son, Baldur. However, she does not make prophecy. Odin had to use other means, such as through his ordeal on Yggdrasil and his sacrifice to Mimir, to gain the same knowledge. Frigga already possesses this knowledge but is for some unknown reason unable to communicate it. Perhaps she knows it is futile because either it cannot be changed or else no one would believe her. Nothing is more frustrating than to know, from whatever source or by whatever means, what is going to happen and not being able to prevent anything because consensus reality rejects it. There is a Cassandra element here, which I too am very familiar with. She knows everything in advance, but she does not speak out, because by doing so she still cannot change or prevent the unavoidable fate or orlog. In Frigga's silence there is a lesson, for the heroism of Frigga is that, although she knows she cannot change Baldur's destiny, she nevertheless tries to do so. Frigga is as powerful as Odin, but she is an introvert. Only when Baldur has a dream foretelling that he is going to Hel does she try in vain to avert it. If we consider this myth from a purely human point of view, taking the story literally, we are looking at a woman who knows that an untimely death will befall her son and that his death heralds the onset of the Ragnarok.

There is a great store of magic in Frigga. The tragic paradox is that, in a way, she engineers Baldur's death. Because Baldur dreams he is going to die, Frigga extracts promises from all living things not to hurt him. Once that is done, the Aesir make a sport of shooting all sorts of weapons at Baldur, whom they suppose to be immortal, until Loki discovers the forgotten mistletoe. Frigga had overlooked it because it seemed so harmless; it is then used at Loki's instigation to kill Baldur. If Frigga had not taken the precaution of extracting the protective oaths, nobody would have considered making a sport of attacking Baldur with weapons, and consequently the mistletoe murder would not have been committed. One action leads to the other one. If Frigga does not act, Baldur will certainly die, but by trying to save him she involuntarily provides the weapon of Baldur's death. She is a very tragic figure. The magical lesson we can extract from this is: do not interfere with anybody else's wyrd, because by trying to change it you might actually set it in motion. Instead of it just happening as a matter of course, by interfering you then take it onto your own wyrd.

Frigga is often portrayed with a distaff, an implement which is used for spinning. There is magical significance here, since spinning is a way of forming thread from a raw material. Spinning has to be done before weaving. The Norns are said to weave the threads of the web of life of each of us. Frigga with her distaff may well be the one who actually does the spinning before the weaving can be done. This assumption would indicate that Frigga is in charge of the *prima materia;* in other words, she spins the substance which the Norns weave.

The goddesses have the knowledge which even Odin himself depends on for counsel. In effect, Odin obtains all his knowledge second-hand. He sacrifices for it and discovers it within himself, although even this assertion is not entirely true: after he has hung on the Tree, he says, "Nine lays of power I learned from Bolthorn." Therefore somebody else taught him. When he goes to the well of Mimir and sacrifices an eye to gain more knowledge, it is Mimir who gives him permission to drink from the well. He conjures up the dead Volva and receives knowledge from her, but he is only able to do so because Freyja has taught him necromancy, which is part of seidr. And mediumship, a traditionally female preserve, is akin to necromancy. Thus all of Odin's occult knowledge is second hand, coming mostly from female sources, while Frigga, Freyja, and the Norns possess knowledge which nobody taught them.

Frigga's animal is the heron and her magical weapon is the distaff. Modern recovered lore suggests the owl as a power animal of Frigga. To my knowledge, at least three independent people have had a visitation of an owl during a Frigga working. My current view is that the owl belongs to both Frigga and Odin. When working magic or divination it might not be a bad idea, before you gather your magical weapons, to invoke Frigga in order to gain access to the prima material.

Freyja

Names ♦	Freyja (Norse), Frija (Dutch), Freia (German), Freo (English)
Main element ♦	fire
Secondary element ♦	water
Colors ♦	gold
Totem animals ♦	cats
Magical items ♦	falcon coat, catskin gloves, Brisingamen
Invoked for ♦	love, sex, war, witchcraft (seith)
Runes to use ♦	Fehu, Pertho, Inguz, Hagalaz, Berkana, Laguz

Most renowned of the Northern goddesses, yet sometimes confused with Frigga, is Freyja. Some scholars, for example Grimm, have been of the opinion that these two goddesses are in fact quite distinct both in origin and function, a view I now support in light of further studies I engaged in after the completion of the first edition of this book. The oldest name for Freyja is Freo in Anglo-Saxon and Frija in Dutch. However, the attributes of the Dutch Frija have more in common with the Scandinavian Frigga. With the possible exception of Friesland, the Vanic Freyja was not known under this name in Holland; there are goddess names such as Gabiae and Aligabea, these names translate as Giver and Allgiver and are a direct equivalent of Gefjn, whom we know to be a version of Freyja. Freyja in some respect, even more that Frigga, is a "Great Goddess" in the modern occult understanding of this term. She is both the giver of life and the giver of death, whereas Frigga is a giver of life solely. Freyja is invoked for childbirth alongside Frigga and the Disir, and Freyja also receives or more properly chooses half of those who die in battle.

The meaning of the name Freyja is simply "lady," indicating either a woman of royal birth or in later days the woman of the house. Freyja's name therefore originated as a title rather than as a personal name. It is not impossible that the oldest names of various goddesses were lost in the distant past, or perhaps lingered on in various names of the Matronae. If we look at the name Frey, which means "Lord" and is clearly a title, while his true name is Ingvy or Ing, perhaps the original name of the goddess he is twinned with could have been something similar, for example, Ingva or something like that. A recent book on Freyja by the Swedish scholar Britt-Mari Nastrom mentions the name Ingagerd which nicely confirms my own feeling that Freyja has had a more personal name at one point in history.

Freyja stands out as the most active figure among the goddesses. She is simultaneously a Valkyrie and a Dis, hence one of her names is Vanadis. She is primarily the goddess of love and war, life and death. She is the opposite polarity of and most compatible with Odin, for both engage in sorcery, both are shamans, and both use animal forms to roam about the worlds. Both have an equal share of the dead slain in battle, and it is remarkable that Freyja has the first choice. Freyja's totem animals are cats. She has been portrayed driving a chariot drawn by two cats, which are either white or gray. Freyja was especially the patroness of volvas, who in olden days in Scandinavia used to wear catskin gloves in her honor. Nowadays Freyja is successfully invoked to curse people who abuse cats. Another one of her animals is the sow, a symbol of fertility. Freyja is the owner of the Brisingamen necklace, which she acquired as a reward for sleeping with four dwarves. These four dwarves represent the four elements, whereas the necklace represents the fifth element, which only can come into existence through the integration of the other four. Brisingamen has been described as a girdle as well, a girdle which was used to help women in labor. Freyja's day is Friday, a day traditionally thought of as being lucky for weddings.

Freyja's name is linked with two Dutch words, *vrijen* and *vrij*. The first word means "to make love" or "to court." A vrijer is a suitor. The second word, vrij, means "free." In later Icelandic tradition, Freyja was regarded as being married to Odr, which, as has been well established, is an alternative form of Odin. Odr may well be an aspect of Odin as wanderer. Odr leaves her, and she seeks after him through all the nine worlds, assuming various names such as Mardoll, Syr, and Gefion, meaning "sea-bright," "sow," and "giver," respectively. She weeps tears of gold during her search for Odr. She also is named Menglad or "necklace-glad" in one of the more obscure myths recorded by Saxo Grammaticus. This story records that she is delivered into the hands of the giants, from whom she is later rescued by Svipdag or Ottar, who is identified with Odr. Freyja is lusted after by various giants, who devise ways and means to obtain her as their bride. She possesses a falcon-feathered coat which enables her to fly. It has been suggested by various scholars of Norse mythology that Freyja is identical to Gullveig. Edred Thorsson adds in *Runelore* that Freyja also is identical to Heid, the Volva whom Odin consults. Robert Graves in *The White Goddess* states that Freyja was associated with a raven before it became Odin's totem animal. This would make sense in one way, as Freyja is the goddess of death as much as she is the goddess of life. In the early medieval period, Freyja was the patroness of a genre of love songs called mansongr, or in German, *Minnegesang*. This practice was obliterated by Christianity, but the later medieval minstrels or troubadours continued this tradition and dedicated their songs to the Virgin Mary. Many of Freyja's attributes and plants, herbs and animals such as the lady-bird, which is named after her, have been transferred to this corrupted version of the goddess. Like most goddesses in Northern mythology, Freyja is a solar goddess, the Sun being seen in the North as feminine.

Iduna

Names ♦	Idunn, Iduna (Norse)
Main element ♦	earth
Color ♦	green
Magical items ♦	apples
Invoked for ♦	longevity, health
Runes to use ♦	Jera, Berkana, Inguz

Another of the goddesses of Asgard whom little is known about is Iduna. She is an almost shadowy figure, but as I will show there is more to her than meets the eye. She is older than the Aesir and possibly even older than the Vanir. Her father is Ivalde, a giant and star-hero, and her brother is Orvandil, who previously was married to Sif. Orvandil, Iduna, and Baldur's wife, Nanna, are all the children of Ivalde and belong to an older race of gods. It is a reasonable assumption that the giants were the oldest family of gods, and that when the new gods superseded them some of the giants became either evil beings or else, like Skadi and Gerd, part of the new divine order. Iduna is normally portrayed as a sweet little maiden, naive and easily led astray by Loki, as when she fell into the hands of the giant Thjazi. She is always portrayed as very young, and she carries a basket laden with golden apples. She does not say much; her husband Bragi does the talking, for he is the lord of poetry. But within her small hands she holds considerable power. She is responsible for the health of the gods, because without Iduna's apples, they age and die. However, she is not prominent in any of the sagas. The apples of Iduna represent prolongation of life rather than immortality, because the gods have to eat them regularly. The inner core of the apple may represent the womb, because it is in the core that the seeds are to be found and it is the seeds that represent new life. Symbolic apples are also found outside of Northern mythology. In Celtic mythology the same concept of apples occurs on Avalon, the mystical island where the golden apples of eternal youth grow. As most occultists know, when an apple is sliced sideways a pentagram is revealed. In Greek mythology, Herakles has to gain golden apples as one of his tasks. The myth of Iduna has been compared to the Kore-Persephone myth. It is only in the Hebrew tradition that apples are connected with evil. But even there it is inadvertently admitted that apples give knowledge of good and evil. Therefore the apple is associated with good and evil and also sexuality as a reproduction principle, because it is only after eating the apple that the biblical Eve conceived children. There is a story that the childless King Rerir in Hunaland sat one day with his queen under a tree, beseeching the gods for a child. Frigga took pity on them and sent her messenger, Gna, to the royal couple. Gna threw an apple into the queen's lap for her to eat, and she thereby conceived a baby. The king and queen's descendants founded the Volsung dynasty. Apples are sacred to the goddess and highly significant in the feminine Mysteries. Symbolically, they carry the souls of the unborn. Iduna is the goddess of vegetation and at the onset of the Ragnarok she sinks down into the roots of Yggdrasil and disappears from the Earth to reappear afterwards with new life.

Hella/Holda

These two goddesses have some features in common. One may pose the question whether they actually are the same or is one derived from the other. Both are associated with the dead. Holda as Frau Gode is like Wodan, a leader of the wild hunt. I felt for a long time that there is a connection between these two. I think they may have been twinned like Ziu and Zisa. Hella is the Scandinavian equivalent of Holda, I think. Holda, however, may have been the oldest death goddess known to us. It always seems to me that Hella is a late arrival contaminated with Christian visions of an unpleasant afterlife. Only once is Hella referred to a hall decked out with flowers and food and drink in anticipation of the arrival of Baldur. A special feature that set Holda apart from Hella is that Holda is the guardian of dead infants; in later Christian time, these were supposed to be unbaptized children. I think that originally she was a death goddess especially in charge of children. This is a specific Germanic view as the Scandinavian Hella seems to be a goddess of death full stop. Everyone who was not fully true to one of the gods or goddesses to whose abode they would fare after death would go to Hella's hall. Hella is described as a being that looks half beautiful-like and half ugly corpse-like. From modern sources we now come to understand her as a kind and wise goddess. Both Holda and Hella are the archetypal ugly witches model as passed on from the Middle Ages. Holda too can appear young and beautiful on occasions, but more often she appears as a kind but severe or ugly old woman, with a deformed foot allegedly due to too much treading of the spinning wheel. This is Dutch folklore and may or may not pertain to other local versions.

At this moment she is making her presence known in the south of England, especially in Greenwich, and enjoys a growing following. Holda's special rune is Hagalaz. She is the patroness of haegetessan or volvas, as is Freyja. A manual of Scandinavian Mythology states that Wodan/Odin was given his ravens by Holda.

Other Goddesses

Here follows a brief description of some of the less well-known goddesses in Northern mythology who are of special interest.

NEHELLENIA

In Holland a specific goddess is associated with vegetation, dogs, and the sea. Her name is Nehellenia. She may well be a friendlier version of Hella, since she is portrayed with a basket of apples which, as described in the section on Idunna, are symbols of life. Dogs, however, are associated with death, often appearing in shamanic tradition as guides to the underworld. Nehellenia may very well be a local version of Nerthus in that case; she may be the goddess whom Tacitus names Isis according to his "interpretatio Romana." The center of worship of Nehellenia was Walcheren, one of the Dutch Friesian islands which now form part of the province of Zeeland. She was invoked by sailors before they attempted to cross the North Sea to England. One of her attributes in addition to the dog and the basket is a ship. Since the writing of this book she has been recognized by the English as the goddess Elen. Nehellenia's element is water; the runes helpful in invoking her are Hagalaz and Laguz. Raido can be incorporated in a working to gain protection when a sea voyage is planned.

SKADI

Another local goddess, this time from Scandinavia, is Skadi. In the myths she has been described as the temporary wife of Niord. He was given to her as a husband as part of the wergild the Aesir had to pay for the killing of her father Thiazi, a giant. As Skadi thus is of giant stock, she may have been part of the elder local divinities worshipped in Scandinavia before the arrival of the Aesir. Scandinavia is named after her, the "land of Skadi." She is a winter goddess, traveling on skates, and as such she has been associated with Uller, who is said to be her husband after she separated from Niord. Alternatively, she might have been involved with Odin himself in his siring of the Skjoldungs, the royal house of Denmark. Her name means "shadow" and she, too, is associated with death. She is the goddess who, after the capture and binding of Loki, fastened a snake above his head in revenge for Loki's part in the killing of her father. Her abode is Thrymheim. Runes that may be associated with her are Eihwaz, Hagalaz, and Isa. Her element is snow.

SIF

Sif, the second wife of Thor, is the lady with the corn-gold hair. Some sources state that she has the gift of prophecy, although this is not mentioned in the Eddas. From older Germanic sources it has been stated that Sif is a swan maiden and can assume this form. Having been married once to Orvandil, she can also be seen as one of the elder race of gods. Sif signifies summer fertility and corn, hence Loki's cutting of her hair is interpreted as a fire destroying a cornfield. Sif's name is cognate with the German *sippe,* meaning "kith and kin." From this we may assume that, like Frigga, Sif is a goddess associated with peace and friendship in a happy family, and with conjugal fidelity. Runes compatible with Sif are Berkana and Inguz.

SAGA

Saga is another name for Frigga; she is invoked for recall and memory She resides by the stream of time and events. Frigga lives in Fensalir ("fenlands") and Saga in Sokkvabek ("sunken benches"). Odin drinks with her every day from golden goblets, and Saga sings the songs of the past and of times gone by. As Frigga has foreknowledge and Saga has all the knowledge of the past, one could say that Saga represents Frigga's memories. She corresponds nicely to the Pertho rune, in combination with Laguz.

EIR, VOR, VAR, AND FULLA

One of Frigga's handmaidens, Eir, is especially involved in healing. The runes I would associate with her are Berkana, Sowulo, and Laguz. Uruz, although also a healing rune, I consider too masculine to be used in an invocation to Eir. Two other handmaidens of Frigga are invoked to witness oaths and to punish oath-breakers: Vor and Var. Of these two, Var has a special significance. The name Var cognates with the German for true, i.e., *wahr,* and survives in English words like "aware" and "beware," which contain the sense of perception, awareness, or realization of the truth. So Var's concern to

maintain the oath can be seen in respect of Var personalizing an ide-
alized concept of truth and honesty. She advises caution and says,
"Beware!" to those who make rash, ill-considered oaths, including
marriage vows, because she, as a representative or handmaiden of
Frigga, who presides over family matters, will avenge those who act
treacherously towards their partners or loved ones. Fulla seems to be
closest to Frigga. She carries Frigga's casket with treasures; she also
is Frigga's confidante.

Outlook on the Future

The feminine perspective of the Northern religion has been overlooked to the detriment of both men and women of our folk. Because
it is the male-oriented Viking Age that bequeathed us most of our
written material, we find scant reference to the goddesses in the
Eddas and sagas, and even less to the feminine Mysteries. To make
matters worse, the Christian scribes, influenced by their own religious views according to which the goddess elements are given no
scope whatsoever, reacted with far greater hostility towards the feminine aspect of the Northern tradition.

Their reluctance to record details of women's Mysteries was
exacerbated by their puritanical disapproval of the fertility-related
nature of these Mysteries. As a result, a vicious circle has come
about. The modern-day restoration of the Northern religion still
appears to suffer from the excessive preponderance of male attitudes
prevalent in Viking times; this religion has not yet totally shaken off
the shackles imposed on it by the Christian monks and priests. Thus,
far too few women are to be found playing a part in restoring a
Northern balance in modern-day heathenism and occult workings,
and so the masculine aspect continues to dominate.

Yet the essence of the Northern tradition should highlight, not
diminish, the function of feminine spirituality. To be true to the original current of the Northern Mysteries means establishing a harmo-
nious balance between both polarities. Without a proper devotion

to the Goddess, without a true understanding of the role of the Norns, Valkyries, and Disir, the Northern restoration will become lopsided and poorly attuned to the modern day; and without the feminine Mysteries viewed as being of equal validity to the male warrior cult, the Northern folk alive today will be much impoverished at a mystical level. Restoring this balance and breaking out of the vicious circle has been the goal of my book. The outlook on the future is not bleak, however. After all, this is the first work on the runes written by a genuine follower and practitioner of the elder Northern faith that has appeared in England, indeed in Europe, for many decades. And it is a woman who has produced it. Women will and women must continue to make their mark in this way. The result will hopefully be a snowballing effect, with many more women prepared to undertake the arduous but rewarding task of bringing the feminine Mysteries to their due position in the Northern heritage.

Of course, given the scarcity of source material which may be helpful in this task, scholarship and intellectual research alone cannot fill in all the gaps. We must resort to our powers of intuition and to imaginative experimentation in order to "feel" our way into the feminine disciplines. This is largely what I have done in my own research. How appropriate it is that the very qualities required— intuition, imagination, and feeling—are those that are particularly well represented in the female psyche.

More qualities than these alone, however, are necessary if the restoration of the Northern Mysteries is to be successfully pursued, for this restoration cannot operate on criteria alien to the folk-soul of our people, and cannot distort or divert that tradition into infectious and strange byways. We Northern women must open our minds and spirits to the stirrings of the collective unconscious of our ancestors' unique contribution to human progress. If the word "necromancy" bears unfortunate or disturbing connotations to many people today, let it be clearly understood that those who have gone before us possessed great wisdom and lore in mystical matters, which we can enter into contact with so as to advance our own knowledge and awareness. We must learn from past generations, whose learning in many ways outstrips our own, and adapt what we learn to present needs; but the means and techniques to arouse that collective memory are hidden deep within each of us in our unconscious minds.

Here again, many women are at an advantage, for the transmission of wisdom has always been a woman's job. It is, above all, women who conserve and preserve the heritage of the past, and it is at their mothers' and grandmothers' knees that the youngsters of a new generation learn their speech patterns, their social customs, their religious insights, and even their old wives' tales, which are so redolent of ancient wisdom. Of course, both men and women function as links in the chain connecting the past with the future, but so often it is women who are most aware of this natural faculty.

Women, therefore, should involve themselves more in their children's schooling. We hear much about classical mythology and Christian mythology, not to mention multi-faith education, but when are children in school ever taught about the Northern gods and mythology? The educational system has been neglecting the Anglo-Saxon and ancient Northern heritage for far too long. Women should take a stand on these issues.

A further argument, however, for a greater balance in the male-female polarity within our tradition is not that it will benefit women only, but that it will be to the advantage of all, both sexes included. The largely feminine arts of healing and divination, for example, can benefit all. The goddesses are for all. They are no more the sole preoccupation for women than are the gods for men. Until this balance is restored, the Northern Mysteries will remain incompletely restored, as well. This book, I hope, will make a contribution, remedy what needs remedying, and heal what needs healing.

Elder Futhark		Anglo/Saxon		Younger Futhark	
ᚠ	Fehu	ᚠ	Feoh	ᚠ	Fe
ᚾ	Uruz	ᚾ	Ur	ᚾ	UruR
ᚦ	Thurisaz	ᚦ	Thorn	ᚦ	Thurs
ᚨ	Ansuz	ᚬ	Os	ᚠ	Ass
ᚱ	Raido	ᚱ	Rad	ᚱ	Reidh
ᚲ	Kenaz	ᚲ	Cen	ᚤ	Kaun
ᚷ	Gebo	ᚷ	Gifu		
ᚹ	Wunjo	ᚹ	Wynn		
ᚺ	Hagalaz	ᚺ	Haegl	ᚻ	Hagall
ᚾ	Nauthiz	ᚾ	Nyd	ᚾ	Naudh (r)
ᛁ	Isa	ᛁ	Is	ᛁ	Is
ᛃ	Jera	ᛃ	Ger	ᛃ	Ar
ᛇ	Eihwaz	ᛇ	Eoh		
ᛈ	Pertho	ᛈ	Peorth		
ᛉ	Algiz	ᛦ	Eolhx		
ᛊ	Sowulo	ᛋ	Sigil	ᛋ	Sol
ᛏ	Teiwaz	ᛏ	Tir	ᛏ	Tyr
ᛒ	Berkana	ᛒ	Beorc	ᛒ	Bjarkan
ᛖ	Ehwaz	ᛖ	Eh		
ᛗ	Mannaz	ᛗ	Man	ᛉ	Madr
ᛚ	Laguz	ᛚ	Lagu	ᛚ	Logr
ᛜ	Inguz	ᛝ	Ing		
ᛟ	Othila	ᛟ	Ethel		
ᛞ	Dagaz	ᛞ	Daeg		
		ᚪ	Ac		
		ᚫ	Aesc		
		ᚣ	Yr	ᛣ	Yr
		ᛠ	Ear		
		ᛡ	Ior		
		ᛢ	Cweordh		
		ᛣ	Calc		
		ᛥ	Stan		
		ᛤ	Gar		

FUTHARK CHART

✦ APPENDIX ✦

Notes on Terminology

In this book certain terms are used that are specific to the Northern tradition but may be unfamiliar to the general public. Following are some brief definitions to aid the reader.

Aesir: Name of one of the principal families or clans of gods described in the Northern mythos. The word *Aesir* has been translated as "pillar." Aesir is the plural form. The singular form is Ass or Aes.

Aettir or Aett: Group of eight runes in a set order. Aett is the singular form and aettir is the plural form.

Anima: A Jungian term meaning the unconscious female part of the male self, composed of all the female influences accumulated in childhood and, possibly, the female content of the ancestral memory. As such, the anima would be part of the hamingja.

Animus: A Jungian term meaning the unconscious male part of the female self, composed of all the male influences accumulated in childhood and, possibly, the male content of the ancestral memory. As such, the animus would be part of the hamingja.

Asatru: This term has been adopted from Icelandic to describe the modern restoration of the Germanic religion of Northern Europe. The literal meaning is "true to the Aesir."

Futhark: The entire sequence of the rune-row in its fixed order. The word "futhark" is derived from the phonetic values of the first six runes.

Fylgja: This term is of old Norse origin. The English equivalent would be "fetch." In occult terms, fylgja corresponds to the astral or etheric body. It can operate independently from the physical body and is used in shape-shifting and "sending." It is thought to survive the physical death.

Galdr: A specific magical discipline involving verbal magic and the chanting of runes.

Germania: The entire area inhabited by speakers of Germanic languages.

Germanic: A branch of the Indo-European language family which includes English, Dutch, German.

Gothic and Scandinavian tongues: Primitive or Common Germanic refers to the early unified form of this language. The common Germanic Futhark originated in this period.

Hamingja: An old Norse term meaning literally "luck." It has a more profound significance than the word "luck" in English, however, and indicates that the amount of luck inherent in the individual is closely related to the deeds of one's ancestors and to one's own behavior and honor. There is a tenuous link with wyrd. The hamingja can be looked upon as a sort of "oversell" in a family or tribe. It can be transferred to descendants and contains genetic memory.

Hugr: The word *hugr* again is old Norse and means "mind" or "intellect." It is not believed to survive the physical death. One of Odin's ravens is called Hugin, meaning "thought."

Jotun: Race of giants or gods who came before the Aesir and Vanir. They can be compared roughly to the Titans of Greek mythology.

Kenning: A poetic metaphor. For example, "the fishes' bath" is a kenning for the sea.

Northern: Throughout this work the term "Northern" or North European refers to a specific tradition indigenous to that part of the world, with its unique mythology, religion, pantheon of gods, languages, customs and laws. A manifestation of this tradition is the runic futhark.

Orlog: *Orlog* is Old Norse for cycle of fate, or for the unalterable destiny of the world. Orlog encompasses all, including the gods. One aspect of orlog is the "Ragnarok." Orlog is the collective wyrd of the world as a whole, whereas "wyrd" is more individual.

Ragnarok: Doom or destiny of the gods; the Northern version of the end of the world. In occult terms it implies the end of an era.

Rede: Statement of the purpose of the working (part of a ritual).

Rune: The original meaning of the word *rune* in most of the Germanic languages is "secret" or "mystery." In this book, rune is used to denote any of the "letters" in the futhark.

Persona: A Jungian term meaning the part of the individual that relates to the external world; the image presented to others.

Self: A Jungian term meaning the potential for wholeness in the individual; in occult terms it is the higher self or "holy guardian angel."

Shadow: A Jungian term meaning the unassimilated content of the personal unconscious.

Sigil: A symbolic representation, usually in the form of a drawing, of a magical principle.

Synchronicity: A Jungian term referring to a coincidence meaningful on various levels, and apparently unrelated by a common cause.

Seidr: Literally "seething." Seidr is the name of a variety of magical and shamanic practices involving sorcery, divination and "soul journeys."

Vanir: Another family of gods. The Vanir are especially connected with fertility.

Wicca: This word is Anglo-Saxon and means literally "wise"; nowadays adopted by practitioners of modern witchcraft.

Wight: A being or entity of any kind with some living quality.

Wyrd: This word is Anglo-Saxon and its meaning corresponds roughly to the Eastern concept of "karma." Although wyrd can be personal, it is often linked to whole families, tribes, and even races. Unlike karma, it is not totally fixed. One can move within one's personal web of wyrd in accordance with the amount of consciousness one commands. The less conscious one is, the more one is subject to the seemingly random workings of wyrd, in contrast to orlog, which is impersonal and cannot be manipulated.

Yggdrasil: The World Tree or Cosmic Axis. Usually seen as an ash; lately it is more correctly identified as a yew. The word *Yggdrasil* means literally "gallows" or "horse of Ygg" (i.e., Odin).

✦ BIBLIOGRAPHY ✦

Esoteric Rune Books

Elliott, R. W. V. *Runes*. Manchester: Manchester University Press, 1959.

Moltke, Erik. *Runes and Their Origin in Denmark and Elsewhere*. Published in Denmark and available through The Viking Society for Northern Research in London.

Page, R. I. *An Introduction to English Runes*. London: Methuen Co., 1973

Recommended Esoteric Rune Books

Howard, Michael. *Wisdom of the Runes*. Published by Rider.

Osborn, Marianne, and Stella Longland. *Rune Games*. Published by Routledge & Kegan Paul.

Essential Esoteric Rune Books

Thorsson, Edred. *Futhark: A Handbook of Rune Magic*. Published by Thorsson.

Thorsson, Edred. *Runelore*. Samuel Weiser, 1987.

On Magic

Carroll, Pete. *Liber Null and Psychonaut*. Samuel Weiser, 1987.

On Shamanism

Bates, Brian. *The Way of Wyrd*. Published by Century Publishing.

On Northern Mythology

Auden, W. H., and P. B. Taylor, trans. *The Poetic Edda*. Published by Faber and Faber Ltd.

Branston, Brian. *Gods of the North*. Published by Thames and Hudson.

The Brothers Grimm. *Teutonic Mythology*. Published by Bell, London, 1884–1888.

Davidson, H. R. Ellis. *Gods and Myths of Northern Europe*. Hammondsworth: Penguin, 1964.

Geurber, H. A. *Myths of the Norsemen*. Published by George G. Harrap.

Gundarsson, Kveldulfr. *Teutonic Magic*. St. Paul, MN: Llewellyn Publications, 1990.

Gundarsson, Kveldulfr. *Teutonic Religion*. St. Paul, MN: Llewellyn Publications, 1993.

Holland, Kevin Crossley. *The Norse Myths*. Middlesex, England: Penguin, 1980.

Rydberg, Victor. *Teutonic Mythology*. Published by Swan Sonnenschein, 1889.

Sturluson, Snori. (Jean I. Young, Trans.). *The Prose Edda*. Berkeley: University of California Press, 1954.

Tichenel, Elsa Brita. *The Masks of Odin*. Published by Theosophical University Press.

On History

Derolez, R. L. M. *De Godsdienst der Germanen.*

Farwerck, F. E. *Noordeuropese Mysterien en hun sporen tot heden.* Published by Ankh Hermes, Deventer, Holland.

Simek, R. *Dictionary of Northern Mythology.*

Tacitus, Cornelius. (H. Mattingly, Trans.). *Germania.* Middlesex, England: Penguin, 1970.

Other Recommended Books

Grundy, Stephan. *Rhinegold.*

Nastrom, Britt-Mari. *Freyja the Great Goddess of the North.* Published by University of Lund Sweden.

Paxson, Diana. *The Wolf and the Raven—Dragons on the Rhine—Lord of Horses.* A trilogy published by William Morrow and Company, New York.

◆ INDEX ◆

☽ REACH FOR THE MOON

Llewellyn publishes hundreds of books on your favorite subjects! To get these exciting books, including the ones on the following pages, check your local bookstore or order them directly from Llewellyn.

Order by Phone
- Call toll-free within the U.S. and Canada, 1-877-NEW-WRLD
- In Minnesota, call (651) 291-1970
- We accept VISA, MasterCard, and American Express

Order by Mail
- Send the full price of your order (MN residents add 7% sales tax) in U.S. funds, plus postage & handling to:
  Llewellyn Worldwide
  P.O. Box 64383, Dept. 1-56718-047-7
  St. Paul, MN 55164-0383, U.S.A.

Postage & Handling
- **Standard** (U.S., Mexico, & Canada)
If your order is:
  $20 or under, add $5
  $20.01–$100, add $6
  Over $100, shipping is free
(Continental U.S. orders ship UPS. AK, HI, PR, & P.O. Boxes ship USPS 1st class. Mex. & Can. ship PMB.)
- **Second Day Air** (Continental U.S. only): $10 for one book plus $1 per each additional book
- **Express** (AK, HI, & PR only) [Not available for P.O. Box delivery. For street address delivery only.]: $15 for one book plus $1 per each additional book
- **International Surface Mail:** $20 or under, add $5 plus $1 per item; $20.01 and over, add $6 plus $1 per item
- **International Airmail:** Books—Add the retail price of each item; Non-book items—Add $5 per item

Please allow 4–6 weeks for delivery on all orders.
Postage and handling rates subject to change.

Discounts
We offer a 20% discount to group leaders or agents. You must order a minimum of 5 copies of the same book to get our special quantity price.

Free Catalog
Get a free copy of our color catalog, *New Worlds of Mind and Spirit*. Subscribe for just $10.00 in the United States and Canada ($30.00 overseas, airmail). Call 1-877-NEW-WRLD today!

Visit our website at www.llewellyn.com for more information.

RUNE MAGIC

Donald Tyson

Drawing upon historical records, poetic fragments, and the informed study of scholars, *Rune Magic* resurrects the ancient techniques of this tactile form of magic and integrates those methods with modern occultism so that anyone can use the runes in a personal magical system. For the first time, every known and conjectured meaning of all 33 known runes, including the 24 runes known as "futhark," is available in one volume. In addition, *Rune Magic* covers the use of runes in divination, astral traveling, skrying, and on amulets and talismans. A complete rune ritual is also provided, and 24 rune words are outlined. Gods and Goddesses of the runes are discussed, with illustrations from the National Museum of Sweden.

0–87542–826–6, 224 pp., 6 x 9, photos, softcover $12.95

NORTHERN MAGIC
Rune Mysteries & Shamanism
Edred Thorsson

This in-depth primer of the magic of the Northern Way introduces the major concepts and practices of Gothic or Germanic magic. English, German, Dutch, Icelandic, Danish, Norwegian, and Swedish peoples are all directly descended from this ancient Germanic cultural stock. According to author Edred Thorsson, if you are interested in living a holistic life with unity of body-mind-spirit, a key to knowing your spiritual heritage is found in the heritage of your body—in the natural features which you have inherited from your distant ancestors. Most readers of this book already "speak the language" of the Teutonic tradition.

Northern Magic contains material that has never before been discussed in a practical way. This book outlines the ways of Northern magic and the character of the Northern magician. It explores the theories of traditional Northern psychology (or the lore of the soul) in some depth, as well as the religious tradition of the Troth and the whole Germanic theology. The remaining chapters make up a series of "mini-grimoires" on four basic magical techniques in the Northern Way: Younger Futhark rune magic, Icelandic galdor staves, Pennsylvania hex signs, and "seith" (or shamanism). This is an excellent overview of the Teutonic tradition that will interest neophytes as well as long-time travelers along the Northern Way.

0–56718–709–9, 264 pp., 5³/₁₆ x 8, illus. $12.95

To order, call 1-800-THE-MOON
Prices subject to change without notice.

SONGS OF YGGDRASIL CD

Shamanic Chants from the Northern Mysteries

Freya Aswynn

SONGS OF YGGDRASIL

By Freya Aswynn
Shamanic Chants from the Northern Mysteries

If you want to experience the power and the beauty of the Norse tradition, rather than just read about it, you must experience this CD! Freya Aswynn, Priestess of Odin and Rune Mistress, presents the history of runes in what can only be called a magical performance. Both powerful and moving, these chants are living, potent *spells*. Included on this extraordinary 40-minute CD is a unique adaptation of the *Havamal*, the ancient myth of the runes and how they were discovered by Odin. Freya also performs an actual invocation of the gods, a circle casting, and more. This is perhaps the only existing recording of a rune practitioner demonstrating the art of Galdr, the magical technique of vibrating runes. With Freya's remarkable vocal range, you can actually *feel* the runic power flow.

1-87542-023-0, 40 min. compact disc $12.95